Correctional Fundamentals

Correctional Fundamentals

A Personal Narrative Approach

O. Hayden Griffin, III
UNIVERSITY OF ALABAMA AT BIRMINGHAM

Meghan Sacks
FAIRLEIGH DICKINSON UNIVERSITY

CAROLINA ACADEMIC PRESS
Durham, North Carolina

Library of Congress Cataloging-in-Publication Data

Names: Griffin, O. Hayden, III, author. | Sacks, Meghan, author.
Title: Correctional fundamentals : a personal narrative approach /
   O. Hayden Griffin III, Meghan Sacks.
Description: Durham, North Carolina : Carolina Academic Press, [2019] |
   Includes bibliographical references and index.
Identifiers: LCCN 2019000924 | ISBN 9781531006952 (alk. paper)
Subjects: LCSH: Corrections—United States—History. |
   Corrections—United States—Administration.
Classification: LCC HV9466 .G85 2019 | DDC 364.60973—dc23
LC record available at https://lccn.loc.gov/2019000924

e-ISBN   978-1-5310-0696-9

Carolina Academic Press
700 Kent Street
Durham, North Carolina 27701
Telephone (919) 489-7486
Fax (919) 493-5668
www.cap-press.com

Printed in the United States of America

Contents

Preface

At one point in time, a discussion of corrections might not have taken too long. Legal codes, if they even existed, were much shorter. The range of punishments was less diverse. Perhaps most importantly, when punishments were imposed, the state generally took no further interest in the offender. As time has gone on, though, corrections have become more complicated. Incarceration, probation, and parole, three of the more modern forms of correctional supervision, are modern inventions. The range of community corrections programs seems to grow by the day. Legal codes are much longer, and the courts have taken a progressively active role in corrections. The growing complexity of corrections is important for two reasons. The first reason is if you want to become knowledgeable about corrections, that takes more time. The second reason is if you want to gain this knowledge, it takes an ever-lengthening textbook to tell this information. Many corrections books approach 20 chapters, and some are even longer. If you want such a textbook, ours is not for you.

When writing this book, we wanted to provide an overview of corrections but a much shorter version. Thus, when we say "correctional fundamentals," we attempted to provide the most crucial information regarding corrections but not the most complete telling possible. In doing so, we present an overview of corrections in 10 chapters. Within these chapters, we believe we cover the most crucial issues. If you need a more comprehensive reading, perhaps you might look elsewhere, but then again, why not start with us first?

In addition to providing an abridged textbook on corrections, we also wanted to provide something else. Corrections, like a great many other things, is made up by people. If there were no offenders, we would not have to punish people. If we did not punish people, there would no need for correctional workers, or at least there would be a lot less of them. Essentially, what we are trying to say is that people are an important part of corrections. If we only told you how many people are under correctional control or how many people work as jailors or correctional officers, you might get a small picture of who these people are, but we wanted to go further. Thus, within the book, we include many people's narratives. These people graciously provided us with many aspects of their life stories, but most importantly, what it is like to be a part of the correctional system. While we are providing a textbook that is shorter on details, we hope these narratives will give you a fuller idea of the American correctional experience. Many textbooks are thick in terminology, or bold terms, that your professors ask you to memorize, but they also seem to have moved away from the human part of this field. The criminal justice system is often viewed as the many parts and agencies that comprise it, but we would argue that it should be viewed through the lens of the people who actually live in it. We hope this book will help to restore the human voice that is too often lost in traditional textbooks about corrections. In doing so, we organized our book into 10 chapters.

In Chapter 1, we will provide a brief history of American corrections. This will include a discussion of historical legal codes and what punishment was like in early America. In particular, we want to provide you some sense of how American corrections has evolved over time.

In Chapter 2, we discuss the different philosophies of corrections. Some of these philosophies are specifically relevant to corrections, but many of them you may have studied in general criminological theory.

In Chapter 3, we discuss the various ways in which legal matters govern corrections. Within this section, we discuss the constitutional rights of inmates, legislation, the courts, and other important legal mechanisms that guide corrections.

In Chapter 4, we discuss incarceration in the United States. Incarceration occurs within two different types of facilities: jails and prisons. Some people seem to use these two terms interchangeably, but, as we discuss, they are quite different.

In Chapter 5, we discuss probation and parole. We will provide some history of how both are treated in the modern day.

In Chapter 6, we discuss community corrections. Community corrections have grown considerably in the United States, both in breadth and scope. While we will not give an exhaustive list of these sanctions, an overview of the most common types will be provided.

In Chapter 7, we discuss life in correctional facilities. This will cover what it is like for inmates who are doing time in jails and prisons.

In Chapter 8, we discuss juvenile corrections. Essentially unknown before the 1900s, the juvenile corrections systems is both similar and different from the adult correctional system.

In Chapter 9, we discuss correctional facility workers. Working in these facilities can be both a trying and rewarding experience. If you are at all interested in a career in corrections, this chapter will give you some idea of what to expect.

In Chapter 10, we discuss rehabilitation programs. The first prison reformers believed that the prison process itself was rehabilitative in nature. Yet, this is not a view that many people have in the modern day. We will discuss some of the different types of rehabilitation programs that are implemented in the American correctional system.

Correctional Fundamentals

Chapter 1

A Brief History of American Corrections

Whenever people think of corrections, they often will think of prisons and jails. In cartoons, various lawbreaking characters, whenever they are finally punished for their transgressions, are usually depicted wearing striped uniforms and having a ball and chain attached to their leg. One of the most common activities they will be engaging in is breaking rocks. While this is just one of many images a person might conjure when thinking of corrections, at a most basic level, the purpose of having a correctional system is to punish lawbreakers. Sometimes, as the name implies, punishment is delivered with the intent to correct what is considered either unlawful and/or deviant (outside of the norm) behavior; however, this is not always the case. Corrections is a truly ancient pastime, and while the focus of this chapter will certainly be on the United States, for at least a few paragraphs, it is necessary to go back a little further in time.

In some ways, one form of corrections has always been around. Indeed, no doubt you have experienced it. Throughout your life, you have most likely had some parental figure correct your actions. Hopefully, these people have taught you right from wrong. When you violated their rules, it is highly likely that there was some form of punishment. From taking away one of your favorite toys or electronic devices, a stricter curfew, withholding an allowance, to confinement in your room, or in some cases, some form of corporal punishment (such as a spanking) are all examples of typical punishments children face during their childhood. If you examine them closely, the punishments you experienced at home are somewhat comparable to punishments criminals have experienced from differing state authorities. Taking away your things or allowance is somewhat comparable to fines, a stricter curfew is comparable to probation, confinement to your room is comparable to jail or prison, and corporal punishment, while no longer practiced in the criminal justice system of the United States, is still practiced in other countries.

Without a time machine, determining when states or other similar forms of ruling authorities began to engage in corrections is seemingly an impossible task. How long humans have been around is an ongoing controversy in the scientific community, and the earliest humans did not read, write, or leave any records behind from which we can decipher when humans began to punish one another for engaging in bad behavior. While we may tend to think of ancient people as primitives, humans have lived in collaborative environments for thousands of years. Our main limitation in understanding them is that time seems to wash many things away. If there is no survivable written record of what they did, we are left to guess, often through pottery and other similar evidence, what their lives were like. It is possible that many groups of ancient people had strict rules to live by and punishments for people who violated these rules. Perhaps some of these traditions were kept orally, most likely by an elder or group of elders. Yet, because there was no written record, we are just left guessing as to how and the manner in which many ancient societies prevented people from behaving badly.

Legal Codes

The oldest documented legal code comes from the first known urban civilization Sumer (in modern-day Iraq). This document is known as the Code of Ur-Nammu and has been dated to approximately 2200 BC.[1] Historians are not exactly sure who wrote the Code of Ur-Nammu. Ur-Nammu was the founder of the third dynasty of Ur and scholars of that period seem to agree that Ur-Nammu was merely the ruler and not the author of the code.[2] To date, only portions of this legal code have been translated because finding a complete legible clay tablet has been elusive. Yet, from the portions scholars have been able to interpret, an interesting picture emerges. Unlike some of the brutal punishments of ancient people we will soon discuss, the punishments of ancient Sumer seem less punitive. Indeed, in three different listed laws, all of which describe the crime of infliction of bodily injury against a person, the punishment is not some form of bodily injury or capital punishment. Instead, in each instance, the perpetrator of the crime was required to pay their victim money for the offense (10 shekels of silver in one instance, 1 mina of silver in another, and 2/3 of a min of silver in the other).[3]

---

1. Good, E. M. (1967). Capital punishment and its alternatives in ancient Near Eastern law. *Stanford Law Review*, *19*(5), 947–977.

2. Kramer, S. N. (1983). The Ur-Nammu law code: Who was its author? *Orientalia*, *52*(4), 453–456.

3. Kramer, S. N. (1972). *Sumerian mythology: A study of spiritual and literary achievement in the third millennium BC*. Philadelphia, PA: University of Pennsylvania Press.

Janelle Diller described this as a "market-based approach" in which a sense of justice is received by obtaining monetary compensation after receiving injury from another person.[4] As Samuel Kramer documented, this is a very different idea of justice from some of the more well-known legal codes of ancient times.[5]

Perhaps the most well-known examples of ancient legal codes is the Code of Hammurabi. Similar to Ur-Nammu, Hammurabi was a ruler of an ancient civilization that was located in what would become Iraq. While Ur-Nammu ruled over Sumer, Hammurabi ruled over Babylon. Hammurabi's reign lasted from approximately 1792 BC to 1750 BC.[6] One of the reasons that the Code of Hammurabi is so well known is that an almost complete and legible copy of it was discovered in 1901 by a French group of archeologists. The researchers found a copy of the code inscribed on black diorite (an igneous rock) in three fragments. Five rows of columns were scraped away, presumably by someone who wished to put some of their own inscriptions on the tablet. One estimate is that the missing portion contained approximately 35 laws. Regardless, the discovery of the black diorite portions revealed that there were 282 laws within the Code of Hammurabi.[7] Whether the Code of Hammurabi was actually intended as a literal legal code to be enforced, a collection of precedents from court authorities, or some version of an ideal legal code has been debated by scholars.[8] The Code of Hammurabi was not just a criminal code but regulated many aspects of commerce and life in ancient Babylon. However, what is most important about this legal code is its philosophy. The Code of Hammurabi is the most complete and first example of the principle of lex talionis—the principle of retaliation and proportion. Most familiar about the code is the principle of an "eye for an eye" and a "tooth for a tooth." While in some instances it is near impossible or at least severely impractical to always include proportional punishment to crimes, the Code of Hammurabi at least seemed to try. In one code portion, if a man injures a pregnant woman and she miscarries, the perpetrator's own daughter may be put to death.[9]

To many people, such a strict code of proportionality seems barbaric. Indeed, why must a daughter pay for her father's crime merely because someone else lost their child? A common response to such punishment is a quote often at-

---

4. Diller, J. M. (2012). Private standardization in public international lawmaking. *Michigan Journal of International Law*, *33*(3), 481–536.

5. Kramer, S. N. (1972). *Sumerian mythology: A study of spiritual and literary achievement in the third millennium BC*. Philadelphia, PA: University of Pennsylvania Press.

6. Nagarajan, K. V. (2011). The Code of Hammurabi: An economic interpretation. *International Journal of Business and Social Science*, *2*(8), 108–117.

7. Edwards, C. (1904). *The Hammurabi Code and the Sinaitic legislation*. London, UK: Watts and Co.

8. Good, E. M. (1967). Capital punishment and its alternatives in ancient Near Eastern law. *Stanford Law Review*, *19*(5), 947–977.

9. Fish, M. J. (2008). An eye for an eye: Proportionality as a moral principle of punishment. *Oxford Journal of Legal Studies*, *28*(1), 57–71.

tributed to Mahatma Gandhi: "an eye for an eye leaves the whole world blind." Yet, thinking beyond such a draconian example of punishment, as we will discuss in more detail later, the principle of proportional punishment is at the very heart of American due process. Furthermore, one of the main reasons that states punish people is not only so that people will follow the law but also so that people will not take vengeance into their own hands and carry out vendettas. If a state does not adequately punish people, you are more likely to have situations like the Hatfields and McCoys, two families in West Virginia and Kentucky who carried out a famous feud, with each side one-upping another and seeking their own justice.

Our understanding of the legal systems of ancient societies, such as Sumer and Babylon, are limited. Yet, a far greater written record exists of the ancient state that began the process of establishing civilization throughout Europe—Rome. Like many places, the founding of Rome is shrouded in myth. From its humble beginnings as a small town in modern-day Italy to a long-standing republic to an empire ruled by dictators who lorded over (or at least affected) the whole of Europe and beyond, as the state grew in complexity, private vendettas as a solution to crime were replaced by a state criminal justice system. Although the source of crimes often involved aggrieved victims, Roman society often saw victims as secondary to the matter at hand. Indeed, the real violation was not that a person had violated another person. Instead, the real violation was that a person had committed a crime against the state. For a great many crimes, the penalty was death, and there was no shortage of ways in which a person under the mercy of the Roman Empire could be executed. Among the more well-known ways in which executions were carried out were crucifixion or being thrown into a pit of ravenous animals. In addition to the death penalty, people in Rome could be exiled from their community (or the state entirely) or fined (all fines went to the state, even if there was a victim), or an offender could incur what is referred to as civil death. Civil death involved stripping away a person's citizenship or status within the empire and included a host of other losses of status or privileges.[10]

While the supremacy of Rome in European politics would eventually fade, beginning in the fifth century, both their motives for and range of brutal punishments would continue. As the renowned historian and philosopher Michel Foucault would argue, punishment was used as a way to not only punish people who committed crimes but also as a way for the state to reinforce its power over its subjects. In many instances, punishment, whether it be the death penalty or lesser forms of corporal punishments, served as a warning to behave and a way to reinforce the primacy of the ruling authority.[11] Such was the case in England as well. Rival ruling families (both domestic and abroad) often plunged the country into civil war, and this fear led to strict punishments. There seemed to be

---

10. Bauman, R. A. (1996). *Crime and punishment in ancient Rome.* New York, NY: Routledge.
11. Foucault, M. (1977). *Discipline and punish: The birth of the prison.* New York, NY: Pantheon.

no shortage of crimes for which a person could receive the death penalty. For this reason, many people in England and Europe, in addition to hoping for freer governments, wanted better justice and religious freedom. These people sought refuge by immigrating to many different places, among which was the land that would become the United States.

In 1607, a group of settlers from England arrived on a peninsula in what would become the colony and later the Commonwealth of Virginia. The settlers would name the settlement Jamestown in honor of King James I of England. Rather than finding a land of riches, the settlers found a land devoid of mineral wealth. They arrived too late to plant crops and were in a land full of understandably hostile residents, natives who had established themselves in the region long before European settlers arrived. Furthermore, the location of Jamestown proved to be an extremely poor location for a first settlement with horrible weather and a great many disease-carrying insects. Large numbers of the settlers died. Many of those who remained were either ill-suited or unwilling to perform the hard labor that was needed to survive.[12]

Thus, something was needed to make sure that the colonialists survived. While they had fanciful dreams of riches, religious freedom, and a freer and just society, that was not reality. Given what was at stake, swift and brutal justice was needed. Furthermore, to ensure their own survival, colonialists as a whole essentially acted as agents of social control and through a kind of peer pressure, they sought to shame others into not only working but behaving. Among the settlers was Captain John Smith who essentially became the leader of the new colony. When settlers stepped out of line, they faced a strict form of military justice that could include corporal punishments (such as whippings or flogging) or the death penalty (usually accomplished by hanging).[13] In the earliest part of the colonial period of America, the crimes for which a person could receive the death penalty included treasons, murder, arson, rape, burglary, robbery, larceny, horse theft, witchcraft, assault, and battery.[14] For a little while, at least, wishes of freedom had to be put on hold.

As more settlers arrived in colonial America, the European population began to stabilize. This led to a relaxation of many harsh punishments. In the place of a system of military justice, the colonies settled into a system influenced by the common law of England. Essentially, the common law system is judge-made law inspired by stare decisis, which is a Latin phrase meaning "let the decision stand." While the system essentially works the same in procedural justice within the American court system, the common law system was largely replaced by legal codes. Such an innovation is important. Although the common law generally

---

12. Friedman, L. M. (1993). *Crime and punishment in American history*. New York, NY: Basic.

13. Jones, M., & Johnstone, P. (2012). *History of criminal justice*. New York, NY: Anderson Publishing.

14. Preyer, K. (1982). *Penal measure in the American colonies: An overview. The American Journal of Legal History*, 26(4), 326–353.

held principles of law and punishment consistent over time, the presence of standardized legal codes ensures that people know exactly what behaviors are prohibited and what range of punishments they can expect for committing a certain crime.[15] Granted, maybe your average citizen is not aware of the presence of every law and punishment, but at least they have the opportunity to find these things out. In a Europe ruled by kings, queens and other groups of nobles, the law was often whatever the ruling authority said at that moment in time. A hallmark of American due process is the predictability of law and punishment.

Punishment in Early America

In one way, the United States was initially an experiment in punishment. One of the oldest forms of punishment is banishment. To banish a person is to either tell them to leave a place or forcibly remove them and either order them not to return for a period of years or, in many instances, stay gone forever. One of the earliest examples of banishment comes from the Old Testament with Adam and Eve being expelled from the Garden of Eden.[16] Although the British had begun their settlement of the Americas in a search of riches, they soon found a dual use for their new colonies. Many criminal offenders or undesirables were told that they could head to the American colonies to avoid punishment, and in some instances, entire ships of offenders set sail for the new colonies. Such a variant of banishment is often referred to as transportation. Only 12 years after the founding of Jamestown, 180 convicts were transported to Virginia. Furthermore, the colony of Georgia was first established as a penal colony.[17]

Today, the punishment of banishment is forbidden by most state constitutions. Yet, some forms of the punishment still exist. Beginning largely in the 1990s, society began to heavily regulate the behavior of so-called sex offenders, a group of offenders who were deemed to be dangerous because they were declared to be highly likely to reoffend and further victimize people. Of special concern was people who might victimize children.[18] Among the variety of laws that were passed that targeted this population were residency restrictions that dictated in what places sex offenders could live should they be released from prison or receive probation for their crime. Typically, sex offenders, regardless of whether they actually targeted children, are restricted from living or going to places in which children may reside, such as schools, playgrounds, churches, and a variety

---

15. Griffin, O. H., Woodward, V. H., & Sloan, J. J. (2016). *The money and politics of criminal justice policy*. Durham, NC: Carolina Academic Press.

16. Ibid.

17. Clear, T. R., Cole, G. F., & Reisig, M. D. (2013). *American Corrections* (10th ed.). Belmont, CA: Cengage.

18. Levenson, J. S., Brannon, Y. N., Fortney, T., & Baker, J. (2007). Public perceptions about sex offenders and community protection policies. *Analyses of Social Issues and Public Policy, 7*(1), 137–161.

of other places. The most common restriction is dictating the number of feet or miles that a sex offender must steer clear of these places.[19] For example, read the following narrative from a convicted sex offender who faces these restrictions.[20]

Narrative: Nowhere to Live in Florida

In 1997, I was living in Fort Lauderdale when I was arrested for downloading 28 child porn pictures. For the record, I knew what I was doing and admit to what I did. I won't go into detail about the hell I experienced through jail, courts, losing my job, etc. After serving 53 days in jail, I found a job and was able to further my career, eventually starting my own company in 2003.

The condo I lived in with my girlfriend was close to an elementary school. I was able, on two occasions, to petition the local court and got the residential distance reduced to 250 feet. This was on the *county* level. I wasn't aware at the time that *cities* have their own separate proximity laws.

Two years ago I landed a great apartment within the permissible area. Recently, the complex was sold, and I was forced to move. This is when I found out just how small the area is in which sex offenders can live in Broward or Miami-Dade counties. It's *literally a small section of one street* in Fort Lauderdale.

After spending hours looking, and hiring my former attorney to scour the county, I got very lucky to find a vacancy in one of several apartment complexes on this street. It's less than ideal . . . In fact, I hate the place. My fear is that if I have to leave this apartment for any reason, I would have nowhere to go in Florida (at least south Florida), as Miami-Dade County is even worse, with thousands of sex offenders living under a bridge.

So now I'm hunting the web for cities anywhere in the United States with the least restrictive registration and residence proximity laws. I am **outraged** over the scarlet letter I wear on my forehead, or rather, the life sentence I and many other "low-level" offenders are burdened with. It's been almost 20 years for crying out loud. My only recourse is to hire an attorney and petition the court to reduce my registration requirement. I consulted one who told me it's essentially up to whoever the judge is at the time—it's a crap shoot.

If you have ever taken a trip to colonial Williamsburg or any other museum/ tourist place that depicts life in colonial America, one of the features of these places is stocks or pillories, devices used to publicly restrain people. Such is a

---

19. Tewksbury, R. (2007). Exile at home: The unintended consequences of sex offender residency restrictions. *Harvard Civils Rights-Civil Liberties Law Review, 42*, 531–540.

20. Tales from the Registry Website. (2016, March 10). *Nowhere to live in Florida.* Retrieved on September 14, 2018 from https://tftr.narsol.org/?s=Nowhere+to+live+in+Florida.

typical example of corporal punishment. This type of punishment essentially serves three purposes. The first purpose is that having to stand in these devices is painful. The second purpose of this type of punishment is that it is meant to embarrass a person. Not only will casual observers gawk at the people, but they also have been known to throw spoiled foods and other objects at the people. The third purpose of this type of punishment is that it is public. Often accompanying a person who is placed in a set of stocks is some sort of sign stating what crime that person committed. Public punishment in this form is meant to serve as a lesson to others. Examples of corporal punishment are nearly limitless; it all depends on the creativity of people and their willingness to cause harm and suffering to other people.

Despite the presentation of corporal punishment in historical accounts of early American justice, perhaps most famously in Nathaniel Hawthorne's *The Scarlet Letter*, corporal punishment was primarily used as a method to punish slaves and the poor. For people of better social standing and wealth, monetary fines were the preferred punishment against those people who did not face the prospect of the death penalty.[21] While corporal punishment is still used today to varying degrees by parents against their children and in a few school systems, it has been abolished for many years from the criminal justice system. Massachusetts was the first state to do so, in 1805,[22] and the federal government followed suit in 1839. Most states enacted similar prohibitions. The last official instance of public state-sanctioned corporal punishment happened in Delaware in 1952. While not practicing the punishment for many years, in 1986, Delaware became the last state to abolish corporal punishment.[23] Fines are obviously still a part of the American criminal justice system today. There is a good chance you may have paid one in the form of a parking or speeding ticket. Yet, besides the punishment of minor crimes or crimes that are essentially civil in nature (such as corporations cleaning up environmental pollutants), the United States has largely resisted the embracement of monetary fines for crimes deemed more serious. To many people, paying a fine is essentially buying your way out of punishment.[24]

In addition to leaving England and other parts of Europe for greater religious freedoms, colonialists also fled to the Americas to avoid what many perceived as an overreliance on draconian punishments in their native lands. England's criminal statutes, which called for the death penalty for seemingly even petty crimes,

---

21. Preyer, K. (1982). Penal measures in the American colonies: An overview. *The American Journal of Legal History*, 26(4), 326–353.

22. Friedman, L. M. (1993). *Crime and punishment in American history*. New York, NY: Basic Books.

23. Hall, D. E. (1995). When caning meets the Eighth Amendment: whipping offenders in the United States. *Widener Journal of Public Law*, 4, 403–459.

24. Ruback, R. B. (2011). The abolition of fines and fees. *Criminology & Public Policy*, 10(3), 569–581.

was so infamous that it was referred to as the "bloody code."[25] While some American colonies (and later states) might allow such crimes as witchcraft or buggery to be punished with the death penalty, the only crimes for which the death penalty was common were murder and rape, the one great exception to this being the punishment of slaves. For them, death could easily come from committing minor crimes or even breaches of social protocol.[26] At the end of 2016, 27 states had the death penalty and four additional states had the death penalty but were under state-imposed moratoriums by those states governors.[27] As a former associate of the director of a prison oversight agency, Gennifer describes her experience visiting death row.

Narrative: Gennifer's Story

Several places I visited over the years were marked by unique cruelty; one was the unit that housed the state's death row inmates. Most striking was the men's unwillingness to talk with us. They were fighting legal battles to save their lives and get off death row—they were not interested in talking with us about their extra-terrible living conditions. The camera on the wall across from their cells meant they were subject to 24-hour surveillance—an intrusive compromise to their dignity. They were watched even while going to the bathroom. The light in each cell on death row, one large fluorescent fixture on the ceiling, was never shut off. Being helplessly subject to 24-hour illumination took a toll on their mental health. These were understandably angry men. While each had been convicted of homicide, there were thousands of men convicted of taking another's life who were fortunate enough (in the eyes of these men on death row) to be living under the conditions of the general population in a maximum security prison. The crimes committed by the men on death row were not necessarily more heinous than others' but due to extralegal factors, such as where the trial took place and the quality of their defense, they were on death row, while other killers were not.

M. Watt Espy and John Smykla, seeking to determine the number of executions in the United States, collected a database of executions that they referred to as the Espy File. From 1608–2002, they estimated that 15,269 executions took

25. Handler, P. (2005). Forgery and the end of the 'bloody code' in early nineteenth-century England. *The Historical Journal, 48*(3), 683–702.

26. Friedman, L. M. (1993). *Crime and punishment in American history.* New York, NY: Basic.

27. Death Penalty Information Center. *States with and without the death penalty.* Retrieved on April 7, 2018 from https://deathpenaltyinfo.org/states-and-without-death-penalty

place in the United States.[28] Calculating a simple average, this is nearly 39 executions a year. However, this is a bit of an oversimplification; nearly 8,000 of those executions occurred between 1900–1972, and slightly more than 4,000 executions took place from 1850–1899. Although the overall number of executions in the 1900s was greater than previous times, part of the explanation for that increase is due to a rapidly increasing U.S. population. However, the number of executions in the United States have been trending downward in recent years. Through the end of August of 2018, 18 people were executed in the United States.[29] In the previous year, 23 people were executed.[30] Considering the high costs associated with the appellate process and problems obtaining lethal injection drugs, some have speculated whether capital punishment may simply die out from the rarity of the punishment and the high monetary costs.[31]

Given that the United States has not greatly utilized the four aforementioned historical punishments, we are led to the question of how does the United States punish the rest of its criminal offenders? As Lawrence Friedman noted, one of the reasons that the United States, very early in its history, was able to largely abandon the use of corporal punishment was the rise of incarceration as a punishment.[32] The idea of incarceration as a punishment is not necessarily new. Many societies, perhaps most famously the Romans, locked offenders in cages or mines. American jails are derived from the English equivalent *gaols*—facilities operated by sheriffs to house people while they await trial and if found guilty, punishment. Furthermore, the British would incarcerate offenders in prison hulks that are sailing vessels that were either decommissioned or no longer seaworthy. This practice began during the American Revolutionary War because the British temporarily lacked a place to send their convicts. Later, Australia would fill the void as a British penal colony. In the late 1700s, various European countries began to construct prisons, facilities designed to house long-term offenders. However, as renowned prison reformer John Howard noted, these places, which almost universally had deplorable conditions, were primarily meant to warehouse bad people away from good people. Indeed, the first prison in America, Old Newgate Prison, was built for this purpose. This began to change, though, when various states began to build penitentiaries, facilities designed to not only punish but also rehabilitate offenders.[33] How well this works, which will be discussed in greater

---

28. Death Penalty Information Center. Executions in the U.S. 1608–2002: The Espy File. Retrieved on June 3, 2018 from https://deathpenaltyinfo.org/executions-us-1608-2002-espy-file

29. Death penalty Information Center. *Execution list 2018*. Retrieved on September 22, 2018 from https://deathpenaltyinfo.org/execution-list-2018

30. Death penalty Information Center. Execution List 2017. Retrieved on September 22, 2018 from https://deathpenaltyinfo.org/execution-list-2017

31. Griffin, O. H., Woodward, V. H., & Sloan, J. J. (2016). *The money and politics of criminal justice policy*. Durham, NC: Carolina Academic Press.

32. Friedman, L. M. (1993). *Crime and punishment in American history*. New York, NY: Basic.

33. Hanser, R. D. (2017). *Introduction to corrections* (2nd ed.). Thousand Oaks, CA: Sage.

detail in Chapter 4, is a topic of conversation, but at least in theory, American justice is meant to both punish and rehabilitate.

A substantial portion of American criminal offenders are housed in thousands of secure correctional facilities in the United States. Yet, slightly more than 30% of the American population that was under correctional control in December of 2016 were incarcerated. The other 70% were living among us and were enrolled in various forms of community corrections. Indeed, the most common sanction that is given to American offenders is probation. In that same month, almost 3.8 million Americans were on probation. Another 870,000 people were paroled from prisons.[34] As we will discuss in Chapter 5, probation is a type of correctional control that allows people to serve their term of punishment within the community so long as they abide by certain conditions. Parole is a system of early release from prison in which certain offenders, so long as they meet certain requirements while incarcerated and after they are released, are able to serve the rest of their term of punishment outside prison walls. Furthermore, along with these two sanctions, there are a variety of other intermediate sanctions that are designed to be alternatives to incarceration. The variety and complexity seem to increase with each coming year.[35]

34. Kaeble, D., & Cowhig, M. 2018. *Correctional populations in the United States, 2016*. Washington, DC: Bureau of Justice Statistics.

35. Clear, T. R., Cole, G. F., & Reisig, M.D. (2013). *American Corrections* (10th ed.). Belmont, CA: Cengage.

Chapter 2

Philosophies of Corrections

One of the problems in studying corrections is that the American correctional system has multiple goals. As if this is not bad enough, many of these goals conflict with one another, and to top it off, different people will have a plethora of opinions regarding which goals are most important. For the most part, we will avoid discussing some of these rivalries between thoughts and theories, but some are simply necessary to describe or may just be patiently obvious when you read the chapter. Nonetheless, we hope at the very least that after reading this chapter, you will appreciate just how difficult administering a correctional system can be when goals differ between the people who administer the system and are inherent within the system itself.

Retribution

We are going to guess that at some point in your life, a friend or a sibling has hit or pushed you. What was your immediate reaction to this happening? Maybe you are a better person than we are, but there is a high possibility that you wanted to hit or push that person back. To many people, this is simply fairness: what happened to you should happen to the other person. This is at the heart of retribution. Most legal codes have retributive elements. For instance, in Chapter 1, we discussed the Code of Hammurabi, a legal code that was almost absolutely retributive. There are many names for retribution. Among them are deserved punishment, just deserts (or desserts depending upon whom you ask), retaliation, revenge, and a host of others. Some people will call retribution "justice." This is where things get tricky. Within a purely retributive code, such as the Code of Hammurabi, the law will try to enforce a literal equivalent punishment for a violation of law. A legal code will do this so that people do not take the law into their own hands. However, in modern societies where a purely retributive code might appear draconian, it is difficult to completely measure what is the proper retributive response. Since the United States mostly relies upon fines, probation, and other forms of intermediate sanctions and incarceration as punishments, it can be difficult to determine what exactly is a proper response. What is the proper retributive sentence for a person who commits a robbery or perhaps a sexual assault? This is the problem with retribution. People can greatly differ as to what is a just retributive punishment. For this reason, relying completely upon retribution as a measure of success in the penal system is difficult.

Deterrence

One of the reasons that many countries have used the death penalty and especially brutal forms of the death penalty, such as crucifixion, disembowelment, or any other form of painful death, was typically done for two reasons. The first reason is that the state (or perhaps a king, queen, or emperor) wanted the person's death to be painful. The second reason is that the state wanted to make an example of that person to everyone else. If you do this type of crime, this is what happens to you. While the punishments may differ, the American criminal justice system still has many hallmarks of deterrence.

The ideas of deterrence have been around for quite a while, but the first person to actually codify such ideas into a criminological theory was Cesare Beccaria, who some refer to as the father of criminology (he lived from 1738–1794). Beccaria lived in Italy during a time in which judges seemingly made up the law as they saw fit, and the death penalty could be used to punish people for even minor crimes. He believed that this was often counterproductive and could have problematic consequences. In what many scholars have since called the brutalization hypothesis, Beccaria argued that if people thought they could get the death penalty for even a minor crime, they would believe that society was unjust, and they would be willing to commit seemingly any crime to avoid punishment since they could rightly expect to die for the commission of any crime. Thus, Beccaria believed that legal codes were needed to tell people exactly what actions were considered crimes, and the legal code should also include the range of possible punishments for these crimes. Given that human beings can have wide-ranging thoughts about punishment, a person might wonder how do you know what is the correct punishment? Beccaria believed that punishment should be guided by three different elements: certainty, severity, and celerity. If a person believed they might be able to get away with a crime (or not), then Beccaria believed that would potentially deter them (or not) from committing a crime. Thus, if punishment is certain, then that has a high likelihood of keeping them committing the action. Regarding severity, if a person was considering committing a crime or if they know the punishment is either very strict or very lenient, then that should have an effect on a person going through with it. Lastly, celerity is a fancy word for swift or fast. One of the reasons that many countries will punish people right after they are found guilty is as an added deterrent. Beccaria believed any added delay might affect a person's willingness to commit a crime. The further in the future that punishment may be, the more likely they are to commit a crime.[1]

Modern scholars have described two different main types of deterrence. If you take our previous example, giving a person the death penalty would ensure specific deterrence. Indeed, that person will not be able to commit that crime again. Separate from the death penalty, Beccaria and other proponents of deterrence would argue that to ensure specific deterrence, you need to find an appropriate and just penalty to ensure that a person does not commit a crime again. This rationale is based upon the belief that if a person is adequately and fairly punished, they are less likely to commit that crime again. Building upon our previous example once again, one of the reasons that many punishments used to be public was to serve as an example to other people of what would happen to them if they committed a particular crime. Within criminology, this is known as general deterrence.[2]

It is hard to say why deterrence has had such a lasting effect on criminology, perhaps simply because it sounds good. While ideas of deterrence are certainly older than Beccaria, no one really bothered to begin testing whether deterrence principles actually work to reduce criminal offending until the 1960s. Generally speaking, criminologists have found support for certainty affecting people's desistance from crime, but the effects of severity and celerity are inconclusive.[3] For the most part, deterrence seems to work for minor criminal offenses. Part of the problem, though, is that many people who seem to fear the legal consequences of the law are unlikely to commit crimes in the first place. People who commit crimes will often commit additional crimes after being caught and punished.[4] Thus, many scholars have found that other factors, and especially other criminological theories, are needed to try to account for why (or not) principles of deterrence fail to prevent people from committing crimes. One of the most common approaches is rational choice theory, which is essentially a variant of deterrence (largely introduced by economists) trying to assign the benefits and costs of com-

---

1. Beccaria, C. (1963). *On Crimes and Punishment*. Translated with an Introduction by H. Paolucci. New York, NY: Macmillan. Original work published in 1764.

2. Bernard, T. J., Snipes, J. B., & Gerould, A. L. (2015). *Vold's theoretical criminology* (7th ed.). Oxford, UK: Oxford University Press.

3. Nagin, D. S., & Pogarsky, G. (2001). Integrating celerity, impulsivity, and extralegal sanction threats into a model of general deterrence: Theory and evidence. *Criminology, 39*, 865–891.

4. Bernard, T. J., Snipes, J. B., & Gerould, A. L. (2015). *Vold's theoretical criminology* (7th ed.). Oxford, UK: Oxford University Press.

mitting crimes.[5] Such an approach is problematic because who is to say whether a person is acting rationally (or not), and if so, different people may value different things, and some punishments may not be that harsh to some people.

Incapacitation

One issue that has arisen when testing the effect of deterrence on criminal offending is that principles of deterrence can overlap or conflict with other goals or limitations of the correctional system. The main goal of the death penalty and incarceration is to prevent offenders from harming people in general society either on a permanent or periodic basis. While the death penalty deters people from forever committing crime, at least on this plane of existence, people can still commit crimes in a jail or prison. However, it is impossible to know how much or if those people would have committed crime had they not been locked away from society.[6] Nonetheless, the goal of incapacitation is simply preventing people from committing a crime again by removing them from society.

Through many different changes in sentencing policy, at times, the United States has heavily embraced incapacitation as a goal of the correctional system. During the 1930s, the United States had rates of incarceration that were comparable or even lower than European countries. By the 1960s, the American incarceration rate was still comparable to European countries. However, beginning in the late 1970s, American incarceration rates began to increase. During the 1980s and 1990s, American incarceration rates exploded, and the United States became the world leader in the rate in which it incarcerated its citizens.[7] According to Malcolm Feeley and Jonathan Simon, the United States has entered had begun a "new penology" that placed an increase reliance on incarceration to remove greater numbers of "dangerous" people from society.[8] This shift in policy was accompanied by many changes, such as longer sentences (especially for drug offenders), mandatory sentencing policies (such as three strikes laws), and stiffening of parole criteria. In many states, parole was abolished. These changes created what many people have referred to as mass incarceration.[9] In 2007, the American incarceration rate peaked with more than 2.3 million people being confined in prisons and jails and a total of more than 7.3 million people under correctional control. That rate has decreased to more than 2.1 million incarcerated and slightly more than 6.6 million people under correctional control in 2016.

---

5. Akers, R. L., Sellers, C. S., & Jennings, W. G. (2017). *Criminological theories: Introduction, evaluation, and application.* Oxford, UK: Oxford University Press.

6. Gibbs, J. P. (1975). *Crime, punishment, and deterrence.* New York, NY: Elsevier.

7. Tonry, M. (1999). Why are U.S. incarceration rates so high? *Crime and Delinquency, 45,* 419–437.

8. Feeley, M. M., & Simon, J. (1992). The new penology: Notes on the emerging strategy of corrections and its implications. *Criminology, 30,* 449–474.

9. Pratt, T. C. (2009). *Addicted to incarceration.* Thousand Oaks, CA: Sage.

Thus, while incarceration rates have trended slightly downward, the United States is still embracing the incapacitation of a large number of its citizens.[10]

Punishment and Rewards

In some ways, this may seem so basic that it does not warrant discussion. There is simply no way you could have made it this far in life without dealing with punishment and rewards. As we mentioned in Chapter 1, you most likely dealt with these concepts growing up. Say, for instance, that you stayed out one night past curfew. A very simple punishment would be to simply ground you and—except for attending school or various other necessary out-of-home places—forbid you to leave the house at all for a certain period of time. Contrarily, if you received a good grade, your parents might allow you to choose a favorite meal at dinner, or they might even give you a sum of money. There are countless other examples of the imposition of these concepts. Within the American correctional system though, the system is built more on the concept of punishment than rewards. In fact, many people would argue that the primary goal of the penal system is to punish people. While some criminal justice programs are meant to rehabilitate or help people who continually break the law (such as drug treatment), these are still instances in which the government mandates that an offender do something they most likely would not have done on their own volition. Furthermore, while you might hear periodic stories about homeless or poor people purposefully committing crimes so that they can be incarcerated during cold winter months, these stories are isolated incidents. Few people actually enjoy being incarcerated, and most inmates would leave if given the chance to do so.

The fundamental reason that we punish people is that we hope that they will learn from the experience and change their behavior. Studying how people learn is an ancient endeavor and it was the Greek philosopher Aristotle who first articulated that people most often learn through association. He argued that humans lack instincts and acquire all knowledge through experience. People learn through mental images and association. To Aristotle, people made four types of associations to learn: similarity, contrasts, succession in time, and coexistence in space. In more modern terms, people who believe that learning through association comes through memory, ideas, or expectations are referred to as cognitivists. Groups of people, often referred to as behaviorists, largely retain the ideas of Aristotle but state that association occurs through observable stimuli and responses rather than mental images. As the field of psychology was established, three major types of learning emerged. The first, classical conditioning, which was first developed by Ivan Pavlov, posits that learning was a passive process.

---

10. Kaeble, D., & Cowhig, M. (2018). *Correctional populations in the United States, 2016*. Washington, DC: Bureau of Justice Statistics.

This was famously demonstrated by Pavlov's dog salivating after hearing a bell rung because the dog associated the bell ringing with being fed. The second, operant conditioning, was developed by B. F. Skinner. He argued that learning is the result of changed behavior through rewards and punishments. The third, social learning theory, was developed by Albert Bandura. He largely retained the ideas of operant conditioning but also noted that people could learn from the rewards and punishments that happened to other people.[11]

The application of learning into criminological and correctional thought essentially began with the work of Edwin Sutherland. Through his research of professional theft and white-collar crime (a term he coined), Sutherland found that many criminal offenders tended to learn how to commit crimes from others. In a theory he referred to as differential association, Sutherland argued that criminal offenders essentially have the same motivations as law-abiding citizens. The main difference though is that criminal offenders learn different ways to behave and make money. Often, these people will see nothing wrong with what they are doing; they were just taught a different way of life.[12] Later, Robert Burgess and Ronald Akers created what they called a differential association-reinforcement theory as a means of testing whether differential association could predict crime.[13] Over the next 40 years, Ronald Akers would add to the original work, and the final product would eventually become known as social learning theory. Essentially, what he did was integrate the concepts developed by Sutherland with the work of Bandura. Rather than just noting like Sutherland that crime was a learned process, Akers argued that those people who became criminal offenders were more likely to have received some form of positive affirmation while observing or engaging in criminality. These associations not only describe why people first commit crime but also why they will continue to do so.[14]

In his narrative, Dexter gives an example of this process.

Narrative: Dexter's Story

I started with robbery, indiscriminately committing strong armed robberies against people for their jewelry (watches and necklaces) since it was a quick way to get some money. Those acts, along with other criminal acts I

11. Bernard, T. J., Snipes, J. B., & Gerould, A. L. (2015). *Vold's theoretical criminology* (7th ed.). Oxford, UK: Oxford University Press.

12. Akers, R. L., Sellers, C. S., & Jennings, W. G. (2017). *Criminological theories: Introduction, evaluation, and application.* Oxford, UK: Oxford University Press.

13. Burgess, R. L., & Akers, R. L. (1966). A differential association-reinforcement theory of criminal behavior. *Social Problems, 14*, 128–147.

14. Akers, R. L., Sellers, C. S., & Jennings, W. G. (2017). *Criminological theories: Introduction, evaluation, and application.* Oxford, UK: Oxford University Press.

> committed, helped me to gain a favorable reputation among the older criminals. The admiration I received bought me favor to borrow their guns, and sometimes I would go along with them to do robberies since they had stolen cars to assist us to travel to different places where we committed crimes.

While the punishment aspects are easy to see within the correctional system, the rewards aspects are not as plentiful. One prominent way that rewards are given is through good time credits in jail or prison and the process of parole. Essentially, through good behavior and completing various correctional programs (such as drug rehabilitation or job training), a state's Department of Corrections or a parole board can grant an inmate early release. Furthermore, in community corrections, researchers have produced evidence that suggests that offenders on probation and parole actually respond to rewards for positive behavior better than sanctions for negatives behaviors and were more likely to successfully complete their supervision term when rewarding good behavior was the primary means of behavior modification tactic. Thus, while sanctions themselves are inherently punishment, rewards can be built in to help offenders behave and hopefully reform.[15]

Control Theories

Ever heard the saying "idle hands are the devil's workshop" or some other variation? That is essentially what control theories argue, that some people have just too much free time on their hands. While many theories argue that people are either blank slates or naturally good, control theories assume that people left to their own devices are either bad or may just act poorly or do stupid things. Thus, the goal of control theories is often to keep people from being their own worst enemies. There are many different variations of control theories in criminology.[16] In perhaps the earliest version of a control theory in criminology, Albert Reiss argued that juveniles who engaged in delinquency had weak personal controls and failed to submit to the various social controls of society.[17] Similarly, Jackson Toby argued that one of the ways to prevent juveniles from offending was for them to develop stakes in conformity. Youths who perform poorly in school often lack

---

15. Wodahl, E. J., Garland, B., Culhane, S. E., & McCarty, W. P. (2011). Utilizing behavioral interventions to improve supervision outcomes in community-based corrections. *Criminal Justice and Behavior*, 38, 386–405.

16. Bernard, T. J., Snipes, J. B., & Gerould, A. L. (2015). *Vold's theoretical criminology* (7th ed.). Oxford, UK: Oxford University Press.

17. Reiss, A. J. (1951). Delinquency as the failure of personal and social controls. *American Sociological Review*, 16, 196–207.

the incentive to behave. Getting suspended or expelled from school is often what they want.[18] Ivan Nye was the first criminologist to actually describe such a theory using the word *control*. He argued that three different types of social control existed that would influence a juvenile's criminality. The first was direct control. Nye argued that direct control of juveniles was done by parents either rewarding or punishing their children. The second, indirect control, is when a juvenile refrains from committing delinquent acts due to fear of pain and/or embarrassment. Basically, they feared direct control. The third, internal control, is when a juvenile refrains from committing delinquent behavior due to the presence of conscience or guilt.[19] A similar idea was developed by Walter Reckless when he proposed what he called containment theory. He argued that juveniles would develop an inner control system and an outer control system. If these controls were strong, people would be more likely to refrain from engaging in crime and delinquency.[20]

The aforementioned researchers were instrumental in the development of control theory, but the most well-known application of control theory in criminology was developed by Travis Hirschi. In his text *Causes of Delinquency*, Hirschi argued that people who were able to develop strong social bonds were less likely to engage in criminality. According to Hirschi, four factors were predictive of whether people were able to develop social founds: attachment, involvement, commitment, and belief. Regarding attachment, people who are able to develop relationships to other people or institutions (such as school or an organization) are more likely to be law-abiding. People who are involved in conventional activities are less likely to have the time or find the opportunities to commit crimes. If people are committed to normative society, they are less likely to engage in behaviors that question or harm society. Lastly, if people believe that they should follow the rules, they are more likely to do so.[21]

You have undoubtedly been subjected to forms of control theory already, whether you realize it or not. While you may have enjoyed any combination of playing sports, scouting, church groups, band, choir, forensics, 4H, Boys and Girls Club, or any other activity you may have been engaged in during your youth, the time you spent doing these activities was most likely not spent engaging in criminal or delinquent behavior. Maybe some of the people in these programs bent the rules, but it is difficult to actually commit a crime while at soccer practice, unless you really want to commit such an action. Within the correctional system, offenders who are on probation or parole are expected to abide by certain restrictions, such as working a job, maintaining contact with a probation or parole

---

18. Toby, J. (1957). Social disorganization and stake in conformity: Complementary factors in the predatory behavior of hoodlums. *Journal of Criminal Law and Criminology, 48*, 12–17.

19. Nye, F. I. (1958). *Family relationships and delinquent behavior*. Oxford, UK: John Wiley.

20. Reckless, W. C. (1961). A new theory of delinquency and crime. *Federal Probation, 25*, 42–46.

21. Hirschi, T. (1969). *Causes of delinquency*. Berkley, CA: University of California Press.

officer, abiding by a curfew, and many other types of restrictions. The whole ideas of these activities or restrictions is to keep people engaged in prosocial activities and to not have too much free time or be hanging out around the "wrong" people.

Rehabilitation

Keeping a similar theme to the previous section, much of the history of criminal justice and punishment, throughout the world, has witnessed countries using punishment as a mechanism of maintaining control over its citizens. Through the public spectacle of executions and corporal punishments, states, often through kings and queens, sought to continually exert their royal dominance over their subjects.[22] As we mentioned when discussing the contributions of Beccaria to deterrence theory, many of the Enlightenment scholars challenged the idea that criminal justice should be about merely controlling its citizens, but the ideas began that punishment should not be only for the sake of punishment. Instead, punish should also seek to improve the people who are being punished.[23] Thus began the idea that rehabilitation should be one of the goals of punishment. Indeed, the gradual shift from calling the study of punishment penology to corrections reflects this idea. Granted some people still use the term penology, but corrections is more common. Within the United States, rehabilitative ideas began with the invention of the penitentiary. Rather than simply calling a correctional facility a prison, the Quakers, a sect of Christianity that is dedicated to principles of peace, imagined penitentiaries as correctional facilities in which inmates would reflect upon the nature of their sins and hopefully turn their lives around. Many correctional facilities require inmates to work. While some people would argue this is merely a case of the state trying to extort cheap labor, at least the less cynical goal of this process is to teach inmates a work ethic or job skills.[24]

As the 1900s began, the American correctional system began to enact many different rehabilitative principles. Inmates in many correctional facilities began to be viewed as both prisoners and patients who needed diagnosing. Probation and parole statutes were enacted in every state so that offenders could be rehabilitated in the community rather than in prisons. A plethora of job training, educational, psychological, and many other programs were enacted to try to better the long-term prospects of offenders.[25] However, along with the punitive turn in American corrections we previously mentioned came the downfall of rehabilitation. One of

---

22. Foucault, M. (1995). *Discipline and punish: The birth of the prison* (2nd ed.). New York, NY: Vintage Books.

23. Bernard, T. J., Snipes, J. B., & Gerould, A. L. (2015). *Vold's theoretical criminology* (7th ed.). Oxford, UK: Oxford University Press.

24. Clear, T. R., Reisig, M. D., & Cole, G. F. (2015). *American Corrections* (11th ed.). Boston, MA: Cengage.

25. Ibid.

the most often cited events was an article published by Robert Martinson, in 1974, called "What works? Questions and answers about prison reform." In the article, Martinson conducted a comprehensive study of many rehabilitation programs and concluded that very few programs seemed to be effective.[26] As renowned criminologist Francis Cullen would note, regarding what would often be referred to as the *Martinson Report*, Martinson's study was not necessarily novel at the time. Many criminologists had already published studies that demonstrated there was limited effectiveness in correctional programming, and improvements needed to be made. What made the report so influential was that it received an unprecedented level of media attention for an academic study and seemed to conform to what many people wanted to hear—that the correctional system was too soft. Rather than trying to improve these programs, many politicians and citizens instead sought to simply eliminate most of these programs and instead more often rely upon incapacitation strategies for criminal offenders. It would not be until the latter part of the 1990s that American society began to embrace rehabilitative principles again.[27]

Before we discuss the reemergence of rehabilitation again, we ask you to consider when rehabilitation is appropriate. For that matter, when are the other punishment rationales most appropriate? Should we only incapacitate those who we deem the most dangerous, or are those individuals the ones we should try hardest to rehabilitate? These questions are difficult, and unfortunately the system does not always get it right the first time, or the second or third for that matter. Consider Jaimie's story below. She describes what she believes was a missed opportunity at rehabilitation in one case and a waste of it in another. What do you think after reading her story?

Narrative: Jaimie's Story

My first day working for the New Jersey State Parole Board was spent in trainings and confidentiality meetings. I was excited to start this new journey where I had special clearance and a fancy new name tag. My faith was restored. My first assignment was to the Edna Mahan Correctional Facility for Women, where I was to assist the parole hearing officer in prepping release meetings. In addition to this, I was allowed to sit in on parole hearings and engage with the members of the New Jersey State Parole Board. This was nothing short of amazing. This was where I wanted to work, and I never

---

26. Martinson, R. (1974). What works? Questions and answers about prison reform. *The Public Interest*, 35, 22–54.

27. Cullen, F. T. (2005). The twelve people who saved rehabilitation: How the science of criminology made a difference. *Criminology*, 43, 1–42.

wanted to leave. My internship opportunity lasted six months, and during that time, I gained valuable knowledge about the justice system and the inner workings of prison life. I saw my fair share of prison fights and even tried my hand in the prison food (surprisingly similar to the taste of my college cafeteria food). Nothing was going to break my dream now.

As the days went on, I was given more responsibilities and tasks, and my boss gained a great deal of trust in me to perform tasks I probably was not authorized to perform. Part of my job was to review all the cases on the log for the day and look through the details of the case: the crime, the arrest, and the sentencing. I noticed that drugs played an integral part in almost all of these cases, which I had expected. What I had not expected was the wide array of women that I would encounter and the variety of their offenses. Two cases that I had in the same week stood out to me; one in particular has changed me forever.

One morning, when I was reviewing case files with the parole hearing officer, who I had grown to love and admire, I started by reading off the names of the incoming inmates, as we liked to keep a running list of how many girls come and go a day. As I was reading them, she would shake her head in approval that she heard me after every name as she was filing and preparing the never-ending paperwork from yesterday's cases that I would later log into the system. How-ever, I read one name that stopped her in her tracks. She asked me to read it back about three times before accepting that she knew this young girl, who we will call Jackie.

Jackie had been in prison three times in the last five years, and no one ever thought they would see her back after her last visit. She was doing well, had got straight, and was ready to be a good mom to her two-year-old child, who she delivered in between prison stays and was left in the care of her relatives. Jackie was a sad story. She had every possible pink slip she could in her file. These slips indicate infractions the inmates have and are basically write up forms that are taken very seriously if the inmate wants any form of early release on probation.

Jackie had got into drugs at a young age after her mom went through as many new boyfriends as she could to find new strands of drugs. She was born into an affluent, White family, but money and friends did not stop her from her addiction; it only made it worse. Eventually, she turned to stealing for money when her family cut her off, and this led her into some extremely dangerous situations. She would steal money from anyone she could and was frankly not good at doing it well. The drugs made her someone she was not.

One night, she found herself in bed with a man for money, and this was just the start of a vicious cycle of prostitution and drug use, until she couldn't take it anymore. Previously, she had been collared for prostitution, drug paraphernalia, possession, and intent to distribute, but this time was different. We knew after reading the charges that Jackie was here to stay. She was convicted of murder. How did this happen? She was not a murderer; she was pushing drugs but never capable of this. Jackie found herself in bed with a man that did not want to leave. She found herself scared and alone, and withdrawing from the heaviest forms of cocaine, she found herself with no other choice but to bash his head in with the nearest object, a lamp, so that he would not touch her again. Jackie was done. She was to live out the rest of her life in this prison.

This is one example of how my faith started on its next downward spiral. I thought the system could have helped Jackie. There must have been something more we could have done than watch her deteriorate until it got to this point. This was the end of the line for so many women, but Jackie had a chance. What were we doing wrong that we were releasing people who were clearly not ready for release or releasing them to nothing but their old lifestyle? What had we done to Jackie? Although, largely, Jackie made her own choices, I saw her file and did not look down and see charges and arrests. I saw opportunities for us to intervene, which we chose not to take.

The next story that still shakes me and is the reason I lost almost all of my faith in the system that year was a story of a woman who we will refer to as Mary. Mary was a mom of seven children, all between the ages of one through eight. She was not equipped to be a mother, and she knew this herself. She started dating a man that did not like children, and so she thought it would be best to keep her children locked in her basement whenever he came over to avoid them being seen or heard. This went on for many months until one night she left on vacation with her boyfriend for two weeks. Her sister, who had three children that she also kept locked in that same basement, agreed to "check on" the children occasionally and make sure they had water. Unfortunately, her sister was hit by a car just days after Mary went on vacation, and she was bedbound in the hospital with no one to check on the children and feared telling the police about it.

When Mary returned, she found the children had been unattended to, and that one of her children was missing. Upon further investigation, she also saw that her nephew had been lying on the cement floor and was not moving. He was dead. Her son had killed him and fled the basement by breaking through and climbing out of a window. Both the deceased boy and her runaway son were seven years old at the time. They were play-wrestling and her nephew had fallen to the ground, cracked his skull, and bled out. The children were terrified. Instead of calling the police, Mary stuck her nephew's body in a laundry basket and kept it in the basement with the children for many more months.

Eventually Mary and her boyfriend bought a place together and they moved. She moved all of the children, including the boy in the basket, into her new basement, but this time things would be different. Her neighbors eventually called the authorities when they had seen all of the children entering the home on move-in day but had not heard or seen them since. Mary was arrested on only seven counts of child endangerment and had a prison sentence of five to seven years. This broke me. I saw this woman in front of me and heard her talk about her children as if they were dogs, and how unbothered she was that her actions almost took their lives, and that they were now entering the foster care system. She was heartless. And yet, somehow, the system did not see her as this careless, cruel being that she was. It decided to help her and wanted her to go into rehabilitation and eventually probation so that she could try and be a better mother for her children. No amount of therapy or parenting classes was going to fix the monster that I saw in front of me, but it could have fixed Jackie.

This injustice I saw, mixed with the large caseloads and lack of governmental support, led me to my final diminished faith in the justice system. I was broken, and everything I had imagined my-self being able to achieve in this field was gone. Eventually, I realized that this drive was what the justice system needed: people who see the injustice and care enough to fix it, no matter how small the fix is. I did not see myself working directly with victims, or even with offenders, but my faith is back. The system is only as corrupt as we allow it to be, and although I wanted to quit many times, I did see the good of what we do. As I saw the young girls commit suicide be-cause of their abuse, I also held the hands of the girls who watched their offenders get a guilty verdict and get locked up. I saw the women in the prison who had been hooked on drugs and prison since they were 15, but I also saw the few who were released and changed their lives. I guess we need to remember that there will always be bad in this world, but we need to fight for the good.

The rebirth of rehabilitation did not come in the exact form as previous iterations. Rather than a rebirth of the idea that offenders could be completely cured of their problems, new strategies of rehabilitation came from stark realities. It began to be generally perceived that locking up as many people as possible was expensive and often ineffective as well. Furthermore, scholars such as Joan Petersilia documented that thousands of offenders were being released from correctional facilities every year. With no hope of parole for early release and a great reduction in the variety and amount of prison programming, many of these inmates had dim prospects upon release and were very likely to reoffend.[28] Petersilia and many other scholars argued that better planning was needed for the reentry of these people into general society. Thus, rather than use the term rehabilitation, which

28. Petersilia. J. (2003). *When prisoners come home: Parole and prisoner reentry.* Oxford, UK: Oxford University Press.

seemed to be an illusory goal, many correctional policies were rebranded with the buzzword of reentry so that better plans could be made. We do not mean to sound derisive in such a description, just describe the difference in terminology that has occurred.

Dexter gives an example of how a positive reentry experience might help an offender returning to the community:

> Besides my family, there are other people who have been supportive of me and my transition back into society. I managed to get my driver's license within a year, went to see a professional football game, went to a Broadway show in New York City, and have eaten at many restaurants. I like driving at night and going to the movies and the mall. I still have not mastered technology as far as using the computer. Without the help of my niece, I would be the worst. It is sister, my niece, and I who reside in this comfortable two-family home.

Labeling

Perhaps no theory speaks to some of the contradictions and pitfalls of the correctional system more so than labeling theory. As Petersilia wrote, unless you execute offenders or sentence them to life in prison, they will eventually make their way back to society. Yet, as you have probably already encountered, anytime you fill out an application for a job, school, or a loan, a person's criminal background is usually part of the application process. For a lot of reasons, this makes sense. We would probably not want someone becoming a locksmith who has a burglary conviction. However, making it in general society can be difficult after having a criminal conviction. In addition to having to report your criminal record, states often put added restrictions, often referred to as collateral consequences, to people with criminal records. Among these restrictions are limits on the right to vote, serve on a jury, live in certain places, and countless other restrictions. In Chapter 1, we discussed the various restrictions for sexual offenders.

Within criminology, the first person to really develop the idea of labeling was Frank Tannenbaum. He led somewhat of a radical youth. Along with his participation in multiple labor strikes, he was arrested on multiple occasions and was even incarcerated for a year. Eventually, after his release, Tannenbaum earned a bachelor's degree and later a PhD.[29] He even taught at Ivy League universities. Perhaps partly based upon his own experience, Tannenbaum noted that many juveniles engaged in delinquency and dabbled in bad behavior, but society could often overdramatize the acts these kids committed over too often describe these

---

29. Bernard, T. J., Snipes, J. B., & Gerould, A. L. (2015). *Vold's theoretical criminology* (7th ed.). Oxford, UK: Oxford University Press.

acts as "evil." While some of these kids may be bad, the majority are not. Tannenbaum did not specifically use the word "label" but instead argued that juveniles could become tagged with a bad reputation. If they could not shake this reputation, they might become known as a bad kid and later commit additional acts in furtherance of this reputation.[30] Later, Edwin Lemert would actually use the phrase "label" to describe this process. In his text *Social Pathology*, Lemert developed two important terms: primary deviance and secondary deviance. Lemert argued that primary deviance are offenses people commit through their own actions. He argued that any number of criminological theories could be used to describe this process of offending. However, if someone became labeled as a lawbreaker and internalized such a label, they might start to believe that they are indeed a bad person. Lemert stated that any crimes that a person commits that are related to the acceptance of this label is a result of secondary deviance.[31] Put a little differently, Howard Becker argued that when certain rule breakers accepted they were deviant, this became their master status.[32]

To avoid the labeling process, many actions can be taken. For one, the number of collateral consequences can be lessened upon offenders' release from correctional facilities or correctional control. However, many proponents of labeling theory argued that actions needed to be taken much earlier when juveniles are first engaged in lawbreaking. Proponents of labeling theory have generally argued that juveniles need to have their behavior corrected, but the criminal justice system should be the last resort when dealing with juvenile offenders. Various types of diversion programs are needed to keep juvenile offenders out of the system. These can take many forms. One example is rather than a juvenile undergoing the normal arrest policy for breaking the law, a police officer will call the juveniles parent(s) or guardian(s) to come pick the juvenile up and take them home. Diversion programs can give alternative sanctions to incarceration or other forms of correctional control. Perhaps the most extreme was suggested by Edwin Schur when he argued that policies of radical nonintervention should be used. As he suggested, kids should be left alone from the criminal justice system whenever possible.[33]

To decrease the likelihood or diminish the harm from labeling, many different ideas have been proposed. One of the most often cited in criminology was developed by John Braithwaite, which he called reintegrative shaming. Braithwaite is Australian and conducted studies of the Maori people, a group of Polynesian people in New Zealand. He described their use of ritual drum circles that were used

---

30. Tannenbaum, F. (1938). *Crime and the community*. Boston, MA: Ginn.

31. Lemert, E. M. (1951). *Social pathology*. New York, NY: McGraw-Hill.

32. Becker, H. S. (1963). *Outsiders: Studies in the sociology of deviance*. New York, NY: Free Press.

33. Schur, E. M. (1973). *Radical nonintervention: Rethinking the delinquency problem*. Englewood Cliffs, NJ: Prentice Hall.

to shame people who broke the rules. However, after the shaming commenced, the person who had broken the people's trust was forgiven and then officially accepted back into the good graces of the people. Braithwaite argued that this should be among the principles of the criminal justice system. People need to be punished, but they also need to be later forgiven and accepted so that they can properly reintegrate within the community.[34] A slightly similar idea is restorative justice. While restorative justice can take many shapes, it is similar to reintegrative shaming in that offenders need to admit their guilt and be admitted back into the community. However, restorative justice also seeks to introduce the victims of crimes into the process so that not only offenders can be healed and forgiven, but also so that victims can be part of the process and have the opportunity to confront their victims but later forgive them. Thus, rather than focusing on forgiveness of the state, the focus is placed on forgiveness by the victim(s) of crime.[35]

Conflict Theory

There are many different proponents and iterations, but many people believe in the idea of the social contract. Essentially, they believe that people willingly cede different degrees of freedom to the state so that they might be protected. Such a belief is often attributed to Thomas Hobbes in his seminal work *Leviathan*.[36] Advocates of conflict criminology argue that these ideas are bunk. While conflict theories can take many forms, they essentially revolve around the idea that the laws of the state are created by powerful people to the detriment of others. These theories can be Marxist in nature, which argues that state laws are just another mode of capitalistic protections of the elite, and prisons are filled with people who justifiably seek to either change or rebel from these polices.[37] Feminist critiques of the criminal justice system have argued that the criminal justice system is patriarchal nature and seeks to exploit and control women. Of particular emphasis is the attempt to control women's sexuality.[38]

Perhaps the most ubiquitous conflict-oriented critique of the correctional system is that it disproportionately punishes minority populations and particularly African Americans. Two examples come from Michelle Alexander and Loic Wacquant. Michelle Alexander has argued that various sentencing and crime policies, particularly mass incarceration and the war against drugs, have specifically been

---

34. Braithwaite, J. (1989). *Crime, shame, and reintegration*. Cambridge, UK: Cambridge University Press.

35. Zehr, H. (2014). *The little book of restorative justice: Revised and update*. New York, NY: Good Books.

36. Hobbes, T. (1982). *Leviathan*. London, UK: Penguin. Original work published in 1651.

37. Bernard, T. J., Snipes, J. B., & Gerould, A. L. (2015). *Vold's theoretical criminology* (7th ed.). Oxford: Oxford University Press.

38. Chesney-Lind, M., & Pasko, L. (2013). *The female offender: Girls, women, and crime* (3rd ed.). Thousand Oaks, CA: Sage.

enacted to place greater restrictions on African Americans. As the title of text indicates, she has dubbed these circumstances *The New Jim Crow.*[39] Loic Wacquant takes an approach that harkens to both the work of Foucault and Marx. He argued that the purpose of the criminal justice system has always been to manage groups of people who are either dispossessed or dishonored. As African Americans were freed from Jim Crow laws and ghettos, the disproportionate punishment and placement of African American males is a means to control them after they have been largely rejected from deregulated wage-labor markets.[40]

Darryl Davis, an inmate at East Jersey Prison, echoes this sentiment in his story.

Narrative: Darryl Davis's Story

I was convicted of murder in the first degree and sentenced on Christmas Eve 30 years to life to run consecutive to a sentence of 30 years with a 10-year stipulation, making my sentence 40 years to life.

Upon entering New Jersey State Prison, the dark garage that seemed to seal my fate, I walked in those painful shackles down those gloomy hallways of Trenton State Prison. I was a young man, age 27 now. Prior to this, when I was initially arrested, I was only 24 years of age and only had one prior experience with the Department of Correction. Now, I had entered into a world I had no knowledge of, and I was fearful due to the rumors you heard concerning prison and all its horrors.

Fast forward, and it is now 2018, and I have served 30 years of my sentence, and I have so much knowledge about myself and the system that was used to purge me, and what the state meant for evil, God used for his good. But first, I had to come to the end of myself, which is what must take place for every individual who enters into the confines of prison. Whether Black, White, Spanish or other, we must come to terms with who we are, what we have done, and what we can do to change our circumstances. I read a portion of the book *Introduction to Criminal Justice: A Personal Narrative Approach.* In this book, authors Alissa R. Ackerman and Meghan Sacks examine personal accounts from inmates and law enforcement concerning the perspectives they have on the prison culture or institutions.

There was a word used, *prisonization*, which means that some inmates not all take on or assimilate to the values, norms, and customs of prison life. And one of the primary questions was does the prison gets its influences

---

39. Alexander, M. (2012). *The new Jim Crow: Mass incarceration in the age of colorblindness.* New York, NY: The New Press.

40. Wacquant, L. (2001). Deadly symbiosis: When ghetto and prison meet and mesh. *Punishment & Society, 3*, 95–134.

from outside sources or does it stems from the structure of prison in and of itself?

To the first issue, prisonization, I was fortunate to have had a spiritual awakening of sorts. God changed my life personally and set me upon a path that would forever change my destiny. When I say personally, I mean that God, through his Son Jesus Christ, taught me the ways in which he would have me live the life he has blessed me with and continues to do so... So my understandings are grounded in the principals of the Bible, yet I will speak on the level that you will understand, at least I pray that you will. For me, I learned after my awakening that it was a bad thing to be in prison; however, it was even worse for the prison to be inside you, which means I would not allow myself to become what I despised. I saw the bullying, the preying on the weak; I saw the beatings that were unjust by officers who were only men when they were inside their uniforms. I witnessed firsthand the dehumanization from both sides that was self-taught and sought after.

This influence was developed within the prison system by those who were supposed to be in charge of the care of the inmates that were being housed within these walls of confinement. But what I learned was that most of the officers male/female have no clue as to what it takes to treat someone like they themselves would like to be treated. For example, there was an officer in New Jersey State Police (NJSP) who exemplified this attitude, Officer Steve A. Miller. He worked in the ad-seg unit in seven wing, a notorious wing that was located in the basement of NJSP where men would get stabbed, knocked out, and even killed. This officer was well respected by prisoners, and he was the only officer who did not have to walk in fear. He was despised by his fellow officers, who called him an inmate lover. He eventually left that job making $60,000 a year to become a pastor, and eventually God opened up the prison doors SO he could come back into the same prison that he worked to facilitate a Bible study that would be the largest in the prison attended by all men whether Christian, Muslim, gang member, whatever. He had the respect of the men who he treated like men and treated them the way he would have wanted to be treated himself. They eventually plotted to get rid of him, not only him but also several men and women who came into this prison with the mindset to help men change their lives spiritually first.

The forces that influence the prison today has the greatest influence from the outside world. The gang culture thrives off of its ability to network within and without the system, and with the innovation of technology that has now come into the prisons, with social media and emails, a kiosk allows inmates to download music and keep up to date with what is happening on the outside world. However, there is a flip side to this culture. You see, I have had the pleasure to take the time and make an effort to get to know these young men who society has deemed unredeemable! But they are far from that. They are largely misunderstood, and when society does not understand something or someone, they classify it as insignificant.

The prison has created classes within the system of those who are allowed to have certain privileges, which causes a divide among the population of prisoners. It is like the Willie Lynch Letter: how to keep a slave a slave for the next 300 years. You pit the young against the old, the light skinned against the darker skinned. In this case, you utilize the same concept, only on a broader scale. The jobs that pay the most are those jobs that not many African American males can do, e.g., plumbing, electricians, and the ones that they can learn such as painting or cementing. They simply won't get them because they are of a different race. The availability of the jobs that Blacks do qualify for are the kitchen jobs in food service, porters, anything that has to do with a different sort of labor. Even in the commissary where they sell goods for inmates, such as food and toiletries, most of those workers are also Caucasian or Spanish but very few Black workers because of the stereotype placed on them as thieves. So when you have this type of structure in the prisons, the only way to combat that is to create a system within a system, which brings into play the gang cultures and fear as a weapon used to equal the playing field. It has come full circle now because in spite of the DOC's best efforts, they cannot control the in-flux of men into who come this system who have made names for themselves on the streets, what officers who they control. Now you're on a higher level of structure that the system deems as wrong; however, when you are battling a corrupt system like the DOC, you find yourself with no real alternatives if you keep your eyes closed.

I opened my eyes, and like I said, realized early on that I knew being in prison was a bad thing, but allowing the prison to infiltrate my mind and character was an even worst ordeal. So at age 50, I set out to get my education. I obtained my General Equivalency Diploma (GED), and after getting my diploma, I set out to earn a college degree. I am currently only four classes away from accomplishing that, and I plan to go further by earning a bachelor's in criminal justice.

So does the outside world influence the prison system? Absolutely, and does the influence also stem from the structure of the DOC? Certainly! The real issue is and has been since the very off-set, what is the answer? In short, like I said, we must first deal with the entire picture of the per-son involved, and this requires time and money as well as work. Instead of simply looking at the crime committed, let's go into why the crime was even thought to be committed in the first place. Every action will have an equal reaction; therefore, if you have an inner city whose young Black men are disenfranchised and living in poverty, what do you expect from them? When you have young Black men being gunned down unmercifully by White men uniforms because they are afraid of Black men, what do you think will be the end results? This system goes all the way back to the systemic practices of slavery in America, when Africans were forced to come to this country and literally build it from the blood and death of a people America never has looked at as citizens. Today, prisons are simply a new form of slavery. Prisons are the new plantations, correctional officers are the new slave masters, and in every area you have a White overseer who implements new policy for the slaves they govern.

This is bigger than what we want to believe, but first we have to be truthful. And any real narrative that is going to speak to this has to come from all the voices, and that costs money and time. There is an African proverb I learned from one of my classes with Professor Ike Methusaleh Dunn out of Philadelphia Temple University:

Until the Lions tell their tale, the story will always glorify the hunter.

Chapter 3

Law of Corrections

Until the middle of the 20th century, once a person was found guilty of a crime, they seemingly lost all of their rights and were often at the mercy of the state. Many Americans languished in correctional facilities, essentially forgotten souls and without any real legal recourse to challenge their punishment. In this chapter, we discuss how the courts became involved in the practice of corrections, the rights of people who have been convicted of crimes, and how the courts can intervene in the process of punishing offenders.

As the very first sentence of the U.S. Constitution indicates, "We the people of the United States, in Order to form a more perfect Union," the framers of the Constitution had largely focused on fixing the problems of the Articles of Confederation. This task largely involved making the 13 former British colonies a unified group of states rather than a loose confederation of essentially autonomous republics. The Constitution laid out the construction of the new federal government, including the three branches of government: legislative, executive, and judicial. Despite these new innovations in more efficient government, a common complaint immediately after the U.S. Constitution was first written and being presented for ratification to the states was that it lacked any description of the freedoms and rights that were vested in the new republic's citizens. This led to the creation of the Bill of Rights, the first 10 amendments to the Constitution.[1] These first 10 amendments are simultaneously a list of complaints about British authorities' treatment of American colonists during colonial rule and a list of basic rights and freedoms that American citizens would have from the newly

---

1. Griffin, O. H., Woodward, V. H., & Sloan, J. J. (2016). *The money and politics of criminal justice policy*. Durham, NC: Carolina Academic Press.

created American federal government. Many of these rights you have most likely heard of such as the freedom of speech, freedom of religion, freedom from being compelled to be a witness against one's self, and a freedom from cruel and unusual punishment.

Despite this progressive new form of government with individual rights and protections, it did little good at the time. While the new federal government solved many problems, such as developing one form of currency for all of the states, the Bill of Rights and new Constitution did little for most people within the criminal justice system at the time of ratification. Why? The United States is guided by a system of federalism, which encourages different levels of government. In the United States, there are many different levels of government, including federal, state, county, and municipal (cities and towns). Such a system, especially for a country the size of the United States, is inherently practical because there are many different problems that are best regulated through different levels of jurisdiction. Within the United States, criminal justice is primarily a state endeavor. In the late 1700s, while there were federal courts, these institutions were rarely used simply because there were so few federal laws to enforce. Crimes such as murder, larceny, robbery and others are state crimes that are most often prosecuted by either state, county, or municipal (city or town) prosecutors.[2]

For much of the United States's history, the federal and state courts routinely ruled that people who were prosecuted in state courts, punished by state authorities, and held in state or local correctional facilities were not entitled to the protections of the U.S. Constitution. To the justices and judges of those courts, whatever protections were found in state laws and state constitutions was controlling, not the federal constitution. Thus began what many people have referred to as the "hands-off" period of corrections. For many years, the federal courts left the oversight of state corrections operations to state courts, regardless of what abuses or brutalities took place.[3]

The decision of the federal courts to not apply the Bill of Rights to the states has always seemed curious to many people. Indeed, within the Constitution is the supremacy clause that states that the document "shall be the supreme law of the land."[4] Yet, at least for a long while, the federal courts simply turned away state complaints to federal courts. This process began to change, in 1884, with a case before the Supreme Court called *Hurtado v. California*. In that case, Joseph Hurtado had been tried and convicted of murder in a California state court and received a death sentence for his crime. From the court records, it did not seem that Hurtado's appellate attorney wasted much time claiming his client was innocent.

---

2. Freidman, L. M. (1993). *Crime and punishment in American history*. New York, NY: Basic.

3. Gideon, L., & Griffin, O. H. (2017). *Correctional management and the law: A penological approach*. Durham, NC: Carolina Academic Press.

4. U.S. Const. art. VI.

Instead, his attorney challenged the process through which Hurtado's conviction and sentencing had been obtained. Before Hurtado's trial had commenced, he was charged by information. This means that rather than have a preliminary hearing or a grand jury review the evidence in the case prior to a trial being held, Hurtado went straight from being arrested to going to trial. This might not seem like a big deal to many people, but typically before a defendant goes to trial, their case is usually previewed by a judge through a preliminary hearing, or a prosecutor will present a case to a grand jury. In either proceeding, if probable cause is found, a defendant will then be tried for their alleged crime. Within a preliminary hearing or grand jury hearing, the burden of proof is probable cause, much less than the guilt beyond a reasonable doubt standard of a criminal trial.[5] Thus, to many people, it might not seem like a big deal that Hurtado's case did not receive either type of preliminary review. Indeed, if he was found guilty in a criminal trial and given a death sentence, a previous judge or grand jury most likely would have found probable cause that Hurtado had committed the crime. However, preliminary hearings and grand jury proceedings are part of a set of checks and balances within due process. Even if a defendant seems completely guilty, it is still necessary to go through the full process.

Within the Fifth Amendment of the U.S. Constitution, it states that "No person shall be held to answer for a capital, or otherwise infamous crime, unless on a presentment or indictment of a Grand Jury." There are a few exceptions to this clause of the amendment; however, none of them were pertinent to Hurtado's case. To many people, this case would seem like a slam dunk. Hurtado's rights were violated, his conviction should be dismissed, and proceedings should start anew. That did not happen, though. Despite Hurtado's objections, the Supreme Court once again ruled that despite a seeming clear protection, the Bill of Rights did not apply to the states. However, within this decision, Justice John Marshall Harlan dissented from the other justices of the Court. At that time, the American Civil War had only been over for 19 years. Within the wake of the war, the Constitution was amended three times. The Thirteenth Amendment was ratified in 1865, the same year the war ended. It abolished slavery. The Fourteenth Amendment was ratified three years later in 1868. While the amendment was long and accomplished several things, the most important of which was that it granted equal protection of law to all citizens who were born or naturalized within the United States. The Fifteenth Amendment was passed in 1870. It guaranteed the right of all citizens to vote regardless of race. To many people, the ratification of these three amendments simply seemed natural in the aftermath of the Civil War and sought to make sure that newly freed African Americans slaves would be treated as full citizens. Despite this intent, Justice Harlan had a new creative use for the Fourteenth Amendment.

---

5. Samaha, J. (2008). *Criminal procedure* (7th ed.). Belmont, CA: Thomson Wadsworth.

Justice Harlan wrote that the Fourteenth Amendment did not just give a new group of people constitutional rights, but that all state citizens should enjoy the rights and protections of the U.S. Constitution. Thus, Harlan ruled that the Fifth Amendment protection should have applied to the proceedings in Hurtado's case. While it did not happen overnight, beginning in the 1940s, more and more justices of the Supreme Court began to accept the idea that via the Fourteenth Amendment, the protections of the U.S. Constitution should be extended to defendants in state courts. This idea has come to be known as the incorporation doctrine. It is not absolute and does not apply to all amendments.[6] For instance, the Seventh Amendment, by its language, only applies to proceedings in federal civil courts; the Third Amendment's protection against the government quartering troops in people's homes simply does not occur (or at least only in the rarest cases); and no one is completely sure what the Ninth Amendment means. However, relevant to corrections, state courts must adhere to the First, Fourth, Fifth, Sixth, and Eighth Amendments of the U.S. Constitution. Later in this chapter, we will discuss these rights and how they are applied to people under correctional control; however, before we do that, it is important to discuss the rights of people under correctional control. This is important because for a long time, people simply believed that people under correctional control, and especially prison and jail inmates, had no rights.

While many defendants in state courts benefited from the so-called due process revolution in which the state courts had to abide by many provisions of the Bill of Rights,[7] the federal courts were reluctant to entertain lawsuits from prisoners, probationers, and parolees. The main reason for such a position was that according to the courts, beyond legal issues, the courts were ill-suited to determine the needs of the correctional system. According to the courts, professionals within the correctional system were best able to understand what was needed to manage correctional clients, and the courts seemed to openly worry that applying many protections of due process to these people might interfere with the ability of the correctional system to manage their clients.[8] However, as an outgrowth of the civil rights, captives within the correctional system increasingly perceived their treatment and their lack of civil rights as unfair. Not only did this lead to an increasing number of inmate activism but also an increase in prisoner lawsuits protesting their treatment.[9]

---

6. Samaha, J. (2008). *Criminal procedure* (7th ed.). Belmont, CA: Thomson Wadsworth.

7. Griswold, E. N. (1971). The due process revolution and confrontation. *University of Pennsylvania Law Review, 119*(5), 711–729.

8. Turner, W. B. (1971). Establishing the rule of law in prisons: A manual for prisoners' rights litigation. *National Black Law Journal, 1*, 99–119.

9. Garland, D. (2001). *The culture of control: Crime and social order in contemporary society.* Chicago, IL: University of Chicago Press.

Inmate Lawsuits

Before we can discuss the individual constitutional rights that inmates have, it is important to discuss how inmates can claim these rights. One of the most common tactics of inmates, when claiming that their rights have been violated, is to file a habeas corpus petition. Habeas corpus, which is a Latin phrase meaning "you have the body," is a legal mechanism that dates back to before the Middle Ages in England. Such a legal challenge was meant to challenge the often arbitrary and indiscriminate rule of monarchs. In particular, a habeas corpus petition is meant to stop the practice of incarcerating people for long periods of time without charging them with a crime. Such a right was so important to the founding fathers that they put it into the Constitution with the caveat that it could only be suspended during times of rebellion, invasion, or if "public safety requires it." The U.S. Judiciary Act of 1789 authorized the federal courts to hear habeas corpus petitions from federal prisoners, and later the Habeas Corpus Act of 1867 empowered the federal courts to hear habeas corpus petitions of state prisoners.[10]

One of the reasons that federal courts did not hear a great number of state inmate lawsuits was that the courts had a very narrow reading of habeas corpus petitions. Typically, the courts would only consider whether an inmate had been tried in the proper criminal court in the appropriate jurisdiction.[11] For instance, in 1941, the Supreme Court, in *Ex Parte Hull*,[12] ruled that prison officials could not take actions against inmates that prevented them from filing habeas corpus petitions. The Court did not necessarily give inmates any new rights but instead just merely stated prisons and jails could not prevent inmates from filing this type of litigation. It was not until the 1960s that the federal courts and the U.S. Supreme Court began to more broadly interpret the scope of habeas corpus petitions and would review many different aspects of inmates' lives under the correctional system. In 1964, the Supreme Court, in *Cooper v. Pate*,[13] ruled that inmates could file lawsuits alleging violations of their civil rights under Section 1983 of the Civil Rights Act.

One example of an inmate complaint in a typical habeas corpus motion comes from Ronald:

> I filed a federal writ of habeas corpus against the Department of Corrections and against the NJ State Parole Board. My sole argument was the lack of a presentence report prevented me from ever being considered for Community Release Programs by the NJDOC, and that I could NEVER get a fair parole hearing without the mandatory presentence report. In August 2017, I filed a petition for a writ of mandamus in the U.S. Third Circuit Court of

---

10. Samaha, J. (2008). *Criminal procedure* (7th ed.). Belmont, CA: Thomson Wadsworth.
11. Ibid.
12. Ex parte Hull, 312 U.S. 546 (1941)
13. Cooper v. Pate, 378 U.S. 546. (1964)

Appeals, seeking them to order the District Court to decide my 2015 habeas corpus petition that had been pending almost two years with no requirement of an answer to be filed by the state. Ten days later, the U.S. District Court issued an angry decision denying my petition for a writ of habeas corpus, finding that the issue was time barred. I am currently appealing this decision in the U.S. Third Circuit.

Yet, while many justices and judges in the federal judiciary have sought to greatly expand the rights of inmates, many people believe that this has come at a cost. While some people believe that inmates simply do not deserve any rights, others have noted that inmate lawsuits have clogged up the courts. For instance, in 2012, 126,714 lawsuits were filed by or on behalf of prisoners that accounted for 9.38% of cases heard by federal magistrates that year.[14] Furthermore, there has been the concern that inmates could potentially file multiple habeas corpus petitions. Within American law, there is the principle of res judicata, which means that once a legal issue is decided, it should not be heard again.[15] As a means to combat the latter point in 1966 and later in 1996, Congress limited the ability of inmates to file multiple petitions and codified in federal law that inmates could only file one habeas corpus petition unless that inmate alleged they suffered a new type of abuse by prison officials that would warrant a new legal action against prison officials. However, what has perhaps been the greatest limitation on inmate litigation has been the Prisoners Litigation Reform Act (PLRA), which was passed by Congress and signed by President Bill Clinton in 1996. The law placed limits on the manner in which inmates could file lawsuits and also limited the circumstances in which the federal judiciary could intervene in matters involving state prisoners. Of particular importance was that PLRA mandated that before state inmates could even file lawsuits in federal courts, they must first exhaust all legal remedies in state courts but must also exhaust all remedies within their prison/jail grievance system.[16]

While filing lawsuits in state courts might not seem especially daunting to inmates, since the main fear with these lawsuits is that state courts are unsympathetic, filing grievances with a prison/jail can make an inmate nervous. While some correctional officers might merely view inmate complaints as part of the job, other officers might have a reason to fear such proceedings because they actually committed some wrong against the inmates. This can cause issues, as Victor noted in his narrative: "Before I once wrote a grievance against a correctional officer, I had to first write two lawyers, the prison ombudsman, the DOC com-

---

14. Griffin, O. H., Woodward, V. H., & Sloan, J. J. (2016). *The money and politics of criminal justice policy.* Durham, NC: Carolina Academic Press.

15. Samaha, J. (2008). *Criminal procedure* (7th ed.). Belmont, CA: Thomson Wadsworth.

16. Gideon, L., & Griffin, O. H. (2017). *Correctional management and the law: A penological approach.* Durham, NC: Carolina Academic Press.

missioner in Trenton, and my family so that everyone would know, if it were to happen this way, why I got jumped by officers, thrown into solitary confinement, or transferred to another prison." However, he noted that a grievance filed by an inmate had produced some good. According to Victor, "One student boldly decided to write a grievance to administration about this issue. In response to this, the officers were even more vigorous in sabotaging this individual's college material and also threatened him with physical violence. After a long and hard battle between him and custody, certain officers were reprimanded, and some were even reassigned to new posts so they could no longer harass college students."

Inmate Rights

As you can tell from the previous section, inmates are guaranteed a right to the courts, but they must go through the proper procedures to get there. If an inmate decides they do not like their prospects in prison/jail grievance procedures or state courts, they still need to go through these procedures; if not, the federal courts will dismiss inmate lawsuits. This is true even if inmates have valid claims. Like so many other things, process matters!

Although inmates do not lose all rights once they enter a jail or prison, inmates certainly have diminished rights and will not receive the same strict scrutiny protections or heightened scrutiny protections that many citizens enjoy while living on the outside of correctional facilities. While it is necessary to not take away all rights from inmates, correctional agencies still have a job to do. For this reason, the courts will in many cases defer to the interests of correctional agencies if regulations are needed that may inhibit the civil rights of inmates. Perhaps the most often cited Supreme Court case that illustrates this principle is *Turner v. Safley*.[17] In that case, the Court ruled that when evaluating inmate rights, courts should use the rational basis test. If a prison/jail rule is reasonably related to a valid penological interest, then the regulation is permissible. On the other hand, if a prison/jail rule inhibits a constitutional right and is not rationally related to a valid penological interest, then the regulation is unconstitutional. While we cannot reasonably discuss all of the rights of inmates in one chapter in an introduction to corrections textbook, in the pages that follow we will try to provide you with the essential highlights of inmate constitutional rights.

First Amendment Rights

The First Amendment to the U.S. Constitution guarantees Americans the freedom of religion and speech, freedom of the press, and the freedom to peaceably assemble and petition the government. The First Amendment is considered

---

17. Turner v. Safley, 482 U.S. 78 (1987).

among Americans as the most important and cherished rights and one of the hallmarks of a free society. While there are many exceptions to the First Amendment for people in general society, such as engaging in speech that causes a clear and present danger or yelling "fighting words," inmates can expect severely diminished First Amendment rights. As you can guess, though, prisons and jails are not free societies. Thus, there will be entirely different restrictions on the First Amendment rights of inmates. For instance, one freedom that inmates would seemingly not be able to assert is the freedom to peaceably assemble. Within prisons and jails, administrators need to be able to regulate the behavior of inmates. There are routines and procedures that must be followed, and it would be folly to allow inmates to gather and protest the actions of correctional administrators as a group of free citizens would, such as various groups of people gathering at state capitals or marching in Washington, DC. Peaceful or not, any such gathering could quickly lead to a disturbance and/or a riot—something correctional facilities seek to avoid at all costs. In a different vein, since prison administrators cannot prevent inmates from filing grievances or lawsuits, inmates will not be able to claim that they are prohibited from petitioning the government. Therefore, this section will largely discuss free speech and religious rights and to a much lesser degree, freedom of the press regarding the correctional system.

As Aaron Caplan has discussed, when the courts consider inmates' freedom of speech rights, comparisons are often made to the rights of children at school. While some people might find such a comparison strange, children and prisoners are both being kept in an environment in which they have limited rights and administrators (whether in school or a prison) need to maintain discipline.[18] Many of the people reading this textbook have never been incarcerated but most will have attended school at some point in their lives. Whether on a bus ride or having class with a substitute teacher, many children have witnessed when a failure to control behavior results in some amount of chaos. Furthermore, talking back to teachers could result in a verbal reprimand, detention, or worse. These things also hold true for inmates. Although prison officials may not discipline inmates every time they utter vulgarity or talk back to a correctional officer (if this happened, prison disciplinary hearings would be overwhelmed), but prison officials are certainly allowed to write up an inmate if a correctional officer believes it is necessary. Yet, school children have some rules of expression that inmates would not be allowed. While some schools require that students wear some form of uniform, most do not. In those schools, students have been allowed to engage in various forms of protest through dress. For instance, in *Tinker v. Des Moines*

---

18. Caplan, A. H. (2010). Freedom of speech in school and prison. *Washington Law Review*, 85, 71–105.

Independent Community School District,[19] the Supreme Court ruled that students could wear black armbands to protest the Vietnam War while they were at school. Yet, beyond mild forms of political protest, schools are routinely allowed to restrict the dress of students if there is a vulgar and/or distracting message—even if a statement is partially political. On the other hand, inmates generally wear uniforms. Aside from a few different types of clothing that inmates can buy in a prison commissary, inmates can show very little expression in their dress. Thus, inmates are typically denied, based upon the grounds of penological purposes, from many free speech protections.

The most protected speech rights of inmates involves their use of reading materials and sending or receiving mail. In the earliest prisons in the United States, inmates were allowed to possess one book: the Bible. As will be discussed later, this was largely due to the Quaker influence of early prisons and the belief that the path toward rehabilitation required inmates be penitent and essentially get right with God.[20] Later, as correctional facilities began to establish libraries, and inmates were allowed to possess personal reading materials, rules needed to be established regulating these materials. One of the most common rules is that inmates can only obtain reading materials from the prison library or directly through a publisher, which is usually done through purchase orders that have to be approved by correctional authorities (typically the warden of a facility). This is due to the fear that visitors might provide reading materials to inmates that may contain contraband. Additionally, the subject matter of reading materials is highly regulated.[21] In *Thornbaugh v. Abbott,*[22] the Supreme Court reviewed regulations enacted by the Federal Bureau of Prisons regarding what were permissible reading materials for prisoners. Within those rules, any reading material that discussed the manufacture of any form of contraband, materials that could be used to help an escape attempt and/or violence, materials that encourage illegal activity or could cause violence, and sexually explicit materials were prohibited. The Court ruled that these were valid restrictions. Upholding the constant theme from *Turner v. Safley*, the restrictions were valid and had a rational basis to penological interests.

Regarding inmate mail, there are generally two different types that have different degrees of protection. If an inmate is corresponding with legal counsel, these materials are marked confidential, and correctional officers can only inspect the contents with an inmate present. Any mail that is sent from an inmate to family and/or friends can be inspected by correctional authorities (many states do

---

19. Tinker v. Des Moines Independent Community School District, 393 U.S. 503 (1969).

20. Clear, T. R., Reisig, M. D., & Cole, G. F. (2016). *American Corrections* (11th ed.). Boston, MA: Cengage.

21. Gideon, L., & Griffin, O. H. (2017). *Correctional management and the law: A penological approach.* Durham, NC: Carolina Academic Press.

22. Thornbaugh v. Abbott, 490 U.S. 401 (1989)

so without inmates being present during the inspection) and can be rejected or withheld for a variety of reasons.[23] For instance, in South Dakota, the Department of Corrections website lists a number of regulations that must be followed when sending inmates mail. In addition to general restrictions that are similar to restrictions on reading materials, mail must have a return address. Cash cannot be sent to inmates. Instead, a money order or check can be sent. Some facilities only accept money orders or checks directly to a correctional administrator. Envelopes must be white, and there are even restrictions on the color and type of writing utensil (no crayons are allowed). Furthermore, only written messages are allowed, but if the writing includes references to criminal behavior, the mail can be confiscated.[24] Despite these regulations, in *Procunier v. Martinez*,[25] the Supreme Court ruled that prison officials cannot be overly broad in restricting the substance of conversations between inmates and friends and/or family members. If there is not a valid penological interest or security concern, so long as inmates and the people with whom they correspond follow a general set of rules and regulations, conversations should not be censored. Mail should not be denied if an inmate or a non-inmate complained about correctional officials in a nonthreatening way. Indeed, in a case before the Fifth Circuit Court of Appeals, the court ruled that an inmate could not be punished for writing in a letter that the correctional staff who read the letter "were masturbating and having sex with cats."[26] According to that court's judgment, no threat was given, and the phrase was not uttered in front of correctional officers or administrators that might cause a disciplinary problem. While inmates are given some latitude in the people with whom they correspond, inmates are not allowed to send and receive mail to inmates within their own or other correctional facilities unless they are codefendants in a case. This blanket restriction is given due to a fear that inmates are engaging in criminal behavior and/or trading coded messages. Some states will make exceptions if another inmate is a family member. Lastly, except for cutting off mail to legal counsel, inmate mail privileges can be suspended for periods of time as a result of disciplinary infractions.[27]

In a day and age when we discuss fake news, which media outlets are biased, and many people get their news from social media, it is easy to lose sight of why the founding fathers regarded the freedom of press as a right that needed to be

23. Gideon, L., & Griffin, O. H. (2017). *Correctional management and the law: A penological approach*. Durham, NC: Carolina Academic Press.

24. South Dakota Department of Corrections. *Frequent questions: Inmate mail*. Retrieved on March 13, 2018 from https://doc.sd.gov/about/faq/mail.aspx

25. Procunier v. Martinez, 416 U.S. 396 (1974)

26. Caplan, A. H. (2010). Freedom of speech in school and prison. *Washington Law Review*, 85, 71–105. Quote on page 85.

27. Gideon, L., & Griffin, O. H. (2017). *Correctional management and the law: A penological approach*. Durham, NC: Carolina Academic Press.

guaranteed in the First Amendment. Indeed, under colonial rule, the British authorities greatly restricted the freedom of press of American colonialists.[28] It was important to the founding fathers to protect this freedom because not only is it an extension of freedom of speech that non-slanderous or non-libelous speech be protected from criminal prosecution but also what has become the media ideally serves as a watchdog of government. For this reason, the media has often been given greater access to places than normal citizens so that they may perform this role. Indeed, among the places that the media has obtained greater access to are correctional facilities. Many state laws will allow journalists to tour correctional facilities.[29]

While not a member of the media, in her narrative, Gennifer Furst aptly described the need for oversight of correctional facilities:

Today, prison monitoring is used as a way to protect the civil rights of incarcerated people and to ensure that legal standards of humane treatment are upheld. Mass incarceration and decreased prison programming, including educational and vocational programs, has resulted in prisons becoming increasingly dangerous places for inmates and staff. Prison administrators are tasked with combating violence, gang activity, and spread of disease with limited resources. Exposing what occurs in prisons is crucial for public accountability and to reduce the likelihood of human rights violations. However, gaining access to prisons remain one of the biggest challenges in meeting these objectives. Prison officials accustomed to operating free from public scrutiny are often apprehensive to open their gates to the wondering eyes of outsiders.

Yet, while state laws may provide such protections, in two cases, *Pell v. Procunier*[30] and *Saxbe v. Washington Post Co.*,[31] the Supreme Court ruled that beyond state law protections allowing greater access to correctional facilities, there is no constitutional guarantees that allows journalists unfettered access to these facilities. Furthermore, correctional authorities can block media organizations from meeting specific inmates for face-to-face interviews. Within many visitation policies for correctional facilities, an inmate can only receive visitors from friends, family, or clergy members. Many correctional facility administrators believed that allowing the media to interview specific inmates often resulted in these inmates obtaining a degree of fame, which, it was believed, could cause jealousy and/or power differentials among inmates. One example of such a situation was

---

28. Kurland, P. B. (1985). The original understanding of the freedom of the press provision of the first amendment. *Mississippi Law Journal, 55*, 225–258.

29. Nimmer, M. B. (1975). Introduction—Is freedom of the press a redundancy: What does it add to freedom of speech. *Hastings Law Journal, 26*(3), 639–658.

30. Pell v. Procunier, 417 U.S. 817 (1974)

31. Saxbe v. Washington Post Co., 417 U.S. 843 (1974)

the killing of notorious serial killer Jeffrey Dahmer. Christopher Scarver, who was already serving a life sentence in Wisconsin's Columbia Correctional Center, carried around a newspaper article detailing the many horrific crimes that Dahmer had committed. One day, Scarver confronted Dahmer with the details of his crimes. When Scarver did not receive an answer he liked, he beat Dahmer to death with a metal bar.[32] To try to minimize such situations, many correctional facilities restrict media members from these face-to-face interviews and only allow journalists to correspond with inmates via mail. In the two aforementioned cases, media organizations attempted to challenge these regulations, arguing that as media members, they needed access to newsworthy events. As they argued, such a right was guaranteed by the First Amendment's protection of freedom of the press. However, the Court did not agree with this assertion. It instead ruled that as long as visitation policies were based upon penological goals and did not block all access, the media did not have a right to interview in person any inmate they chose.

As we have discussed, many of the first correctional facilities in the United States were founded upon religious principles. Correctional facilities are very different today. Criminological and penological theory have evolved a great deal since that time, and a whole host of factors have been identified, beyond a lack of subservience to a deity, that explain why people commit crime. Furthermore, due to various Supreme Court rulings and other factors, religiosity has become less apparent in many state-sponsored activities. Yet, in correctional facilities, religion and spirituality still have a heavy presence. One of the reasons, as we will shortly discuss, is that the courts have routinely ruled that inmates should not be stopped from participating in religion and/or spiritual activities.[33] The other reason is that a plethora of research has demonstrated that for inmates, religious and spiritual activities can increase prosocial behaviors, which in turn are likely to encourage inmates to behave while they are incarcerated and reintegrate into society upon release.[34] Evidence that religion and spirituality could cause prosocial behaviors was a big factor in President George W. Bush and his administration advocating for more faith-based initiatives in America's correctional facilities.[35]

---

32. Schram, J. (2015, April 28). Why I killed Jeffrey Dahmer. *New York Post*. Retrieved on May 20, 2018 from https://nypost.com/2015/04/28/meet-the-prisoner-who-murdered-killer-cannibal-jeffrey-dahmer/

33. Gideon, L., & Griffin, O. H. (2017). *Correctional management and the law: A penological approach.* Durham, NC: Carolina Academic Press.

34. Kerley, K. R., Matthews, T. L., & Blanchard, T. C. (2005). Religiosity, religious participation, and negative prison behaviors. *Journal for the Scientific Study of Religion, 44*(4), 443–457.

35. Gideon, L., & Griffin, O. H. (2017). *Correctional management and the law: A penological approach.* Durham, NC: Carolina Academic Press.

First Amendment

Within the First Amendment is the free exercise clause. The First Amendment states "Congress shall make no law respecting an establishment of religion, or prohibiting the free exercise thereof . . ." While the establishment clause protects Americans from being compelled to join a state-sponsored religion, the free exercise clause protects most religious activities from state interference. That being said, there are limitations. For instance, the state would not allow a religion that believes in human sacrifice to practice this belief. However, as Michael McConnell noted, the courts have never been able to completely agree on whether to grant exemptions for people from laws if they have a sincere religious belief or whether legal authorities are only forbidden from strictly targeting certain religions and their belief from legal discrimination.[36] In some instances, the Supreme Court has created exemptions for people from laws, such as ruling that Amish parents cannot be punished for refusing to send their children to school.[37] In other cases, the Supreme Court has refused. Such was the case when the Supreme Court ruled that members of The Church of Jesus Christ of Latter-Day Saints could not engage in polygamy.[38] One example in which the Supreme Court struck down a law that in their opinion purposefully targeted a religion is *Church of Lukumi Babalu Aye, Inc. v. City of Hialeah*. In that case, a group of people in Hialeah, Florida, practiced Santeria. During worship, members of the religious group would, on occasion, sacrifice animals, a recognized practice within their faith. The Supreme Court overturned a state statute that outlawed the possession of animals if the purpose of possessing those animals was to sacrifice or slaughter the animals.[39] Yet, while the Supreme Court allowed members of the Santeria religion to sacrifice an animal, the Court had ruled in *United States v. Seeger* that religious beliefs must be sincere and a meaningful part of a religion.[40] One problem, at least regarding the general public, is deciding whether a group of worshipers belong to a "legitimate" religion. Many different people have attempted to organize religions around behaviors that would ordinarily be impermissible, or a group of people might use the creation of a religion to avoid paying taxes.[41] Such questions are indeed murky. Yet, within correctional institutions, many of these questions become simplified because once again, the courts will consider whether the penological interests of a correctional facility outweigh the constitutional rights of an inmate.

---

36. McConnell, M. W. (1990). The origins and historical understanding of free exercise of religion. *Harvard Law Review, 103*(7), 1409–1517.

37. Wisconsin v. Yoder, 406 U.S. 205 (1972)

38. Reynolds v. United States, 98 U.S. 145 (1878)

39. Church of Lukumi Babalu Aye, Inc. v. City of Hialeah, 508 U.S. 520 (1993)

40. United States v. Seeger, 380 U.S. 163 (1965)

41. Choper, J. H. (1982). Defining religion in the First Amendment. *University of Illinois Law Review, 1982*, 579–613.

As we previously documented, religion can be important to the rehabilitation of many inmates, but it can also be an opportunity for some enterprising prisoners to try to get extra privileges. One example of this comes from the popular television show *Orange is the New Black*. During the television show, Sister Jane Ingalls, despite being a nun, requested kosher meals since they were of better quality than the meals that everyone else were eating in the prison cafeteria. Upon learning this, another Cindy Hayes, an African American inmate, began to request kosher meals as well. Due to the rarity of African Americans practicing Judaism, this caused prison authorities to question Cindy's meal choice, which ultimately ended with an interesting conclusion (we do not want to give spoilers). For this reason, correctional authorities may seek to determine both if a claimed religious group actually constitutes a religion and if a claimed religious practice is necessary to the practice of that religion, and then they determine if such practices can be implemented in a correctional facility without upsetting the operations of that facility. Prior to the 1960s, many correctional facilities only recognized sects of Christianity and Judaism as legitimate religious faiths. Cases like *Fulwood v. Clemmer*[42] and *Cruz v. Beto*[43] changed this, allowing members of Islam and Buddhism to practice their faith in correctional facilities. Other cases, such as *Kahane v. Carlson*,[44] have ruled that inmates who have religious dietary restrictions should be accommodated, and if a correctional facility refuses to do so, the facility should explain why a request cannot be accommodated. Beyond simply allowing inmates the opportunity to practice their faith and eat a diet that complies with that faith, other issues are a little bit more complicated and probably are best saved for a text specializing only in the law of corrections.

Fourth Amendment

While some people have argued these protections are being eroded, the Fourth Amendment of the Constitution remains one of the most important mechanisms to guard Americans' freedom and privacy. This amendment protects us from both "unreasonable searches" and demands that all warrants must be justified by "probable cause." Passage of the Fourth Amendment was extremely important to the founding fathers due to the British practice of using general "writs of assistance" that essentially allowed colonial authorities to search whoever and whatever they felt like at any time.[45] If this was a discussion of free citizens' rights, a much longer explanation would be necessary describing all of the different permutations of the Fourth Amendment and the varying circumstances that may lead to exceptions to various search and seizure protections. Yet, considering

---

42. Fulwood v. Clemmer, 206 F. Supp. 370 (1962)
43. Cruz v. Beto, 405 U.S. 319 (1972)
44. Kahane v. Carlson, 527 F.2d 492 (1975)
45. Samaha, J. (2008). *Criminal procedure* (7th ed.). Belmont, CA: Thomson Wadsworth.

prisoners, probationers, and parolees have limited rights, the Fourth Amendment provides very few protections for people under correctional control. The reason why is easy to understand. Correctional facilities are dangerous places, and correctional authorities and officers need to always ensure the security of these facilities. Additionally, probationers and parolees, as conditions of their being allowed to serve their time outside a secure facility, agree to essentially waive their Fourth Amendment protections.[46] That being said, there are some rules about the manner in which people under correctional control can be searched.

Regarding people's homes, the courts often refer to people's homes as their castles a phrase that means people's property should be treated with sanctity. This is not the case with inmates. In *Hudson v. Palmer*, while acknowledging that inmates have limited rights, the Fourth Amendment essentially did not apply to inmates. The only real protection the Court provided inmates was that correctional authorities and officers could not search inmates merely to harass them. However, random cell searchers were deemed by the Court as important for the security of the institution. Beyond random searches, inmates can be searched with reasonable suspicion, a much lower standard than probable cause.[47] In addition to periodic cell searches, inmates can expect to not only be subjected to a strip search but body cavity searches as well. While the Supreme Court did not completely define the parameters through which these searches could be done, in *Bell v. Wolfish*,[48] the Court ruled that these searches were necessary to maintaining institutional security. The complete circumstances through which these searches can be carried out has been largely left to lower courts, but in general, there must be a reasonable suspicion for these searches to take place except for when an inmate first enters a correctional facility.[49] Strip and cavity searches being done upon admission to a facility does not require any level of suspicion and is a common experience for new inmates. In *Florence v. Board of Chosen Freeholders of the County of Burlington*, the Supreme Court ruled that even people who were arrested for minor offenses and showed no propensity of violence or suspicion of carrying contraband could be searched in this manner.[50] As well as being subject to search at any time, inmates can also expect to have any phone calls they make or receive recorded. The Supreme Court ruled that inmates (or the people who talk to inmates) have no expectation of privacy when talking on the phone.[51]

Although the courts will often lump the rights of probationers and parolees together, that is not the case when considering the Fourth Amendment protec-

46. Gideon, L., & Griffin, O. H. (2017). *Correctional management and the law: A penological approach*. Durham, NC: Carolina Academic Press.
47. Hudson v. Palmer, 468 U.S. 517 (1984)
48. Bell v. Wolfish, 441 U.S. 520 (1979)
49. Gideon, L., & Griffin, O. H. (2017). *Correctional management and the law: A penological approach*. Durham, NC: Carolina Academic Press.
50. Florence v. Board of Chosen Freeholders of the County of Burlington, 566 U.S. 318 (2012)
51. Lanza v. New York, 370 U.S. 139 (1962)

tions of these two different groups of people. In *Griffin v. Wisconsin*, the Supreme Court ruled that so long as a probation officer has a reasonable suspicion that a probationer was likely to have some form of contraband, then that person's home could be searched without a warrant.[52] Later, in *United States v. Knights*, the Supreme Court ruled that police officers, so long as they had a similar specified reasonable suspicion, could search probationers' homes without warrants.[53] When considering parolees, the Supreme Court ruled that as a group, they had less rights than probationers. Indeed, in *Samson v. California*, the Court ruled that since parolees had just been released from prison, were serious offenders, and were at a high risk to reoffend, police and parole officers were provided the justification to search parolees without any direct evidence that there was reasonable suspicion they were engaged in a crime. The mere fact that parolees are on parole can justify a search of their persons or home.[54]

Eighth Amendment

While there are three clauses to the Eighth Amendment to the Constitution, the last clause essentially has two purposes and has spawned considerably more litigation. According to the language of the amendment, "Excessive bail shall not be required, nor excessive fines imposed, nor cruel and unusual punishments inflicted." As we will discuss in the next chapter, jails were originally designed as places to detain people until their trial and if found guilty, their punishment. People have been allowed to put up bail, either money or property, so that they can be released and reside in their home until their trial. More than 90% of people will receive bail. Bail is important for two reasons, ensuring that people will later appear at trial and to allow a release mechanism for defendants (all of whom are presumed innocent) from overcrowded jails. It is important to note that bail is not a guarantee by right; rather, the Eighth Amendment simply guarantees that bail should be proportional to the alleged crime.[55] In *Stack v. Boyle*, the Supreme Court established several criteria that should be utilized in determining if a defendant should receive bail and if so, the proper amount. These factors include the seriousness of the alleged offense, the evidence against a defendant, a defendant's ties to their community and the length of time in which they have resided in that community, a defendant's criminal history, and whether a defendant has ever failed to appear in court.[56] In the Bail Reform Act of 1984, Congress established that if evidence existed that a defendant was likely to harm others or flee the jurisdiction,

---

52. Griffin v. Wisconsin, 483 U.S. 868 (1987)

53. U.S v. Knights, 534 U.S. 112. (2001)

54. Samson v. California, 126 S.Ct. 2193 (2006)

55. Gideon, L., & Griffin, O. H. (2017). *Correctional management and the law: A penological approach*. Durham, NC: Carolina Academic Press.

56. Stack v. Boyle, 342 U.S. 1 (1951)

that evidence could be used to deny a person bail, a practice often referred to as preventative detention. In *United States v. Salerno,* the Supreme Court ruled that preventative detention was constitutional.[57] In case you are not entirely familiar with American organized crime, Anthony Salerno was, at that time, the boss of the Genovese crime family. Part of the reason he had avoided prosecution for such a long time was that he had intimidated and killed (or ordered the killings) many people. Thus, the courts had a good reason for not allowing Salerno to be out on bail during his trial. The second clause of the Eighth Amendment, which prohibits excessive fines, is not a major issue in the United States. As previously mentioned, while many European countries use monetary penalties as a way to punish a great many crimes, in the United States, fines for violations of criminal law are typically small in nature and reserved for minor infractions.[58]

The third clause of the Eighth Amendment, which prohibits cruel and un-usual punishment, has been interpreted by the courts as essentially having two purposes. The first purpose is to make sure that punishment is proportional to a crime. The second purpose of this clause is to make sure that people who are incarcerated are not kept in inhumane conditions. Both purposes are important and cover a range of issues.

The primary punishment that has been litigated before the Supreme Court is the death penalty. The death penalty has been controversial since the founding of the United States. Among the founding fathers, many sought to place restrictions on imposition of the death penalty, and some argued it should even be prohibited altogether.[59] Modern death penalty litigation essentially began in 1972 with the Supreme Court case *Furman v. Georgia.* In that case, five justices of the Supreme Court ruled that as constituted, the death penalty in the United States, at that time, was unconstitutional.[60] As a result, every person on death row, at that time, had their death sentence commuted to life in prison.[61] Yet, the decision in *Furman* did not end the death penalty in America. The case had been decided by a 5–4 margin. Two of the justices in the majority, Justices Brennan and Marshall, argued that the death penalty itself was unconstitutional. Justice Douglas did not go that far, but in his legal reasoning he essentially ruled that any imposition of the death penalty would be unconstitutional. Justices White and Stewart, who voted in the majority, took a different tactic. Rather than state that the death penalty was unconstitutional, they instead argued that the imposition of the death penalty in the United States at that time was unconstitutional. Justices White and

---

57. United States v. Salerno, 481 U.S. 739 (1987)

58. Ruback, R. B. (2011). The abolition of fines and fees. *Criminology & Public Policy, 10*(3), 569–581.

59. Friedman, L. M. (1993). *Crime and punishment in American history.* New York, NY: Basic.

60. Furman v. Georgia, 408 U.S. 238 (1972)

61. Clear, T. R., Reisig, M. D., & Cole, G. F. (2016). *American Corrections* (11th ed.). Boston, MA: Cengage.

Stewart noted there was a great variation in different state death penalty statutes, the crimes in which a person could be eligible for the death penalty, and the legal process surrounding the death penalty. Both justices seemed to indicate that the death penalty could be considered constitutional if the federal and state governments changed their laws.[62] Such a view was mildly prophetic.

Four years after *Furman*, the Supreme Court, by a 7–2 margin, ruled in *Gregg v. Georgia* that, essentially, the death penalty was again constitutional in the United States. However, that is a bit of an oversimplification. In *Gregg*, the Supreme Court ruled that death penalty statutes could be ruled constitutional, but these statutes must comply with a variety of requirements.[63] The list of requirements has continued to grow throughout the years. Essentially, as the Supreme Court would rule in *Woodson v. North Carolina*, which was decided in the same year as *Gregg*, defendants who could potentially be punished with the death penalty deserved "super due process" given the finality of the death penalty over other punishments.[64] Thus, the Supreme Court requires that before a person is given a death sentence, certain safeguards are enacted that defendants who merely receive a sentence of life in prison without parole are not necessarily entitled to.

In *Gregg v. Georgia*, the Supreme Court made three major requirements. The first was that for a person to receive the death penalty, their trial must be bifurcated—meaning the trial must have two parts. The first part is known as the guilt phase. During that portion of the trial, only a defendant's guilt may be considered. If a death-eligible defendant is found guilty, then the second part of the trial will commence—the penalty phase. At this portion of the trial, it will be determined whether a defendant will receive the death penalty or some other form of punishment (most often life in prison without a chance of parole). The second requirement of *Gregg* greatly affects the penalty phase. While states can have different mechanisms of how to consider them, a court must consider both the aggravating and mitigating factors that might indicate if a person should or should not receive the death penalty. The third requirement from *Gregg* is that there must be some automatic form of oversight of death sentences. In most states, this is accomplished by an automatic appeal to a higher court.[65] An essential fourth requirement comes from *Woodson v. North Carolina*. In that case, the Supreme Court ruled that no crime, no matter how heinous, can have an automatic death sentence. Such a decision should always be decided during a trial.[66] Furthermore, in *Ring v. Arizona*, the Supreme Court ruled that for a person to receive the death penalty, that question must be determined by a jury and not by a judge.[67] While the evidence against

62. Furman v. Georgia, 408 U.S. 238 (1972)
63. Gregg v. Georgia, 428 U.S. 153 (1976)
64. Woodson v. North Carolina, 428 U.S. 280 (1976)
65. Gregg v. Georgia, 428 U.S. 153 (1976)
66. Woodson v. North Carolina, 428 U.S. 280 (1976)
67. Ring v. Arizona, 536 U.S. 584 (2002)

a defendant can easily point toward their guilt and almost render the first part of a trial mere formality, the decision whether to live the rest of their lives in prison or be executed often becomes the most important and controversial part of a trial. One example of this was the bombing of a federal building in Oklahoma City that caused the death of 168 people and injured hundreds more. Among the dead were 19 children, who were in a daycare within the federal facility. After a criminal trial in federal court, Timothy McVeigh, the main perpetrator of the crime, was found guilty and given the death penalty. He was executed many years ago. However, his accomplice, Terry Nichols, received life without parole. To some people, the decision to spare Nichols life was unacceptable, and as a result, Terry Nichols was later tried in state courts for 161 counts of murder. All told, estimates for the cost of the trial were about $10 million; however, it may have very well been a waste. Once again, Nichols was given life without parole.[68]

Separate from the questions of the proper process for the death penalty and what crimes are death eligible, there are also a few groups of people who cannot be subjected to the death penalty. Depending upon the severity of psychosis, some people who suffer from mental illness either during their trial or develop mental illness while on death row may be exempted from the death penalty.[69] In *Atkins v. Virginia*, the Supreme Court ruled that defendants who are developmentally disabled should be exempted from the death penalty,[70] but the Court in *Hall v. Florida* declined to establish a clear threshold of what IQ score would specifically disallow a person from receiving the death penalty. In that case, the Court struck down a Florida law that had mandated that a defendant must prove she or he had an IQ of 70 or below to avoid the death penalty.[71] Lastly, in *Roper v. Simmons*, the Supreme Court ruled that people who were under the age of 18 at the time they committed a death-eligible crime could not receive the death penalty.[72] Such a ruling was important because it strictly set an age limit rather than individual circumstances of the case. Indeed, Christopher Simmons, who was 17 at the time, along with another young man, Charles Benjamin, premeditated a plan in which they broke into Shirley Crook's home, bound her with duct tape, and put her in her own minivan. The two young men drove in Crook's van to a state park where they threw Crook off a bridge, and Cook would ultimately die by drowning. The young men only collected $6.[73]

---

68. Griffin, O. H., Woodward, V. H., & Sloan, J. J. (2016). *The money and politics of criminal justice policy.* Durham, NC: Carolina Academic Press.

69. Ford v. Wainwright, 477 U.S. 399 (1986)

70. Virginia v. Atkins, 536 U.S. 304 (2002)

71. Hall v. Florida, 572 U.S. ___ (2014)

72. Roper v. Simmons, 543 U.S. 551 (2005)

73. Raeburn, P. (2004, October 17). Too immature for the death penalty? *The New York Times Magazine.* Retrieved on May 29, 2018 from https://www.nytimes.com/2004/10/17/magazine/too-immature-for-the-death-penalty.html

While the courts have seemingly given a lot of time and consideration to varying permutations of the death penalty, with the exception of juveniles, which will be discussed in Chapter 8, the courts have not readily inserted themselves into the constitutionality of sentences that do not involve the death penalty. The Supreme Court has continually stated that sentences should be proportional to the crimes committed and even noted in a purely hypothetical situation that giving a defendant a life sentence in prison for a parking ticket would be unconstitutional. Yet, the Supreme Court has routinely upheld or failed to consider cases in which offenders have received lengthy sentences for relatively minor criminal actions. Among these cases are so-called three strikes, or habitual offender, laws that punish offenders in a harsher manner after repeated criminal activity. While these law were often enacted to target violent offenders who escaped severe punishment, many nonviolent offenders have received lengthy prison sentences from these laws. In *Rummel v. Estelle*, the Supreme Court upheld a life sentence for a defendant who had committed three thefts that, in total, netted $229.11.[74] Similarly, in *Lockyer v. Andrade*, the Supreme Court approved two sentences of 25 years to life for a defendant who had stolen $150 worth of videotapes from a department store.[75] In both cases, the Supreme Court reasoned that it was not necessarily the value of products taken that justified the lengthy sentences, rather laws punishing repeated criminal behavior.

Although the Supreme Court seems to only have problems with lengthy sentences in hypotheticals, the Supreme Court has stepped in when considering aggravated sentencing factors. One example of this is hate crime laws, which allow for people to receive greater punishments if they committed crimes for racial intimidation or bigoted purposes. However, for such a sentence to be handed down, a jury must decide, by a preponderance of the evidence, that a defendant had such a bigoted purpose beyond just committing a crime. In *Apprendi v. New Jersey*, the Supreme Court ruled that a judge alone could not make such a ruling.[76]

As stated earlier, the Eighth Amendment's protection against cruel and unusual punishment mandates that people who are incarcerated in prisons and jails must be kept in a humane and safe environment. The courts acknowledge that prisons are not necessarily supposed to be nice places to live. Indeed, living in more basic conditions is viewed by many people as part of both the deterrent and retributive aspects of incarceration as a punishment. Yet, prisons are supposed to be rehabilitative environments as well, and if inmates are kept in completely deplorable conditions, the courts have noted inmates will not be able to properly rehabilitate offenders. This process began in *Jones v. Cunningham* when the Supreme Court ruled that inmates could file habeas corpus petitions to challenge the conditions in which they were held as cruel and unusual. In three successive

---

74. Rummel v. Estelle, 445 U.S. 263 (1980)
75. Lockyer v. Andrade, 538 U.S. 63 (2003)
76. Apprendi v. New Jersey, 530 U.S. 466 (2000)

cases, *Holt v. Sarver, Ruiz v. Estelle,* and *Pugh v. Locke,* the Supreme Court ruled that federal courts could take over entire state prison systems and mandate that conditions be improved in those state prison systems. While the aforementioned Prison Litigation Reform Act has placed some limitations on the period of time that federal courts can oversee state prison systems, such a power is still allowed. Typically, federal courts will consider the totality of conditions in penal facilities before taking such dramatic actions. Among the corrective actions federal courts and the Supreme Court have allowed are forcing states to spend more money on penal facilities, fixing broken infrastructure, improving the quality of food, hiring more correctional staff, and reducing overcrowding in correctional facilities.[77]

Whether these plans have actually worked is debatable. Victor describes his correctional facility:

> Paint is peeling everywhere (usually as a result of black mold); buildings have been renovated and closed down as a result of asbestos. There seems to be a drinking water advisory every other month, the ventilation is terrible, and any structure that breaks is 'made pretty,' much like a fat hog is made pretty by someone adorning it with beautiful jewelry. The most blatant and reckless Band-Aid was that which I saw on a loading dock. Right beneath the surface of the dock, the cement was hollowed out, from wear and tear, in the shape of a half-circle with a radius of about three feet. It looked like someone had chiseled out most of the cement underneath the platform but left the platform intact. Right before the DOC commissioner and other politicians were scheduled to appear at a college graduation ceremony in our visit hall, a piece of plywood was nailed over the cave and the whole thing was spray-painted yellow. To me, this is symbolic of New Jersey's practice of corrections: if something is broken and it doesn't affect us, leave it alone, but if someone important comes around, let's make it look like it's not broken so we don't get in trouble.

Along with providing a humane environment, correctional facilities are responsible for the health care needs of inmates. In *Estelle v. Gamble,* the Supreme Court coined the controlling phrase "deliberate indifference" that controls how states and correctional authorities must act. Correctional authorities do not necessarily have to provide the most current or best care, but they must provide the necessary medical treatments.[78] It is not always easy to determine when states have violated inmates' rights in this regard. Similar to conditions of confinement, the courts have often interpreted the adequacy of inmate health care on a system-

77. Gideon, L. & Griffin, O. H. (2017). *Correctional management and the law: A penological approach.* Durham, NC: Carolina Academic Press.

78. Estelle v. Gamble, 429 U.S. 97 (1976)

wide basis. One or two instances of medical malpractice are usually viewed as state tort actions and not Eighth Amendment claims.[79]

Due Process

Due process is mentioned in two different amendments to the Constitution. Within the Fifth Amendment, it is stated as "nor be deprived of life, liberty, or property, without due process of law," and in the Fourteenth Amendment, it guarantees that all native born or naturalized citizens are guaranteed equal protection and due process of law. Essentially, due process means that people are entitled to fundamental fairness of process within the courts. For defendants at trial, this would require that such things as the right to an attorney, the protection against compelled self-incrimination, and many other protections. People in prison have already been convicted of crimes. If they are charged with a new crime, they are entitled to the same protections as any other defendant; otherwise, due process typically applies in two different circumstances to inmates. Furthermore, the Sixth Amendment guarantees several protections that the courts have often lumped into due process claims of defendants. Among these protections is the right to a speedy and public trial, a trial by an impartial jury, to be informed of the charges a defendant is facing, to confront one's accuser, and the right to an attorney.

Much like other areas of law, people under correctional control who are not facing the death penalty often have diminished due process rights. Except in death penalty cases, most inmates do not have the right to appeal their conviction. They may file an appeal, but there is no guarantee that any appellate court will actually hear the appeal. Furthermore, except in death penalty cases, most inmates do not have the right to have an attorney to help them file an appeal. There are a few ways in which states must aid inmates in preparing for appeals. In *Griffin v. Illinois*, the Supreme Court ruled that inmates could not be denied the ability to file an appeal if they could not afford the cost of a trial transcript.[80] Furthermore, while inmates do not have the right to an attorney for appeals, correctional facilities must provide some legal assistance to inmates. However, the Supreme Court has not been definitive in determining how such assistance should be provided. Some correctional facilities allow "jailhouse lawyers," inmates who seem to have legal knowledge to provide advice to other inmates. One example of this comes from Ronald when he said "Not boasting, but I became one of the best so-called jailhouse lawyers in the state. I have written hundreds of legal briefs for others and have had a slew of criminal convictions overturned, including a dozen murder convictions. I get mail from people all over the state, seeking help on their cases, based on reputation and the 2006 YouTube piece from NJTV (dueprocesstv/

---

79. Gideon, L., & Griffin, O. H. (2017). *Correctional management and the law: A penological approach*. Durham, NC: Carolina Academic Press.

80. Griffin v. Illinois, 351 U.S. 12 (1956)

jailhouse lawyers)." Another tactic and a common feature in many prisons is a law library. Yet, the Supreme Court has declined to set standards for how either should be definitively governed or how even the adequacy of assistance should be defined. The Court seems to do so on a case-by-case basis.[81]

Melanie McGuire has been incarcerated since 2007 following her conviction in New Jersey for murdering her husband and dismembering his remains. Her case received a lot of notoriety, and she has been referred to in many media outlets at the "suitcase murderer," which she believes has had a negative impact on her appeals. Melanie adamantly maintains her innocence, and in her story, she discusses the many challenges she has faced in the appellate process. Melanie was hopeful in the beginning that her appeals would prevail, but she is no longer that optimistic. Though she technically enjoys due process rights because she can file appeals, does it matter to those whose appeals are never be granted? You decide.

Narrative: "Harmless Error"

It is a cliché that nearly all criminal offenders protest their innocence. Stereotypically, television, movies, and other media portray convicts claiming wrongful conviction. In the not too distant past, that idea would be anathema to the justice system. There has not yet been a paradigm shift in our society's understanding of conviction integrity, but the advent of DNA evidence has helped irrefutably prove innocence where it would once have never been possible. Even the biggest skeptics have to acknowledge wrongful conviction does occur and needs to be addressed. It may seem farfetched but in fact, wrongful conviction and its aftermath play out every day in our communities, and innocent people languish in prison with uncertain futures.

I should know. I'm one of them.

In 2007, after a high profile trial, I was wrongfully convicted of the murder of my husband, William. How did that happen? What went wrong, I'm often asked? Wrongful conviction is really a team effort. It requires a concatenation of events including, but not limited to, prosecutorial misconduct, ineffective assistance of trial counsel, questionable judicial rulings, misstatements and mischaracterizations sworn to by experts and civilian witnesses, and juries that are technologically unable to avoid media contamination in high profile cases without sequestration. Some of these errors occur in varying degrees; some are inadvertent rather than deliberate. Some are a result of active malignment. However, unlike many appellate courts opine, these errors are far from harmless, and the cumulative effect of them is devastating.

---

81. Gideon, L. & Griffin, O. H. (2017). *Correctional management and the law: A penological approach*. Durham, NC: Carolina Academic Press.

My trial was based on circumstantial evidence—admittedly, quite a bit of it. At first, guilt might have seemed obvious. Judges instruct juries about circumstantial evidence using the example of snowfall. You might not have witnessed the snow falling, the judge tells jurors, but when you wake up in the morning with snow on the ground, you know, without directly witnessing it, that snow has fallen. On its face, the analogy makes sense in circumstantial cases. But what if you're at a ski resort and the snow is man-made? There are sometimes other plausible explanations—they simply require context. Defendants are frequently prohibited from presenting evidence that would lend such context. What if the defendant cannot tell the jury the victim used to work at that ski resort? The court excludes certain information that might disparage the victim. How can a defendant show context and present alternative explanations when she is barred from presenting that contextual information? She is not legally obligated to present a plausible explanation, of course, but it is naive to believe that juries do not expect a version of events from a defendant. Without it, they will believe she doesn't have an explanation to offer.

For example, at trial, much was made of items found with the body—blankets, black trash bags, and suitcases that were ours. They corresponded to things from my home and employer. It seemed like an 'Aha!' moment, but the explanation was simple and rudimentary. My husband left after an argument and most likely packed items in the suitcases—suitcases that ostensibly went into his car. Aside from that, we were moving in two days and were packing. I borrowed blankets from the OR at work to wrap the fragile granite inlays on our furniture. He bought a box of contractor bags; those boxes contained two rolls. One went in my car and was used in the course of moving; the other went in his car. None of the bags containing his body matched sequentially to those found in my home, but they were thought to have come from the same production run. To me, and the people who knew my story, this was obvious, not incriminating. The aspects of evidence the prosecution contended were demonstrative of my involvement were actually irrelevant if my husband's body was disposed of using the items he already has in his car—not a stretch, no matter who you believe committed the crime. The "evidence" was presented as demonstrative of guilt in a case where a gruesome dismemberment occurred, although the prosecution could never say definitely where or when it took place. Instead of answering for things like the complete absence of DNA evidence in the home despite of multitude of forensic investigations, this critical gap of real evidence was ignored in favor of blankets and bags—anywhere the prosecution could state a similarity and spin a story.

Make no mistake—it's all about the story. Mine had all manner of salacious details, used against me and recounted inside court and out, relayed on social media, reenacted on true crime programs, and written about in books. I had been engaged in an affair for the last two years of my marriage. My husband gambled and had indiscretions as part of his life I knew nothing about. A television producer told me very simply one day: it was a sexy story. It was the complete antithesis to me. My husband lost his life; my children their father. I filed for divorce in my husband's initial absence, and I obtained a restraining order to prevent him from taking our children. This was all a ruse, the prosecution asserted. Again, I point to the importance of context. The prosecution even told the jury I drugged my husband for days with a prescription for chloral hydrate filled in the name of a patient at my practice. Sounds damning, until you heard Bill's sister testify she believed he was taking steroids. Chloral hydrate is often utilized by users of GHB and other steroids, but the jury never heard that. It would also have been physiologically impossible to drug my husband for days with the single dose missing from the bottle as the state purported. The prescription itself? A number of patient records were found under Bill's username on our home computer, a computer with remote access to my entire patient database. Bill had nearly graduated from pharmacy school several years earlier until a felony precluded him from practice. None of this obviated his training—I am not the only person in my home who knew how to write a prescription, and pads were often available in some of the work I brought home. Bill also worked as a computer programming analyst and was conversant in remote access.

More context.

The gun my husband had me buy two days before he left has never been found, though interesting information has evolved regarding the firearm. A coworker of Bill's had a conversation with him about wanting me to buy a gun for him—testimony he was never permitted to give fully to the jury. This verified my version of events. Next, the number of lands and grooves on the bullets taken from my husband's body do not correspond with the gun manufacturer's specifications. These specifications were later altered by the company on their website, and we have never been permitted to question company officials as to why because the court would not order a postconviction evidentiary hearing to clarify this information. When we eventually learned that there were myriad more relevant computer searches than the state identified, we were denied a hearing on that matter as well. It seems the postconviction process and its participants aren't particularly interested in context or, by extension, justice.

When someone is sentenced to spend their life in prison, is it too much to request a review of facts that have evolved post-trial? I know people who have taken plea bargains and got evidentiary hearings in the postconviction stage. Those aren't whodunits. I'm not denying the need or right for people who take plea bargains to have access to this type of relief—I'm merely wondering why said relief seems so difficult to get in a case where the convicted protests their innocence and there are salient issues to be heard. I cannot help but feel the high profile nature of my case has made relief difficult to obtain, at least within my state. I cannot fathom another reason why it would do harm to at least hear about these things. The prosecution's response is predictable—they will never let a petition for postconviction relief go unopposed. Their record and reputation are at stake. Reviewing courts deem misleading statements by prosecutors' "harmless error."

Nothing changes the fact that a victim is dead, and someone needs to be held responsible by the prosecutor—not even the truth, it seems. There has become more widespread acceptance of the notion of wrongful conviction, both within the legal community and society. Why, then, do people seem so afraid to hear what a convict has to say, particularly when they can put forth viable issues at least worthy of questions? Are our citizens—for that is what convicts still are—at least entitled to the opportunity to raise essential, though perhaps uncomfortable, questions? Is the hubris of the legal community so pervasive that its outcomes cannot withstand scrutiny? When it comes to the question of real justice, there is no such thing as harmless error.

Beyond filing legal appeals, the other way in which people under correctional control enjoy due process is through the various hearings they may request or to which they may be subjected. These hearings can include when a prisoner is charged with a disciplinary infraction or if a person with the community who is on probation or parole is threatened with being sent to a correctional facility. Before any of these people are disciplined or incarcerated, they are entitled to a hearing first unless they have been charged with a new crime. People under correctional control may hire an attorney, but the state does not have to provide one if a person cannot afford one unless they have been charged with a new crime. As part of their due process rights, offenders are entitled to hear the charges against them as well as any evidence against them. One limitation to this, though, is that people under correctional control have a limited right to face their accuser. It is often feared that if a person is victimized by a person who is under correctional control and then has to publicly testify in front of that person, the accuser could be severely victimized and/or suffer various forms of retaliation. Thus, many victims would not report when they are victimized. If correctional authorities can present other evidence to prove their claims and assert that a complaining witness is under danger, then a person under correctional control will not be able to face their accuser. Lastly, if a person under correctional control is found guilty in a hearing, they are entitled to a statement outlining the evidence against them and what punishment they will face.[82]

---

82. Ibid.

Chapter 4

Incarceration

As we have discussed, the United States chooses to punish most of its serious, and especially most of its violent offenders, by incarcerating them in correctional facilities. While the idea of incarceration as punishment is not especially novel, it is more of a modern punishment. In this chapter, we will discuss how the practice of incarceration has evolved in the United States and particularly the differences between jails and prisons, two different types of correctional facilities that people often mix up and refer to interchangeably.

Jails

If you can, try to imagine a world without cell phones, computers, the Internet, or any other modern technology that allows people to communicate quickly with other people. In this world, how do you keep track of people? This is, at its core, one of the primary reasons that the criminal justice system began to rely upon jails. If you charge a person with a crime, in most instances, you want to ensure that they appear at trial. Furthermore, if a person is convicted of a crime and say, for instance, that their punishment was a date with the hangman, if they were allowed to remain in their home until this date, what is they likelihood that they would show up? With a lack of alternatives, many people would probably try to flee. This is the primary purpose of a jail, ensuring that people accused of crimes appear at trial and, if necessary, receive their punishment. However, as time has gone on, jails have become more multifaceted. Before we discuss these innovations though, it is important to go back in time a little.

In colonial America, there was little need for correctional facilities. By 1760, only seven "cities" in the United States had a population of more than 3,000 people. The most populous American city of the time was New York City, which had barely more than 23,000 people. You might think, "well, the world was a lot less populated back then," but that is not completely the case. At that time, more than 900,000 people lived in London.[1] Within colonial America, this was a time of the common law, informal criminal justice process, and community justice. People who committed bad acts usually received swift punishment, typically corporally or through fines. Trials were informal proceedings, most often without attorneys, and formal due process or rules of evidence were generally unknown. Several trials could take place in one day. Holding people until their trial was not typically necessary because there was no backlog of cases like we see today. Furthermore, in newly settled colonies, people needed to work. Having people sit in a correctional facility was an inefficient system. In one historical study of criminal justice within New York, only 19 cases were found (from 1691 to 1776) that administered incarceration as a primary punishment.[2]

Like so many other things, the United States based their jail system on the British model. While their antecedents go back further, *gaols*, as they were known in medieval England, were facilities administered by a shire reeve (later known as sheriff) in their shire. If you have ever watched a Robin Hood movie, no doubt you have heard of the nefarious actions of the Sheriff of Nottingham. In the United States, the system is pretty much the same. States are broken up into counties (except for Louisiana, which has the much cooler name parishes), and a sheriff presides over each county. Within each county, there is usually a jail. One of the sheriff's duties is overseeing the jail(s) within their county.[3] While not as bad as the Sheriff of Nottingham, many sheriffs in early America exhibited similar behavior. In New York, many sheriffs neglected their duties, which resulted in reprimands and, in some cases, prosecution. In Pennsylvania, many sheriffs saw their job as a money-making opportunity. Under the guise of recouping the costs of housing inmates, sheriffs would often extort money from them. As if that were not bad enough, many sheriffs would also sell alcohol to occupants of their jail. Apparently, these problems were so widespread that the colony of Pennsylvania, in 1730, had to prohibit sheriffs from engaging in both behaviors.[4]

The establishment of jails in England began in the early part of the 11th century, and in 1166, King Henry II declared that all sheriffs who did not have a jail in their county needed to build one. As John Irwin argued, at that time in England, feudalism was beginning to break down. While feudalism had essentially required that all people who were not part of the nobility or royalty be serfs belonging to

---

1. Preyer, K. (1982). Penal measures in the American colonies: An overview. *The American Journal of Legal History, 26,* 326–353.

2. Friedman, L. M. (1993). *Crime and punishment in American history.* New York, NY: Basic.

3. Clear, T. R., Reisig, M. D., & Cole, G. F. (2015). *American Corrections* (11th ed.). Boston, MA: Cengage.

4. Friedman, L. M. (1993). *Crime and punishment in American history.* New York, NY: Basic.

the land they were required to work, increasing numbers of people would wander about the country visiting different towns and cities. Some of those people were looking for work, and others were often looking for trouble. At that time, a system of bail was already in place in which people would put up money or property to ensure that they appeared at their trial. Upon completion, if they were not executed for their crimes or had to pay fines, they would get their money or property back. However, with an increasing number of people traveling throughout the country and continually breaking a growing criminal code that included many minor offenses (such as vagrancy statutes), more people were being arrested who did not have the money to pay for bail and were not likely to appear at trial. Such circumstances are what primarily led to the rapid expansion of jails in England.[5]

The earliest jails in the United States, the first of which was built in Jamestown in 1608, lacked any signature style of architecture. Most often it was a facility built in or around the center of town, usually close in proximity to wherever punishment was carried out. Inmates in jails, rather than being in an individual cell, where typically crowded into rooms. Men, women, and children were crammed in together, and how many people were stuffed into the facility all depended upon how many people needed to be. Conditions within were deplorable. While sheriffs could not flat out extort money from inmates, they could still charge them for food and any other amenities they might need. If the prices for these goods were exorbitant, it might effectively be the same as extorting inmates. Friends and family were allowed to provide these items to inmates, but if an inmate had no money or no support, spending time in jail was a truly awful existence.[6]

Today, although jails have more modern design and are secure facilities, their mission is still very similar. Their primary purpose is to hold people until their trial. In 2017, of the roughly 630,000 people who were inmates of a local jail, approximately 443,000 of those people were in jail awaiting trial.[7] So who are the rest of the people serving time in jail? As we mentioned before, the United States did not really embrace corporal punishment beyond the colonial era and only used fines for minor offenses. People convicted of misdemeanors and some felonies may receive less than one year of incarceration. Furthermore, until long-term inmates can receive an assignment to a prison, they will await their transfer to a prison in jail.[8] Thus, approximately 187,000 inmates in jails have been convicted of a crime. Among the largest group of inmates, roughly 57,000 people are serving time in jail for public order offenses (such as prostitution, driving un-

5. Irwin, J. (1985). *The Jail: Managing the underclass in American society.* Berkeley, CA: University of California Press.

6. Hanser, R. D. (2017). *Introduction to corrections* (2nd ed.). Thousand Oaks, CA: Sage.

7. Wagner, P., & Rabuy, B. (2017). *Mass incarceration: The whole pie 2017.* Prison Policy Initiative. Retrieved on July 8, 2018 from https://www.prisonpolicy.org/reports/pie2017.html

8. Irwin, J. (1985). *The Jail: Managing the underclass in American society.* Berkeley, CA: University of California Press.

der the influence of alcohol, vagrancy, loitering). Yet, simply saying that 630,000 people who were in jail on any given day does not really completely portray the chaotic and high-turnover nature of jails in the United States. Last year, more than 11 million people were processed in American jails.[9] This number may seem especially high given that slightly more than 6.6 million people were under correctional control in 2016.[10]

Within 48 hours of being arrested, defendants are entitled to an initial appearance before a judge or magistrate. Not to be confused with an arraignment, in which a defendant will usually enter a plea to the charges against them, at an initial appearance, a judge or magistrate is required to merely inform a defendant of the charges against them.[11] Many jail inmates will be released because police officers do not officially file charges against a recent arrestee. In some instances, this may be that a complaining witness decides not to go through with pressing charges against another person. One example of this would be if two people got into a fist fight and later declined to press charges. Police officers may have arrested the two combatants to prevent a drunken brawl at the bars one night, but the next day, with the incident and perhaps argument over, there was no need to pursue the incident further. Other people may get caught up in a seemingly never-ending battle of control over the streets. As John Irwin noted, many of the people who end up being arrested are simply members of a group of people he nonjudgmentally referred to as "the rabble." Many cities and urban areas are filled with the homeless, drug users, and mentally ill people. These people are often society's castoffs, and while many will not cause trouble, their presence can cause problems either by hanging out in front of businesses or hassling "respectable" people. In some instances, police officers will have legitimate reasons to arrest people from the rabble class for acts of violence, drug possession, or other illegal acts. In other instances, police officers may simply arrest these people to briefly get them off the streets. When it comes time for their initial appearance, there may not have been any actual crime committed, and these people are simply released. This cycle is often repeated because members of the rabble class lack the means to challenge the behavior of the authorities. In many instances, they will simply accept the constant hassle and see going in and out of jail as simply a part of their existence.[12]

Most people (more than 90%), will receive bail or some form of release after being arrested and formally charged with a crime.[13] Some people are not even re-

9. Zeng, Z. (2018). *Jail inmates in 2016*. Washington, DC: Bureau of Justice Statistics.

10. Kaeble, D., & Cowhig, M. (2018). *Correctional populations in the United States, 2016*. Washington, DC: Bureau of Justice Statistics.

11. Hartley, R. D., Rabe, G. A., & Champion, D. J. (2018). *Criminal courts: Structure, process, and issues* (4th ed.). New York, NY: Pearson.

12. Irwin, J. (1985). *The Jail: Managing the underclass in American society*. Berkeley, CA: University of California Press.

13. Gideon, L., & Griffin, O. H. (2017). *Correctional management and the law: A penological approach*. Durham, NC: Carolina Academic Press.

quired to post bail. If a person is charged with a misdemeanor or some other minor offense, they might be simply released on an unsecured bond or what some states refer to as release on their own recognizance (ROR). Some defendants, if they are wealthy or have significant ties to the community, may even be released for minor felonies on ROR. For those defendants who are not considered to be significant flight risks or are not arrested for serious charges, such as capital murder, a cash bond will be given. Some people will simply pay money for the bond or may offer a deed to property to satisfy the bond. Others will go to a bonding company. While terms may vary, the typical arrangement is that a defendant will pay 10% of the bond to a bonding company, and the bonding company will put up the full amount of the bond to the state or federal government. However, rather than get that 10% back, a defendant will simply pay the 10% as a fee for the bonding company. If a defendant decides to flee the jurisdiction before the conclusion of their trial, a bonding company will often send bounty hunters to find the fleeing defendant.[14] Perhaps you have heard of the television show "Dog the Bounty Hunter," which appeared on the A&E Network from 2004–2012. While the show more often focused on Duane "Dog" Chapman and his fellow employees looking for wayward defendants, the reasons Dog did so was that he was afraid of losing the bond he had put up for these defendants to be released from jail.

Many critics of the way bail is administered in the United States have noted the rapid growth of the bonding company industry. While many people have simply argued that requiring bail is simply a way to ensure that defendants appear at trial, many people have argued that the accompanying rise of the bonding industry has subverted justice and has morphed into an apparatus that is more interested in profit than people's potential as a flight risk. If a person cannot afford bail, it is difficult to imagine that they could scrape together the funds needed to flee the jurisdiction.[15]

So, who is in jail today? As we mentioned, there is a mixture of people who are charged with serious crimes, cannot afford bail, and are serving short sentences as punishment and inmates awaiting transfer to prisons. Most often, these are also people of the rabble class Irwin described.[16] Many of those who cannot afford bail will take a guilty plea simply to get out of jail, but for some, pleading guilty is never an option. Read what Ronald had to say about pleading guilty and the consequences of turning down plea bargains.

Furthermore, jails are often filled with people who are mentally ill. For a variety of reasons, during the 1960s, the states and the federal government began

---

14. Hartley, R. D., Rabe, G. A., & Champion, D. J. (2018). *Criminal courts: Structure, process, and issues* (4th ed.). New York, NY: Pearson.

15. Dabney, D. A., Page, J., & Topalli, V. (2017). American bail and the tinting of criminal justice. *The Howard Journal of Crime and Justice, 56*, 397–418.

16. Irwin, J. (1985). *The Jail: Managing the underclass in American society*. Berkeley, CA: University of California Press.

Narrative: Ronald Long's Story

The only function of the courthouse was plea bargains. The public defender had already started the jury challenge by calling in an ACLU Philadelphia Lawyer, David Kairys, and a statistician from Carnegie Melon University, Professor Jonathan Kadane. The judge became more and more agitated by me. We had several more complicated legal issues, and the case got more complicated as it went along. The state had used three subpoena duces tecum and illegally seized my Veterans Administration (VA) hospital records. Judge Porreca first ordered that anyone who read the rec-ords would have to be recused from the case because they were tainted. The judge later ruled that I would have to allow him to read my VA hospital records in order to be able to decide. I wouldn't agree to it.

The plea bargains then kept coming more and more intense. I eventually lost trust in Barry Cooper. It seemed like he was doing the bidding for the prosecutor. Cooper also became annoyed by me getting so many others to join my jury challenge. He started trying to pressure me into taking a plea bargain. I would not accept a plea bargain, no matter what it was! First it was life—serve 30 years on the Compton murder charge and a concurrent sentence on the Carmichael charges. Next, the state offered 40 serve 20 on the Carmichael charges, and the Compton charges would be DISMISSED. Next, 20 serve 10 on the Carmichael case, DISMISS the Compton case. Next, 10 years, serve 3 on the Carmichael case, DISMISS the Compton case. (By then I had almost two years inside, awaiting trial.) Finally, the state offered me an NGI, not guilty by reason of insanity. There was never any intention of defending me because Mr. Cooper was so sure that I would take a deal.

On January 7, 1985, two years to the date of my arrest, Judge Porreca ruled the jury selection procedures were statutorily illegal. He refused to make a constitutional ruling. He ordered the jury commissioners to fix the jury selection system forthwith. No new grand jury presentations could be made to the current system, and no trial could proceed under the current petit jury system. The judge's decision would be prospective only. No indictments would be dismissed or it would "collapse" the criminal justice system in Atlantic County. This decision is reported at *State v. Long*, 204 N.J. Super. 469 (Law Div. 1985). Barry Cooper had me interviewed by no less than 10 psychologists and psychiatrist, all ready to testify that I was insane. I found myself in the odd predicament of trying to disprove a negative—that I'm not crazy.

Cooper really lost my trust when he started asking my family to get me to accept a plea bargain that promised I would be able to get out of jail right away. I eventually fired Barry Cooper. Even though Judge Porreca gave his decision "prospective application only," in April 1985, I was reindicted. This time, instead of a 9-count indictment, the prosecutor added four additional counts. The state denied that this was revenge because of the jury challenge. All of the other death penalty cases were reindicted as well.

what has been referred to as the deinstitutionalization movement. Due to scandals such as those depicted in the book and movie *One Flew Over the Cuckoo's Nest*, most of the state-run secured mental health facilities in the United States, often referred to as asylums, shut down. The hope was that most of these patients could receive better treatment in community mental health centers. Unfortunately, most of the newly desired community treatment facilities were never built. Thus, many of the people who would have been admitted to these centers or many of the now shuttered asylums do not receive the proper treatment. Many of these people end up homeless, others are constantly shuffled in and out of jails, and others end up in prison. Therefore, many occupants in jails are mentally ill. This is especially problematic since jails are not intended as treatment facilities, only short-term holding facilities.[17]

In 2017, there were 3,163 jails operating in the United States.[18] While these facilities may have the same basic mission, they can diverge widely. In general, most jails in the United States are built using one of three designs: linear, podular, or direct. Linear jails have some form of central office and then a traditional cellblock that extends down from that office. Cells are placed along the row. Depending upon your university or placement in student housing, your dormitory might not look a whole lot different, hopefully with a door instead of bars, though. In a podular design, groups of living units are spread out from a central booking office. Rather than one or two inmates sharing an individual cell in the linear design, inmates in a podular design will share a pod with several other inmates. Again, some of you may have had such a dormitory arrangement. In the direct supervision design, correctional officers will be right among the inmates. In this type of model, inmates are essentially herded together in massive cells.[19] To picture such a design, just think of what people would refer to as a "drunk tank." Inmates are simply thrown into a large room among other inmates. In some instances, there are bunks within the cells and in others just benches on which inmates can either sit or sleep. These cells will also have a toilet and sometimes a sink. If you need to use the bathroom, you may have a large audience.

Perhaps the biggest difference between jail facilities is not necessarily the design of the facilities but the size. A ubiquitous phrase is that the United States is a diverse nation, and one of the countless ways this manifests is in jail facilities. While there are more than 3,100 jails in the United States, many of these facilities are small. In fact, just more than 1,000 jails in the United States hold 49 or fewer inmates. By contrast, only 30 jails in the United States hold more 2,500 in-

17. Slate, R. N., Buffington-Vollum, J. K., & Johnson, W. W. (2013). *The criminalization of mental illness: Crisis and opportunity for the justice system* (2nd ed.). Durham, NC: Carolina Academic Press.

18. Wagner, P., & Rabuy, B. (2017). *Mass incarceration: The whole pie 2017*. Prison Policy Initiative. Retrieved on July 8, 2018 from https://www.prisonpolicy.org/reports/pie2017.html

19. Siegel, L., & Bartollas, C. (2016). *Corrections today* (3rd ed.) Boston, MA: Cengage.

mates or more. Slightly more than 100 jails have 1,000 to less than 2,500 inmates.[20] One common example of a small rural jail comes from *The Andy Griffith Show*. Whether you watched the show on purpose or were merely subjected to it by parents or grandparents, Andy Taylor (played by Andy Griffith) was the sheriff of the fictional town Mayberry, North Carolina. A lot of his time was spent at the jail he was entrusted to run, which had two whole jail cells. Most of the time, the cells were empty. On a few occasions, one of the cells would be occupied by the town drunk Otis Campbell. For the most part, Otis was not actually under arrest, rather he would sleep in the cell as a form of self-inflicted punishment or as a means to not get yelled at by his wife. While both the sheriff and the town were fictional, many small towns throughout America have somewhat similar, if not only slightly larger, facilities.

For small communities, maintenance of jails can be difficult. Most days of the year, having a jail (or a large jail) is unnecessary. Yet, a few days a year, whether there are criminals passing through town or a reason for a mass arrest, small jails can quickly be overburdened. For this reason, many small counties have started to band together to form regional jails.[21] Given the unpredictability of jail populations and that many of these small places have small budgets, pooling resources is attractive.[22] While small communities may find consolidation attractive, it belies a problem that many jails face. These facilities are usually run by a sheriff who in turn is an elected official. Politics are often infused with the maintenance of jails, and these institutions are just about always underfunded. Conditions are usually different degrees of terrible, and there is not much incentive to improve them since inmates typically do not stick around for very long.[23] As we mentioned in Chapter 3, prisoner lawsuits have had a dramatic effect on the correctional system, but jails have largely remained untouched because jail inmates are usually more worried about their trial, appeals, or finishing their short sentence to take the time to sue a jail. One recent example of such a controversy is in Alabama. In that state, due to ambiguities in state laws governing the administration of jails, many sheriffs were pocketing any money that was not spent on food for inmates. Due to this incentive, sheriffs often spent as little on food for inmates that they could get away with. In one instance, a federal judge sent a sheriff to jail for repeated failures to adequately feed inmates. Recently, Governor Kay Ivey ordered the state comptroller to send food payments for inmates to counties, rather than

---

20. Zeng, Z. (2018). *Jail inmates in 2016*. Washington, DC: Bureau of Justice Statistics.

21. Ruddell, R., & Mays, G. L. (2006). Expand or expire: Jails in rural America. *Corrections Compendium, 31*, 1–5.

22. Ruddell, R., & Mays, G. L. (2007). Rural jails: Problematic inmates, overcrowded cells, and cash-strapped counties. *Journal of Criminal Justice, 35*, 251–260.

23. Gideon, L., & Griffin, O. H. (2017). *Correctional management and the law: A penological approach*. Durham, NC: Carolina Academic Press.

sheriffs, as a way to combat the practice.[24] This is one of many different examples of how politics and budgets can corrupt the process of jail maintenance. All of which short changes inmates who, as discussed, are often from among the poorest and most marginalized segments of society.

Jails in large jurisdictions do not always fare much better. In fact, some of the larger jails experience conditions akin to "hell," according to the inmates and correctional officers. One such famous, or infamous rather, jail is Rikers Island. Located on the East River of New York City between the Queens and Bronx boroughs, Rikers Island was once home to a pig slaughterhouse and then a landfill that attracted an uncontrollable rat infestation that could not be contained. Despite the obvious health hazards, Rikers opened its first jail in 1935, and today it is home to an average of about 10,000 inmates, though conditions do not seem to have improved since 1935. The following narrative comes from a 19-year-old held in Rikers on first-degree assault and first-degree robbery charges for almost two years on $20,000 bail.[25]

Narrative from a 19-Year-Old

In the box, the bed is on the wall, so it's lower to the floor. You've gotta be careful because there's a lot of roaches and mice running around. You'll be lying down with your eyes closed, and you'll hear all of them making noises, going through your bags on the floor, ripping up pages from the books.

They don't got no air conditioner [in the box]. Sometimes you be in your cell like nude, because it be hot and the windows don't open up, and you'll be complaining like, "I need my window fixed." And the officers will say, "We'll put in a work order." But it never gets done.

What I'd do, I'd grab paper, and I'd make a fan out of it. Sometimes the paper gets worn out because I'd use it a lot, and sometimes there won't be no more paper, so I'd fan myself with my shirt.

The box—it's like you're locked up twice as much as you're locked up now. It's a small room, so you really don't move around a lot. You wake up, and there's a toilet right next to your head. You look out the window, and you see birds flying, and that only leads your mind into wanting freedom more. And since it's a small room, it makes you think crazy.

I'm not gonna lie; I felt like hanging myself. I felt like committing suicide because of the things that run through my head when I'm in that thing:

---

24. Blinder, A. (2018, July 11). Alabama moves to limit sheriffs from pocketing jail food money. *The New York Times*. Retrieved on July 15, 2018 from https://www.nytimes.com/2018/07/11/us/alabama-jail-food-money.html

25. Chammah, M., Weichselbaum, S., Tabor, N., Hager, E., & Goldstein, D. (2015, June 29). Inside Rikers island, through the eyes of the people who live and work there. *New York Maga-*

Why me? Why am I in jail? Why do I have to go through these things for this long? Why am I in the box? I hate it here. I hate my life. I have no life. I hate freedom. I can't taste freedom. I can't hold freedom. I miss my family. I miss my friends.

In the middle of the night, people be yelling. People be singing, people be rapping, people be banging. You talk to people under the door. You lie on the ground, which is dirty, so you put a sheet on the floor. And you put your mouth close to the door. You gotta yell at them so people can hear you. And sometimes you get tired, and sometimes your throat hurts. Hours. 'Cause there's nothing else to do. We talk about our lives. We talk about being in jail. Changing our ways. We talk about what are we gonna be when we get out.

Some people are scared, and they find the box safer for them. I've seen inmates—when they get into fights—they'll be like, "Can you please send me to the box, because I can't be anywhere else but the box." A lot of people go in the box calm, and they come out crazy.

Right now, I'm five-foot-seven. I grew. I came here when I was five feet tall. In the beginning, I kept getting into all these fights because I wanted attention. So I was in the gang. You need people that's gonna help you out. You're repping that gang, and you come to jail; other gangs have problems with that gang. That's why I got jumped. Hospitalized like four times.

It was a little bit serious. But that's how you get your little freedom, too. Because when you're in the hospital, you see people from the outside. They give you the attention that you been dying to get. Your family comes to visit you because you're in a serious problem, you understand? Once you in the hospital, you wouldn't want to leave the hospital. It's just like a little bit home.

I've been incarcerated for so long, and I've fought so many people; they know not to bother me anymore. I've been jumped plenty of times and got into a lot of fights and got stabbed a lot, so they know who I am, and they leave me alone. Sometimes you gotta go in the shower and go knife-to-knife, right? So when I visualize who runs the show, I walk up to that person and tell 'em, "Listen, my name is this, my name is that. I don't want no problems. I just want my respect."

Whoever makes it out the shower gets the crib, gets to own the housing area.

[Since they restricted solitary], a lot of people taking advantage, so now they're like, "Oh, we can't go to the box. We can do what we wanna do now." The only thing that's going to happen is just a $25 ticket. Right now, I owe $183. So I'm actually working it off at commissary.

When you get clothes sent up, that means a lot to other people. People see that and they be like, "Oh, he got support." The guards bring things in for the gangs. Like drugs. Lotion from home. Cologne. And they pay the officers. One time, a female guard had sexual intercourse with an inmate in exchange for money, drugs, and a phone.

One female officer, she'll sit down and explain to me what to do, what not to do. She'll help me out sometimes when I need a new pen. She'll tell me to do good. That I shouldn't be here. She makes my day go by. She brings me books when she's not supposed to. She does things that she's not supposed to do. And she goes out of her way and does it for me because she knows deep inside that I deserve those things. One time I felt like having sex with her. And I told her, "I respect you, but I'm gonna fall back a little bit because I feel like I'm catching a lot of love for you. And I know that's not gonna happen here." Her response was like, "I understand. You've been locked up for a long time. You know I respect you; you know I wouldn't do that."

I be lonely a lot. I'm lonely now, actually. I just be sleeping most of the time. I'll take the drugs they gave me. Seroquel. Benadryl. I'll save that up so the times I don't have nothing to do, I'll take it and just wait until it hits me. And then I'll fall asleep and just wake up the next day and keep moving. It's like, fuck. I can't do this.

This story is not uncommon to the inmates who reside at Rikers Island. The jail is notorious for violence and death. The death of Kalief Browder garnered a lot of attention in 2015. Browder, accused of stealing a backpack, hung himself after spending three years at Rikers awaiting a trial. The recent HBO series, *The Night Of*, tells the story of a young man who is accused of a violent crime, and while he eventually was freed, the years he spent at Rikers awaiting a trial ruined his life. Kalief Browder tried to hang himself once at Rikers but was unsuccessful. He successfully hung himself after he was released. He could not recover from his three years at Rikers. This is a common problem among former inmates. Though not unique to Rikers, inmate violence and inmate-officer violence is exacerbated at Rikers. The sheer volume of prisoners at Rikers makes it more problematic than other jails, but these problems are found at many jails. Jails are different than prisons, in that there is frequent population turnover and prisoners are not yet acclimated to life behind bars. This contributes to a chaotic atmosphere in jails. Unfortunately, jail reform does not fall high on the priority list of policymakers.

zine. Retrieved on September 6, 2018 from http://nymag.com/daily/intelligencer/2015/06/inside -rikers-island-interviews.html

Prisons

As Gresham Sykes noted, the United States has often struggled in determining what prisons are supposed to be. Some people believe they are supposed to rehabilitate prisoners, while other people believe time spent in prison is supposed to be punishment. Still, other people believe the mission is a combination of the two ideas. This is a never-ending ideological struggle that may never be settled.[26] These two tensions play out in very real ways for prisoners on a daily basis, though not always in the ways early experts might have anticipated. Take, for example, the following narrative, part of a longer narrative written by Victor Muglia, a young inmate serving life at East Jersey State Prison in New Jersey for murder.

Narrative: Victor Muglia

Fortunately, I came into the prison culture at a time where things were better in some respects but much worse in others. At the first prison I went to, Garden State Youth Correctional Facility (a.k.a. Yardville), there were many vocational programs—probably more than any other prison in New Jersey—but the officers were incredibly disdainful toward me because of my crime, whereas other prisoners really didn't care or were interested only for the sake of nosey curiosity. I didn't have a charge that was in the category of "morally debased crimes," so I didn't and wouldn't face any persecution from prisoners because of my crime. This was a new concept to me—the idea of a moral hierarchy in prisons. However, it wasn't a very complex concept. It seemed to be stratified like this, from the lowest moral standpoint to the highest: baby killers, child molesters, rapists, people who killed senior citizens, and then everyone else. If you weren't "everyone else," you would be given three options: enter into protective custody, pay rent, or get jumped by two or more people.

The administrator had disdain for me, but it was much more subtle than that of the officers. He told me that I couldn't go anywhere near the vocational area because there were too many objects similar to a crowbar that I could use to beat someone. Nevertheless, I signed up for an introductory shop class, and a month later, I was shipped out to East Jersey State Prison (a.k.a. Rahway or "The Dome").

That entire month at Yardville was hell. The officers had continually threatened me with violence and did physically "rough me up" without doing any real damage. Every day, without fail, I was encouraged by one particular of-

---

26. Sykes, G. M. (1958). *The society of captives: A study of a maximum security prison.* Princeton, NJ: Princeton University Press.

ficers to kill myself; I told the prison psychiatrist they shouldn't let officers try to encourage people, especially those who actually have a history of suicide, to go kill themselves, but she said she could do nothing about it. The officers were incredibly racist, and this shocked me because I never had met people so overtly racist. There was one incident where I had approached an officer incorrectly upon a pat-frisk request—I was supposed to face away from him and walk toward him backward with my arms spread, but I walked directly toward him with my arms at my side. He gave me a hard turn and said, with three officers by his side, "If you had been a nigger, we would've sprayed you and beat the shit out of you." During the movements, a sergeant would routinely shout, at Black inmates, epithets like "gangbanger," "bastard," "monkey," and "nigger."

In spite of all this negativity, there was a positive aspect to the whole experience: I developed incredibly thick skin. In that prison, I never once responded with aggression or even back talk, and I gained humility in the face of abuse. It was so multitudinous that it would be impossible to respond to all of it—I probably would have been killed if I had aggressively responded to every bit of abuse that I endured. It was so overwhelming that I wasn't even emotionally affected by it anymore. It had made me "numb," so to speak. The abuse also taught me something about the attitudes of correctional officers: they take it upon themselves to add to the predetermined punishment of the state. I know this because it wasn't only me that faced this disdain. Some prisoners faced this disdain because of their crimes, while others faced it because of their ethnicity.

I have got along with 99% of the prisoners that I have come into contact with. There have been petty disagreements and some heated arguments, but we usually learn to move past these; very few people like to be immersed in social tension. As for the 1% of prisoners that I have come into contact with, I had either fought them or had almost been in an altercation that was broken up just in time. But these were rare occurrences. Believe it or not, violence is a rare thing in this prison these days, much more rare than it is on the outside. I can't speak for all prisons in New Jersey, but I can speak for the two prisons in which I've been housed—Garden State Youth Correctional Facility and East Jersey State Prison. The lack of violence in the prison in which I'm currently housed has astounding implications; along with the New Jersey States Prison in Trenton, this prison was one of the most notorious prisons in the state, known for its frequent rapes, fights, and stabbings (which still do happen but on a drastically smaller scale). It is hard to pinpoint exactly what may have caused the shift in prisoner-on-prisoner violence, but the facts nevertheless speak volumes.

This lack of violence seems to have an inverse effect on the correctional officers: the less violent that we are as prisoners, the more hostile the officers becomes. Moreover, the more propitious activities we engage in like vocational training and college education, the larger the chips on the officers' shoulders. For instance, at the inception of the NJ-STEP college program, the officers were literally throwing away student's textbooks for no reason. One student boldly decided to write a grievance to administration about this issue. In response to this, the officers were even more vigorous in sabotaging this individual's college material and also threatened him with physical violence. After a long and bard battle between him and custody, certain officers were reprimanded, and some were even reassigned to new posts so they could no longer harass college students.

Seeing this happen to a fellow student and friend was the straw that broke the camel's back when it came to my opinion of correctional officers, and I'm still wrestling with my own understanding of their attitudes on a psychological level. It's as if there is a cognitive dissonance taking place within the psyche of the officers—we're not measuring up to their stereotypes of us as violent animals who must be caged at all times, we are not giving of the supposedly recognizable signs of moral inferiority, and therefore something must be terribly wrong. Or perhaps they think we're violent animals who are putting up a false front of nicety to "manipulate the system," and this makes them angry. I'm just hypothesizing here.

Judging by the actions of officers along with the prison conditions, it would seem that the general philosophy of punishment is this: it is not simply your lack of freedom for a determined amount of time but also whatever negative things come with "being in prison." In addition to abuse from correctional staff, this also includes environmental factors: paint is peeling everywhere (usually as a result of black mold), buildings have been renovated and closed down as a result of asbestos, there seems to be a drinking water advisory every other month, the ventilation is terrible, and any structure that breaks is "made pretty," much like a fat hog is made pretty by someone adorning it with beautiful jewelry. The most blatant and reckless Band-Aid was that which I saw on a loading dock. Right beneath the surface of the dock, the cement was hollowed out, from wear and tear, in the shape of a half-circle with a radius of about three feet. It looked like someone had chiseled out most of the cement underneath the platform but left the platform intact. Right before the DOC commissioner and other politicians were scheduled to appear at a college graduation ceremony in our visit hall, a piece of plywood was nailed over the cave and the whole thing was spray-painted yellow. To me, this is symbolic of New Jersey's practice of corrections: if something is broken and it doesn't affect us, leave it alone, but if someone important comes around, let's make it look like it's not broken so we don't get in trouble.

> Because of my incarceration at such a young age, I was forced to raise myself. I got some pointers here and there from seasoned prisoners, but I had to either become a self-sufficient survival machine or perish both mentally and physically. All the life lessons that I learned were not principles gleaned from sitting on Grandpa's lap while he told me the key to living a successful life—they were all lessons that, especially if I made a mistake, I had to suffer by myself. Everything that I know to be right and wrong as a mature adult was learned by painful trial and error.

The idea that incarceration as a punishment could be an enlightening and humanitarian practice began with the Enlightenment thinkers such as Cesare Beccaria and Jeremy Bentham. Beccaria argued as an extension of his assertion that the death penalty was inhumane; sending criminals to prison for life imprisonment was preferable.[27] Jeremy Bentham went so far as to design the panopticon, an ideal prison in which a single correctional officer could watch any inmate at any time. Bentham believed that inmates would feel that since they could be watched at any time, it was important to behave.[28]

The first prison in the United States was not built upon ideals of reformation. Indeed, it was not even originally designed as a correctional facility. Old Newgate Prison, which operated in Connecticut as a correctional facility from 1773 to 1827 started as an underground copper mine. The first prisoners were kept underground to work in the mine. To some people, this might resemble the idea that the prisoners were supposed to learn a work ethic, but that was really an ancillary outcome. Prisoners in Newgate were meant to be punished. Not enjoying the conditions, several inmates escaped from the facility. To prevent these escapes, a crude prison, including walls and guard towers, were built around the mine.[29] In addition to facilities like Newgate, prison facilities in the United States, before the era of incarceration became the norm for punishments of criminal law, had two main purposes: to house debtors or to serve as workhouses. Essentially, these facilities were targeted at the poor. If people could not pay their debts, they were sent to prison until they did—a somewhat counterintuitive idea. In some instances, these facilities doubled as workhouses, an idea that once again was borrowed from England in which poor people or people who committed property crimes were supposed to learn a work ethic and pay for their misdeeds. Debtors' prisons, as they became known, were largely abolished in the 1830s due to changes

---

27. Beccaria, C. (1963). *On Crimes and Punishment*. Translated with an Introduction by H. Paolucci. New York, NY: Macmillan. Original work published in 1764.

28. Fyfe, N. R., & Bannister, J. (1996). City watching: Closed circuit television surveillance in public spaces. *Area*, *28*, 37–46.

29. Hanser, R. D. (2017). *Introduction to corrections* (2nd ed.). Thousand Oaks, CA: Sage.

in federal law and especially the evolution of bankruptcy laws. Workhouses largely disappeared as the first true prisons took shape in the United States.[30]

Two groups of people are often credited with the major shifts in penological thought that began to diminish the implementation of capital and corporal punishment in the United States and the evolution of penitentiaries as the primary mechanism of punishment for serious offenders: the Philadelphia Prison Society and the Quakers. The Philadelphia Prison Society was a group founded by Dr. Benjamin Rush, a founding father of the United States and a proponent of many different reforms, such as the abolition of slavery and the abolition of capital and corporal punishment among others. The Religious Society of Friends, or more often referred to as the Quakers, is a sect of Christianity that preaches modesty and nonviolence. Collectively, the two groups were appalled by the horrible conditions in jails and the general environment of what they considered brutal punishments in the United States. Furthermore, the groups believed that attempts to use hard labor as a means of correctional action, as practiced at that time, were brutal and exploitive.[31] It was with these thoughts in mind that a new system of punishment through incarceration was proposed, which is commonly referred to as the Pennsylvania system. In the ideal, prisoners would be kept in isolation in separate prison cells. Isolation was important for two reasons: to keep convicts from associating with other convicts and give them time to reflect on their misdeeds. Additionally, inmates were encouraged to develop a spiritual nature and essentially get right with God so that they could be reformed. Inmates were encouraged to read the Bible, the only book allowed in their cell. The only conversations inmates would have with human beings were when employees of the prison came to check up on the inmates or counsel them.[32] This form of incarceration was first implemented within a wing of the existing Walnut Street Jail in Philadelphia and later, in perhaps its most grand form, at the specially built Eastern State Penitentiary that was also located in Philadelphia. Opened in 1829, Eastern State was the most expensive building in the United States at that time. It was designed by the prominent architect John Haviland, and unlike many prisons and jails that have notoriously modest conditions, the prison had many amenities that were novel at the time, such as heat and running water. Even though inmates at Eastern State had the use of an exercise yard, inmates were prohibited from being in the yard at the same time as another inmate who was in an adjoining yard.[33]

Around the same time that the Pennsylvania system of incarceration was being established, in 1816, the state of New York opened the Auburn Correctional Facility in Auburn. The facility established what is known as either the Auburn

---

30. Friedman, L. M. (1993). *Crime and punishment in American history.* New York, NY: Basic.
31. Bosworth, M. (2010). *Explaining U.S. imprisonment.* Thousand Oaks, CA: Sage.
32. Clear, T. R., Reisig, M. D. & Cole, G. F. (2015). *American Corrections* (11th ed.). Boston, MA: Cengage.
33. Bosworth, M. (2010). *Explaining U.S. imprisonment.* Thousand Oaks, CA: Sage.

system or congregate system of incarceration. Unlike the Pennsylvania system, which placed inmates in solitary confinement, the Auburn system allowed inmates out of their solitary cells during the day to work. While inmates were supposed to stay silent and not communicate with other inmates, the system did allow inmates some level of interaction with other human beings that was lacking in the Pennsylvania system.[34] The Auburn system had no qualms against corporal punishment. The warden of the facility was Captain Elam Lynds, a former soldier who, in the words of Mary Bosworth, ruled the facility with an "iron fist" and expected that his militaristic style training would be effective in reforming prisoners. Corporal punishment in the facility varied from whipping inmates to placing them in stocks and pillories.[35] Additionally, since a lot of the work inmates engaged in was outside correctional walls, inmates were dressed in striped uniforms for easy identification and were expected to walk in lockstep.[36]

While prisons in the northern United States experimented with systems of solitary confinement or variations of the congregate system, states in the south and west primarily relied upon a leasing system in which private individuals would either operate prisons, or convicts sentenced to some period of incarceration were leased to individuals or companies looking for workers. With little oversight, these inmates were often treated in a brutal fashion, which included being expected to work long hours in horrible conditions and subject to corporal punishment. Later, both regions would establish penitentiaries as well, but within the south, many prisoners worked as part of chain gangs or prison farms. Some of these farms survive to the present day.[37]

Despite what seems like the best of intentions, the Pennsylvania system of incarceration quickly proved a failure. While limitations of budgets and facilities certainly decreased the effectiveness of the system, the bigger problem was that solitary confinement as a strategy of rehabilitation seemed to cause more problems than it solved. Long periods of solitude seemed to make inmates with mental illness deteriorate, and some inmates, who had no history of mental illness, started to develop some of these troubles.[38] This is not to say that the Pennsylvania system disappeared from American corrections; instead, it evolved. As punishment for a variety of offenses, problematic inmates are either placed in solitary confinement, commonly referred to as either administration or disciplinary segregation, for short periods of time, or to supermax prisons, for longer periods of time. In both of these forms of incarceration, inmates spend 23 hours

---

34. Hanser, R. D. (2017). *Introduction to corrections* (2nd ed.). Thousand Oaks, CA: Sage.

35. Bosworth, M. (2010). *Explaining U.S. imprisonment*. Thousand Oaks, CA: Sage.

36. Freedman, E. B. (1981). *Their sisters' keepers: Women's prison reform in America, 1830–1930*. Ann Arbor, MI: University of Michigan Press.

37. Bosworth, M. (2010). *Explaining U.S. imprisonment*. Thousand Oaks, CA: Sage.

38. Sykes, G. M. (1958). *The society of captives: A study of a maximum security prison*. Princeton, NJ: Princeton University Press.

a day in isolation and are only allowed 1 hour outside of their cells. Much like the original Pennsylvania system, inmates in these more modern forms of solitary confinement often suffer from the same mental health issues.[39] In a narrative titled "Memoirs of a Lost Soul," Kevin Stout, serving a lengthy term of incarceration for murder in a New Jersey prison, said the following of his experience in "the hole" or solitary confinement.

Narrative: Memoirs of a Lost Soul, by Kevin Stout

My crime happened around the time of fear that everyone in the world would recognize, even though they may not celebrate it. It was Christmas time. A time of bliss, a time of love, and a time where families of all creeds are gathered together as one.

The guilt and shame of that has haunted me ever since. I have been remorseful since that dreadful day, yet I could not wrap my mind around being forgiven for such a horrible crime. It took me fears before I came to grips with the fact that God forgives, and that in order for me to heal, I must also forgive myself.

I continued to mask my shame and pain with getting high. I knew no other way to deal with the atrocities that I had inflicted upon others. My real pain was the fact that it was an elderly woman, age 64, and all I had to do was wrestle the money away, not shoot her point blank in the face. To this very day, this very moment that I write this, it still bothers me.

Fast forward my life 20 years. I was still using drugs to mask my shame while in prison. In November 2000, I was busted for drug use and sent to the hole as punishment.

The hole is a place of loneliness, which is cold, dark, damp, and noisy. The walls are dirty, smothered with the previous occupants' feces alongside frivolous writings.

I was a pillar of the prison community because I was in the lifers' group "Scared straight" program and thus looked upon in a different and favorable light. My being a pillar also helped me hide the pain and shame through self-promotion.

This was important to me because all my life I had struggled with feelings of being neglected and rejected.

When I went to courtline my name was plastered and strewn all over the door of the courtline entrance for all to see. There was a collective gasp as my name was called louder than all the other names.

---

39. Arrigo, B. A., & Bullock, J. L. (2008). The psychological effects of solitary confinement on prisoners in supermax units: Reviewing what we know and recommending what should change. *International Journal of Offender Therapy and Comparative Criminology, 52*, 622–640.

I remember my darkest moment was when a social worker was making her rounds in the hole area. She was very much surprised to see me in the hole, let alone for what I was in there for.

I had taken a few of the group therapy sessions that she ran, and we had a rapport, which caused me more embarrassment.

I was standing, at my door earing through the bars, contemplating, my ruin when she appeared out of nowhere.

It had to be a godsend because that moment of deep acute embarrassment led me to never want to feel like that ever again and played an intricate role in my sobriety.

I had an epiphany that burned deep within my soul. I was through with the pain, through with the masking of agony, through with getting high.

That epiphany was challenged the moment I got out of the hole, where I spent 15 whole days, in utter darkness. I was immediately approached with a chance to get high by one of my friends. I finally, for the very first time in my life, refused, even though it was free of charge.

The very next morning, I was called to provide a urine sample, which was a prerequisite to go along with the hole time. You had to void a urine sample at least once a month for a year as part of your punishment.

I said to myself, "see, what if you had not changed your thought patterns while in the hole?" I would have been on zero tolerance for life, which meant that you neither partook in the visit room or other programs conclusive to strengthening family ties.

I was proud of myself for one reason and one reason only!!! That was the first time in my entire life I passed a urine analysis. In the last, I was either dirty, or I avoided prosecution by refusing to give a sample, which was punishable by hole time, as well as an extensive stay in the hole, which is called administrative segregation, spending anywhere from 90 to 365 days in the hole.

Kevin's experience in the hole was more helpful than harmful, though he mentioned that he was housed in filthy conditions while in solitary confinement. In fact, Kevin has now been proudly sober for over 17 years. His last sentence to the hole came at the right time to preempt his sobriety. Solitary confinement is a regular feature of most prisons. It is supposed to be used on a short-term basis, though we know of many cases in which prisoners were kept much longer, suffering severe mental health problems as a result.

Much like the Pennsylvania system, the leasing system has not completely disappeared, but it has evolved. While private companies are no longer able to simply rent a convict, a growing number of private companies are entering the corrections marketplace and have built prisons, jails, and detention centers and operate some community corrections programs. In some instances, these companies flourished in the short term when limits of state budgetary procedures did not allow states to build enough correctional facilities to house the burgeoning inmate populations of the 1980s and 1990s. In other instances, private correctional facilities flourished as an extension of the philosophy that some people hold that anything the government accomplishes, the private industry can do better or cheaper. To many critics of this occurrence, corporations should not profit from human misery in this manner.[40] Today, about 8% of inmates within the state and federal prison population are held in private facilities. While this has been an 83% increase since 1999, the population of inmates in private facilities seems to have stagnated, and in most recent years, has been declining slightly.[41] Despite this increase, the effectiveness of privatized corrections is still very much an open question.[42]

Thus, we are primarily left with the Auburn system, which is essentially the dominant model of American corrections today. Yet, some things have changed. Inmates no longer have to remain silent, except perhaps during certain short-term situations where they are specifically directed to be silent, and by the 1970s, formalized policies of corporal punishment disappeared from correctional facilities. Many inmates work in prisons doing a variety of jobs, from daily maintenance and operation of the facilities (such as janitorial, cooking, and laundry services), some industrial work, and as previously mentioned, some prisons still operate farms.[43] However, inmate labor has always been controversial. In many instances, it is simply deemed exploitative or akin to slavery, but perhaps the real problem is simply competition. Organized labor in the United States has always viewed prison labor as a threat, and many labor groups have successfully obtained restrictions on the forms of labor in which inmates can engage.[44] Furthermore, common restrictions are that prisons are not supposed to provide their goods to anyone but state agencies.[45] Yet, some corporations have seemingly found loopholes to these policies and are able to profit from prison labor.[46] It is hard to com-

---

40. Griffin, O. H., Woodward, V. H. & Sloan, J. J. (2016). *The money and politics of criminal justice policy*. Durham, NC: Carolina Academic Press.

41. Geiger, A. (2017, April 11*). U.S. private prison population has declined in recent years.* Pew Research Center. Retrieved on July 25, 2018 from http://www.pewresearch.org/fact-tank/2017/04/11/u-s-private-prison-population-has-declined-in-recent-years/

42. Lindsey, A. M., Mears, D. P., & Cochran, J. C. (2016). The privatization debate: A conceptual framework for improving (public and private) corrections. *Journal of Contemporary Criminal Justice, 32*, 308–327.

43. Bosworth, M. (2010). *Explaining U.S. imprisonment*. Thousand Oaks, CA: Sage.

44. Krisberg, B., Marchionna, S., & Hartney, C. (2015). *American corrections: Concepts and controversies*. Thousand Oaks, CA: Sage.

45. Sykes, G. M. (1958). *The society of captives: A study of a maximum security prison*. Princeton, NJ: Princeton University Press.

46. Sliva, S. M., & Samimi, C. (2018). Social work and prison labor: A restorative model. *Social Work, 63*, 153–160.

pletely imagine the debate between how to balance how inmates should repay the state for their incarceration, the importance of inmates developing a work ethic, and the importance of not exploiting inmate labor ever being solved.

While the system of silence and reflection of the Pennsylvania system and work ethic development of the Auburn system were intended to be rehabilitative, prisons have incorporated a variety of rehabilitation into correctional programming. We will discuss this in greater detail in Chapter 10. Among the more common programs are educational (such as training for GED) and treatment programs (such as drug treatment or anger management). Yet, for a time, some prisons were essentially run on what has been referred to as either the reformatory era or medical model of incarceration. The most well-known example of this was the Elmira Reformatory in Elmira, New York that was administered by Zebulon Brockway and began operations in 1876. Brockway treated inmates as if they had a disease that caused their criminality. Thus, he tried to treat them through a variety of methods and made use of recently enacted parole statutes so that he could build a reward-based structure that would allow inmates to earn early release if they were deemed reformed. This was completed through the use of indeterminate sentencing. Although inmates would generally have a maximum amount of years they could serve in a correctional facility, there was great variability in how early they could be released. While Brockway repeatedly claimed that he was able to cure criminals, there was a lack of reliable data to support such claims. Some correctional facilities and states enacted similar programs. Yet, the tactics of Brockway were very much a product of the progressive era, and while many states still have parole, sentencing in most states is no longer on an indeterminate basis. More states use determinate sentencing, which has a much smaller window of time toward the end of a sentence in which an inmate can be released. Furthermore, many states either employ mandatory minimums or truth-in-sentencing laws, which greatly restrict the ability of inmates to earn early releases from prison.[47]

Before we discuss prisons in the modern day, it is important to discuss the evolution of women's prisons. Prior to 1840, women were very rarely found in America's prisons. Part of the reason for this is most women were highly controlled and not allowed to stray too far from home. Even as more women came into contact with the criminal justice system, they committed far fewer felonies and a miniscule number of violent crimes. The only crime that they even closely committed at a ratio similar to men were property crimes. Thus, most women who were convicted were either released or served short sentences in jails. However, as the 18th century progressed and American rapidly changed from a largely agrarian and mercantile economy with large numbers of people in rural areas to

---

47. Clear, T. R., Reisig, M. D., & Cole, G. F. (2015). *American Corrections* (11th ed.). Boston, MA: Cengage.

a more industrialized economy with greater numbers of people in urban areas, more women came into contact with the criminal justice system. Furthermore, limited legitimate opportunities for employment led many women into theft and/ or prostitution. This combined with very strict laws governing women's chastity created the concept of the fallen woman, a heavily stigmatized status of women who were considered society's outcasts and deemed beyond hope. These circumstances essentially created a criminal class of women who not only went to prisons but also did not receive any meaningful form of correctional treatment.[48]

While men at Auburn prison often suffered from brutal conditions, the 20–40 women who were incarcerated in the same facility had it much worse. Although they were segregated from the male prisoners, they were essentially locked into the attic of the prison together, which was boarded up. No correctional treatment was given, and it was documented that one prisoner managed to get pregnant while in solitary confinement. Eventually a matron was hired to supervise the women, but this did not substantially improve their plight behind bars. Women were often brutalized by male correctional officers, and in one prison in Indiana, the prison administrators actually created a brothel using coerced women inmates.[49]

There were two barriers to reform of women's prisons. First was that compared to men, women make up a much smaller portion of the inmate population.[50] In 2017, 99,000 women were confined in state prisons, 96,000 in local jails, and 14,000 in federal prisons.[51] Even to the present day, the smaller portion of inmates and that so few women commit violent acts makes them a low target for correctional programming.[52] The second problem was the heavily stigmatized concept of fallen women. With women in general society so heavily controlled and with a more Victorian sense of morals, many women seemed to fear being associated with these women. That began to change with Elizabeth Fry. Fry was a Quaker minister in England. Somewhat of a novel concept at the time, since the Quakers were one of the few religions, especially then, was to provide more equal opportunities in leadership in religious organizations. As we have discussed, the Quakers have been heavily involved in the evolution of correctional policy. Fry, as an outlet of her ministry, began to enter women's correctional facilities in En-

---

48. Freedman, E. B. (1981). *Their sisters' keepers: Women's prison reform in America, 1830–1930*. Ann Arbor, MI: University of Michigan Press.

49. Freedman, E. B. (1981). *Their sisters' keepers: Women's prison reform in America, 1830–1930*. Ann Arbor, MI: University of Michigan Press.

50. Clear, T. R., Reisig, M. D., & Cole, G. F. (2015). *American Corrections* (11th ed.). Boston, MA: Cengage.

51. Kajstura, A. (2017, October 19). *Women's mass incarceration: The whole pie 2017*. Prison Policy Initiative. Retrieved on July 27, 2018 from https://www.prisonpolicy.org/reports/pie2017women.html

52. Clear, T. R., Reisig, M. D., & Cole, G. F. (2015). *American Corrections* (11th ed.). Boston, MA: Cengage.

gland. Similar to the state of women in American prisons, Fry was appalled by the conditions. She then called for more women to not only volunteer at women's correctional facilities but to also administer them as well. She began to debunk the image of fallen women both in that most inmates were not beyond hope, but that many were victims of circumstances, and rather than being seducers of men, they were more often victims of them.[53]

Fry's work was largely limited to the 1820s, and eventually, through family misfortunes and the growing belief among English correctional administrators that Fry was soft on inmates, she had a diminishing role in English corrections. Yet, her writings and example inspired many women, both in England and the United States. As a result, throughout the 1800s, a growing number of middle- and upper-class women began to visit incarcerated women and advocate for better conditions. Additionally, women would have not only a growing influence on policy but in the administration of correctional facilities as well. In the 1860s, women's prison reformers sought three demands. First, they demanded that women be placed in separate correctional facilities. Second, that women inmates received differential and specialized care. Third, that the administration of women's prisons be conducted by female staff and administrators. While the first separate prison building for women was built at Sing Sing Correctional Facility in 1839, the first separate facility, the Indiana Woman's Prison, opened in Indianapolis in 1874. By the 1890s, many women were employed in women's correctional facilities. Among the many women who advocated for changes in the treatment of incarcerated women, also important was the design of women's facilities. Since most inmates were not typically violent and did not need the same oversight or security, many women's facilities were built as separate cottages. This designed was first implemented for juvenile offenders.[54] While conditions in women's facilities today are not ideal and some inmates suffer sexual abuse from male staff and a lack of specialized programming, their plight has improved considerably.[55]

In 2017, approximately 1,330,000 inmates were held in 1,719 state prisons, and 197,000 inmates were held in federal prisons.[56] Prison construction has evolved considerably over time, and the targeted inmate population often is reflected when designing a prison. The earliest prisons in the United States were designed to be intimidating facilities and often resembled castles. These facilities were typically cell block facilities in which wings or rows of cells radiated from a central office or around a courtyard. Many people have referred to these facilities as the

53. Freedman, E. B. (1981). *Their sisters' keepers: Women's prison reform in America, 1830–1930*. Ann Arbor, MI: University of Michigan Press.

54. Freedman, E. B. (1981). *Their sisters' keepers: Women's prison reform in America, 1830–1930*. Ann Arbor, MI: University of Michigan Press.

55. Hanser, R. D. (2017). *Introduction to corrections* (2nd ed.). Thousand Oaks, CA: Sage.

56. Wagner, P., & Rabuy, B. (2017, March 14). *Mass incarceration: The whole pie 2017*. Prison Policy Initiative. Retrieved on July 29, 2018 from https://www.prisonpolicy.org/reports/pie2017.html

telephone pole design. Today, this type of facility is typically reserved for inmates who need to be in a maximum-security facility. Inmates need to be kept separate when the occasion is needed, and these facilities are also built like fortresses to prevent escapes. In many of the facilities, bunks, desks, sinks, and toilets are placed in every cell and are built to be nearly indestructible. Guard towers, razor lined fences, and flood lights are common features on the outside of the facilities. Medium security prisons will have some of the same security features, such as walls around the facility, but often lack the intimidating guard towers and razor wire. Furthermore, inmates more often live in a communal fashion, and many inmates will often share bathrooms. These facilities will more often use pods than cellblocks. Minimum security facilities have very little security and are in some cases work camps or farms. Some facilities will have a guarded fence, and others in rural areas might have none at all.[57]

---

57. Hanser, R. D. (2017). *Introduction to corrections* (2nd ed.). Thousand Oaks, CA: Sage.

Chapter 5

Probation and Parole

n the last chapter, you learned about the era of mass incarceration that has resulted in the imprisonment of almost 1% of the U.S. population. Mass incarceration has had devastating consequences for individuals, families, and communities. It has placed the United States at the forefront of incarceration, in that we hold 25% of the world's prison population. This is a staggering number, one that has been well documented in movies, documentaries, and books. We show many of these documentaries to our classes to help students understand the evolution of the phenomena of mass incarceration. Recent films such as *The House I Live In* and *13th* portray very well the causes of the prison population explosion in the United States over the last 30 years. The focus of prisons is justifiable, but the long reach of mass incarceration extends way beyond the prison walls. While over 2.3 million people are incarcerated, far more Americans are serving a criminal justice sentence involving community supervision. In short, at least 4.6 million Americans are serving a sentence of either probation or parole, doubling the prison population.[1]

In this chapter, we will discuss probation and parole in depth. We will explain the differences between these two punishments, the historical origins of both, and the current ways in which these sentences are applied to offenders. We will provide you with true accounts from the people who are subjected to these criminal justice sanctions and those whose job it is to enforce these sentences in the community. To begin, most people, even many of our students in the beginning of their studies, think that probation and parole are the same sentence. They

---

1. Bureau of Justice Statistics (2016). Retrieved from https://www.bjs.gov/index.cfm?ty=pb detail&iid=5784

are not, but they do involve many of the same conditions. To begin this section properly though, we will define probation and parole for you. Probation is a sentence served in the community in lieu of a term of incarceration. An individual sentenced to probation must abide by conditions specified by the court and enforced by a probation officer. The same is true of those who are on parole, but parole is an early release from a prison sentence that allows an offender to serve the remainder of his or her sentence in the community. Again, they must abide by many conditions, and we will discuss the ramifications of breaking these rules in this chapter, but first we will look at the history of probation.

Probation

History of Probation

The modern-day practice of probation can be traced to the work of a Boston shoemaker named John Augustus. Augustus unofficially began the practice of probation by agreeing to help one man who begged the court not to incarcerate him. The man was charged with public intoxication but claimed that he would never drink again so long as he did not have to go to jail. Known now as the "Father of Probation," Augustus was a religious man who took pity on the man and decided to help him. He asked the court to release the man under his supervision and wait on sentencing him. In doing so, Augustus took responsibility for this man, and in the several weeks that followed, true to his word, the man did not drink. The court was convinced of the man's reform under Augustus' supervision and so began the unofficial beginning of probation in Massachusetts in 1841.[2] From 1841 to 1859, when he died, Augustus bailed out and supervised close to 2,000 offenders, most of whom had alcohol-related offenses. Augustus supervised the offenders and helped them find employment and housing, often times allowing them to stay in his home. He kept careful case notes and reported his findings back to the court at the end of the community supervision. Despite the personal financial cost to himself, Augustus had great success with the offenders he supervised.[3]

In keeping with Augustus' innovation, Massachusetts became the first state to formally adopt probation for juveniles in 1878. Support for juvenile probation came first, with every state but Wyoming adopting juvenile probation laws by 1927 and all states by 1954. New York was first to adopt probation for adult offenders in 1901, and by 1956, all states had probation for adult offenders.[4] There is a federal probation system as well. In fact, one of the authors of this book served as a federal probation officer in the Southern District of New York, which covered Manhattan and Bronx, New York (the federal system uses districts to establish

---

2. Petersilia, J. (Spring 1998). Probation in the United States Part I. *Perspectives,* 31–40.
3. Ibid.
4. Ibid.

jurisdiction). Federal judges were divided over the use of probation. but President Calvin Coolidge signed the Probation Act of 1925, authorizing the probation system in the federal government.[5]

The driving force behind probation was rehabilitation. Augustus believed that proper guidance and supervision could lead to reform and early probation volunteers often came from charitable church groups. The focus on rehabilitation was particularly fitting as well during the period when probation fully flourished in the 1950s. As you have probably learned in the last few chapters, the period from the 1950s to early 1970s was a time characterized by a focus on rehabilitation in the criminal justice system. However, the focus on rehabilitation drastically changed in the 1970s when the United States experienced an increase in crime rates. Changing politics and reports that rehabilitative programs were failing prompted our switch to the crime control model of the 1980s, whereby incarceration and punishment became the main focus of our criminal justice system. You read about mass incarceration in the last chapter, so you should be familiar already with the changes that accompanied our "tough on crime" movement. These changes had implications for the "three P's" of corrections—prisons, probation, and parole. We are going to explain how probation works now, be we want you to keep the changing nature of our criminal justice system in mind as we get into the modern-day practice of probation.

Modern-Day Probation

This is generally the section students love! The historical roots of probation are important of course, but those of you interested in this field want to know how it works on a daily basis. What do probation officers do? What are the rules of probation? Who gets probation? What happens when the rules are broken? In this section, we will answer all of these questions and more. We will provide a narrative from a former federal probation officer to help you better understand the realities of the job and the ways in which the officers and offenders are affected. The system is made up of real people, and that is what we want you to take away from this book and what we hope you will keep in mind if you choose to work in this field.

Let us begin with the two typical functions of probation officers. You probably already know one of them—supervision of offenders serving a sentence of probation. Most students are familiar with this part of probation, but probation officers also conduct presentence investigations. This is an investigation that occurs on the "front end" of sentencing, in that it occurs before a defendant is sentenced but after he or she is convicted of a crime. The investigation is conducted by the probation officer, who collects all information about an individual's offense,

---

5. United States Courts. Retrieved on September 12, 2017 from http://www.uscourts.gov /services-forms/probation-and-pretrial-services/probation-and-pretrial-services-history

criminal history, educational background, employment, family history, medical history, financial background, and other relevant factors. After the investigation is complete, a probation officer uses all of this information to make a sentence recommendation to the judge. Now, we should explain the caveat. Perhaps we can let Meghan explain it in her story.

Narrative: Presentence Investigation—Meghan's Story

An interview with the U.S. Department of Probation—I couldn't have been more excited about any job prospect! I had just graduated with a master's degree in criminal justice, and I had been fortunate to get a number of interviews, but this one was the "money" one in our field. What I mean is that federal jobs are often the goal. We consider them the "cream of the crop," generally. I was nervous but prepared. The interview consisted of six federal officers, including two deputy chiefs, firing questions at me while I sat in a semi-circle. They were not necessarily difficult questions, but they came at me fast and furious. It was a stress interview, meant to gage how I handled stressful situations. I held my own and I got the job. I was asked on the interview if I wanted to work in the presentence division or supervision unit. I said supervision confidently. I was assigned to the presentence division promptly. It was the right choice.

The presentence unit handles all presentence investigations for offenders convicted in federal courts. Once an offender has been convicted, an investigation commences and culminates in a sentence recommendation to the judge. I was introduced to my supervising officer, a female who would become a true mentor and role model, and she trained me in how to conduct presentence investigations. Unfortunately, I still had a misperception about my job. I thought the presentence investigation was one in which I would be able to assess a fair and just sentence for an offender based on all of the circumstances, but the sentencing guidelines thwarted the process in ways I hadn't anticipated. Let me explain. I had learned a lot about the changes to our criminal justice system while earning my master's degree at John Jay College. I knew that the "War on Crime" and "War on Drugs" of the 1980s led to substantial changes in sentencing. We had mandatory minimums, which mandate a minimum sentence for certain crimes, mainly drug crimes. Most states and the federal system had developed truth-in-sentencing schemes, whereby offenders must serve 85% of a sentence before becoming eligible for parole. Parole was abolished in many states and so was the discretion that judges once retained. And then there were the sentencing guidelines.

The Sentencing Reform Act (SRA) of 1984 made sentencing guidelines mandatory in the federal government. Many states followed as they often do when federal legislation is passed. What does this mean? It means that for every crime, there is a corresponding offense level, and for every criminal history category, there is a corresponding criminal history category. When you put the two together, you calculate a mandated sentencing range. Let me give you an example. If John was convicted for illegal possession of a firearm, his base offense level, according to the U.S. guidelines would be a 26. This level might be increased by certain circumstances of the crime, but for this example, let's stick with a 26. After calculating this offense level, the probation officer handling this case calculates the criminal history category. This is done by assessing former arrests, convictions, and sentences and assigning a total criminal history score, which corresponds to a criminal history category. Let's say that John had two former petty convictions that places him in Criminal History Category II. Now, the sentencing range can be calculated. If the offense level is 26 and Criminal History Category is II, the sentencing guidelines chart proscribes a sentencing range of 70 to 87 months. The only discretion the probation officer and/or the judge ultimately has is where in that range to sentence an offender.

The investigation into an individual's employment, family, and financial obligations was helpful in that determination, but that was the extent of it. It was not a true sentence recommendation so much as it was simply a guidelines calculation. The fate of human beings and their families came down to chart of sentences and our ability to apply it. It did not feel like what I signed up for. The hours I spent meeting with offenders and their grieving families, the digging into employment and community service, the sorting through medical and psychologic records, this part of the job had very little impact in the sentencing of offenders. It was disheartening, not only to me but to many federal judges. When the SRA of 1984 passed, some federal judges retired, and many were outraged that their judicial discretion they worked so hard to earn would be downgraded to a systematic calculation of impersonal sentencing ranges.

To make matters worse were the types of offenders I dealt with. I had anticipated that we would convict and sentence serious offenders, such as the "drug kingpins" and murderers, those who committed large-scale white collar offenses and other substantial crimes. In all of approximately 150 cases I handled, I had less than two handfuls of these types of offenders. In reality, the drug kingpins were usually low-level drug mules, who were caught making drug runs in order to support their families. Most offenders I handled were poor, minority, uneducated offenders who lived in and came from terrible backgrounds. These were not the criminal masterminds I thought I would be working so diligently to put behind bars. These were unfortunate people who made bad decisions, usually because of bad circumstances. I had to visit most of the offenders on my caseload in federal jails because they could not afford bail. They were stuck and usually forced into a plea agreement because they had no resources, and the mandatory minimum sentences and sentencing guidelines would result in the harshest of punishments if they did not agree to plead guilty. I began to see the realities of our "just" system and the reality was that it was a highly prejudiced, coercive system that all but mandates that poor people plead guilty to offenses to avoid spending the rest of their lives in prison. Yay for justice!

After two-and-a-half years, I began planning my escape. It was more than just my own upset at working in a system I saw as totally unjust, though. It was also the attitudes of the people around me. I found that most officers were either totally burned out and just waiting on their pensions to come, or the ones that were enthusiastic were usually the ones who had no interest in rehabilitating or helping people, which was in fact the original goal of probation. These officers were enthusiastic about arresting people and seeing them go to prison. It was a perverse system that in turn perverted the people who worked in it. I knew I had to leave. I applied for the PhD program at John Jay College and after exactly three years as a U.S. probation officer, I retired. That chapter closed and a new one began. The irony was that shortly after I left in 2006, the U.S. Supreme Court ruled that the sentencing guidelines were no longer mandatory but rather advisory. I was pleased that it was a step in the right direction, but I still knew that my time as U.S. probation officer was over.

Meghan's story highlights the role of presentence officers but also gives us a look at the inner workings of probation. Meghan did not work in the supervision division, but she worked with those officers often. The supervision division is found at the "back end" of the sentencing process. Once Meghan closed her case, it meant that an offender would either go to prison or perhaps to probation supervision. Even if a person is incarcerated, eventually they might be given a term of supervised release. Supervised release is essentially the same as parole, but we will hold off on this discussion until we turn to parole. For now, we will focus on probation supervision. If an offender is sentenced to probation (Meghan had some offenders who received probation), he or she is assigned to a probation officer.

Probation supervision means that a court has granted an offender a sentence of probation to be served in the community under the supervision of a probation officer. A probationer is no longer a defendant. Once a defendant is convicted, he or she becomes an offender. We often hear people refer to offenders as criminals, which is common outside of our field, but inside our field you should learn the proper ways to discuss the people with whom you will work. A probationer is allowed to serve a sentence in the community so long as the offender abided by the conditions of probation. These are rules that fall under two categories: standard conditions and special conditions. The former, standard conditions, are those that are applied to all probationers. For example, probationers cannot possess a firearm, associate with felons, or leave the state without permission. They must report to a probation officer on a regular basis and provide truthful information to their officer. Meghan did not deal with offenders as you recall, but many of her colleagues did, and Meghan worked on a special team that helped deal with noncompliant offenders, or those who broke their conditions. We will discuss the consequences of doing so shortly. In addition to standard conditions, there are often special conditions imposed by the court.

Special Conditions

Special conditions are those conditions assigned to a specific offender based on the crime, criminal history, or social history of an offender. For example, if a person commits a fraud using the Internet, a judge may order no Internet usage as a special condition of probation. If an offender has a history of drug abuse, the court will order drug rehabilitation and drug testing as special conditions of probation. Examples of other special conditions can include paying restitution, abiding by a curfew, and performing community service. Sex offenders often have to abide by a number of special conditions, including restricted computer usage and restricted residency, meaning that they cannot live within a certain proximity to schools and/or other locations where children congregate. In sum, the court can choose from a variety of special conditions to protect the community and aid the offender in his or her rehabilitation. Maybe this brings us to another important question. Why probation?

Why Probation and Who Is Eligible?

By now, you know that probation is rooted in rehabilitation. Augustus began the practice of probation with the goal of helping offenders to reform their behavior. Rehabilitation is certainly still one of the goals of probation, but is it the only one? This is not a simple question, but we think we can shed some light on this issue for you. First, let us turn to the numbers to help place our answer in the appropriate context. There are currently close to 3.8 million adults on probation in the United States,[6] compared with a prison population of approximately 2.2 million Americans.[7] Probation is now most commonly used form of punishment in the United States, and while rehabilitation explains the popularity of probation in the beginning, it does not provide the full picture.

As we said earlier, the introduction of the "tough on crime" movement of the 1980s resulted in radical changes to the criminal justice system. The result of

6. Bureau of Justice Statistics. (2017). *Probation and parole in the United States, 2015*. Retrieved from https://www.bjs.gov/index.cfm?ty=pbdetail&iid=5784

7. Bureau of Justice Statistics. (2017). *Correctional populations in the United States, 2015*. Retrieved from https://www.bjs.gov/index.cfm?ty=pbdetail&iid=5870

mandatory sentencing and other punitive policies was a prison population explosion. In our field, we refer to this explosion as mass incarceration, whereby the number of Americans incarcerated went from approximately 200,000 in the early 1970s to 2.2 million today. It is now a well-established fact that while the United States holds just 5% of the world's population, we incarcerate roughly 25% of the world's prisoners. We are currently the world leader in incarceration. Let that sink in a bit. We do not lead the world in education or technology but rather in the rate at which we incarcerate our own citizens.

The result of mass incarceration is prison overcrowding and a massive strain on state budgets to keep up with the costs of incarcerating so many people. The average cost of incarceration is approximately $33,274[8] per inmate per year, though these costs range from a low of $14,870 to a high of $69,355[9] in New York. The costs are high, but they are even higher when we factor in the aging prison population. After all, mandatory prison sentencing means that people stay in prison longer, and the prison system must accommodate the rising medical costs of an aging prison population. In comparison, the average cost of probation per year is much lower, ranging from about $1,300 to $2,800.[10] The use of probation therefore has two positive outcomes: it relieves prison overcrowding and lowers correctional costs. That being said, not every offender is eligible for probation.

A person convicted of a misdemeanor is a much stronger candidate than one convicted of a felony. Typically, probation is used for those nonviolent offenders who have little to no criminal history in their past. These offenders are considered nonserious offenders for whom getting caught and punished by the criminal justice system will serve as a deterrent to future crime (also important that you understand the concept of deterrence, so please read back on this one as well if you do not). Most states and the federal government do not allow the use of probation for violent felons or those with a history of felony convictions. For example, a person convicted of armed robbery would never be a candidate for probation, but an individual convicted of theft might be a candidate for this type of sentence. Though the type of crime and an individual's prior criminal history are the strongest predictors of probation, judges also consider factors such as a defendant's employment or educational status, familial obligations, and standing in the community. These factors are part of the presentence investigation conducted by probation officers, as discussed earlier in Meghan's story.

A judge does not always have the freedom to decide between probation and prison, though. In states with mandatory minimums, certain offenders are prohibited from receiving probation. Also, sentencing guidelines based on offense

---

8. Mai, C., & Subramanian, R. (2017). *Price of Prisons 2015: Examining State Spending Trends, 2010–2015.* New York, NY: Vera Institute of Justice.

9. Ibid.

10. Schmitt, J., Warner, K., & Gupta, S. (2010). *The high budgetary cost of incarceration.* Washington, DC: Center for Economic and Policy Research.

type and criminal history may also result in mandatory prison terms, whereby probation is not an option. Probation eligibility is therefore determined in one of two ways: by legally proscribed sentencing policy or at the discretion of a judge. When a judge decides, typically the offense type and criminal history of an offender are the most important factors, followed by other social ties related to information about an offender. Once a person is sentenced to probation, he or she is mandated to follow the conditions we discussed in the previous section, which brings us to our next question: what happens if a person breaks the rules?

Probation Revocation

There are many conditions of probation, and it is a probation officer who must enforce these rules. Traditionally, probation officers were considered social workers who helped in the rehabilitation of offenders, but the 1980s brought with it many changes to the work of law enforcement and correctional officers. In particular, probation officers became more aligned with traditional law enforcement in many ways. They are responsible for monitoring their probationers for compliance with the conditions of probation, which involves different modes of surveillance. Surprise home visits are part of the officer's job, and with the advent of mandatory drug sentencing, many probationers are subject to random drug testing in the office and at their homes. When a probationer breaks the conditions of his or her probation, this is referred to as a violation of probation. So, what happens when someone violates their probation?

Not every person who violates a condition of his or her probation is going to see a judge or a prison time. There are two types of violations: a technical violation and a new arrest. A technical violation is a violation of a condition of probation, such as a broken curfew or failure to report to one's probation officer. A new offense is a new arrest, which is both a technical violation (because it is a condition not to sustain any new arrests) and a new offense. A new offense will almost always trigger a violation hearing, which is a hearing to determine whether a person will lose their right to remain on probation in the community. The probation officer handling the case decides whether to file a request for a violation hearing, and when it comes to technical violations, probation officers have a lot of discretion. For example, if a probationer fails to report one week to his or her officer but has an excuse, it is unlikely that the probation officer will initiate a violation hearing. Why do you think that is? Well, think back to the issue of prison overcrowding and lack of resources. Judges are not fond of hearing cases in which minor technical violations are the issue, unless these technical violations are recurrent. If they are or if there is a new arrest, a violation hearing is requested by the probation officer.

What happens at a violation hearing? Is it the same as a trial? The answer is yes and no. Probationers do not have a right to probation, as it is a privilege, but a person's liberty is at stake when there is a probation revocation hearing. The first step, the preliminary hearing, is a ritual step, really. In this hearing, the court decides if there is enough probable cause to move to a full revocation hearing. The court almost always finds that there is enough evidence, as the probationer (defense) is not allowed to submit refuting materials at this stage. Therefore, most probationers waive their right to a preliminary hearing to save time and move straight toward the revocation hearing. In this phase, the court has established that probationers have certain due process rights, though they are not as extensive as afforded to individuals in criminal courts prior to conviction.

In *Mempa v. Rhay*, the U.S. Supreme Court ruled that probationers are entitled to have counsel at revocation hearings. In this 1967 case, 17-year-old Jerry Mempa had his probation revoked after he was found guilty of a burglary, but he was not afforded the right to counsel at his hearing. The Court found this unconstitutional and ruled for the first time in favor of giving probationers due process rights.[11] In a second Supreme Court case, *Gagnon v. Scarpelli,* Gerald Scarpelli had his probation revoked after his conviction for an armed robbery and was sentenced to serve a full turn of his original 15 year's incarceration. Scarpelli appealed his decision, arguing that he had a lack of due process protections, and the U.S. Supreme Court agreed. In their 1973 decision, they declared that probationers have a right to a revocation hearing at which the probationer can call witnesses and present evidence.[12] One feature of the probation hearing, however, seriously distinguished it from a criminal trial, and that is the standard for conviction at a revocation hearing. A probationer may have a hearing with counsel and present evidence and call on witnesses, but at the end of this hearing, the standard for conviction is much lower than the criminal court's proof beyond a reasonable doubt. The standard for the probation revocation hearing is that which is used in civil court and is known as a preponderance of the evidence, which means that the court just needs to be a bit more certain than not that a probationer is guilty. In numerical terms, beyond a reasonable doubt comports to a 99% standard, whereas a preponderance is much lower, at 51% certainty. This standard obviously does not benefit the probationer, but the incarceration rate of probationers who violated their probation has remained fairly stable in recent years at approximately 5.4%.[13]

Does Probation Work?

Does that last number mean that probation works? At first glance, that number seems encouraging, but it does not provide the full picture. When it comes to probation, the "what works" part usually refers to recidivism, or reoffending. Do probationers reoffend while on probation and if so, at what rate? This is the first

---

11. Mempa v. Rhay, 389 U.S. 128 (1967)

12. Gagnon v. Scarpelli, 411 U.S. 778 (1973)

13. Herberman, E. J., & Bonczar, T. P. (2015). *Probation and Parole in the United States, 2013.* Washington, DC: Bureau of Justice Statistics.

question, but the answer is not straightforward. We will do our best to explain. A national overview indicates that 60% of probationers complete their probation successfully, while 40% fail due to technical violations or new offenses.[14] Additionally, another 15% of those who have served a term of probation will go to jail or prison at some point.[15] You will read Amanda's story in the next chapter to see how failure and success in probation play out. That does not mean that all of these probationers will return to prison though. Often, one of the remedies to violations is to extend a probationer's term of probation. That being said, probation is now the most widely used criminal sanction with an increasing number of standard and special conditions and an increase in mandatory fees for probationers to pay, which places probationers at a higher risk of failure.

The second issue in addressing the effectiveness of probation is the cost. The rise in incarceration and prison overcrowding has made probation an appealing alternative for the courts. The cost of probation is approximately $1,250 per year compared with the average cost of incarceration, which is approximately $30,000 per year.[16] Probation is a much cheaper option, and therefore proponents argue its merits on the cost savings it provides. While part of that statement is true, we have to consider that critics of the current probation system note that probation is affordable because it is the most severely underfunded criminal justice agency.[17] The resources required to address the serious economic, mental health, and educational issues faced by probationers does not exist. The fees this disadvantaged group must pay (court costs, supervision costs, fines) mainly go to the basic costs of supervision, such as probation officer salaries, drug testing, and court costs, with little by way of resources for actual rehabilitation. So, is probation as successful as proponents would like you to think? Well, we want to answer that question with a 2014 quote from the White House Council of Economic Advisers:

> Fines and fees create large financial and human costs, all of which are disproportionately borne by the poor. High fines and fee payments may force the indigent formerly incarcerated to make difficult trade-offs between paying court debt and other necessary purchases. Unsustainable debt coupled with the threat of incarceration may even encourage some formerly incarcerated individuals to return to criminal activity to pay off their debts, perversely increasing recidivism. Time spent in pre-trial detention as a punishment for

14. Jacobson, M. P., Schiraldi, V., Daly, R., & Hotez, E. (2017*). Less is more: How reducing probation populations can Improve Outcomes.* Cambridge, MA: Harvard Kennedy School.

15. Herberman, E. J., & Bonczar, T. P. (2015). *Probation and Parole in the United States, 2013.* Washington, DC: Bureau of Justice Statistics.

16. Jacobson, M. P., Schiraldi, V., Daly, R., & Hotez, E. (2017). *Less is more: How reducing probation populations can Improve Outcomes.* Cambridge, MA: Harvard Kennedy School.

17. Ibid.

failure to pay debts entails large costs in the form of personal freedom and sacrificed income, as well as increasing the likelihood of job loss.[18]

Parole

History of Parole

Probation and parole are often lumped together because they are the two main forms of community corrections, and often probationers and parolees are supervised by the same officers. However, they are not the same, and it is essential for students in the field of criminal justice to understand both the differences and the similarities between probation and parole. Probation, as you just learned, is a sentence in lieu of a prison sentence to be served in the community with conditions. Parole is an early release from a prison sentence to be served in the community under the supervision of an officer and in compliance with conditions set by the court. We will talk about the various issues surrounding parole, and you will read the story of Dexter Tyson, who was recently paroled after serving a 31-year prison term for murder. But before we get to these topics, we will begin with the history of parole.

The practice of parole can be traced back to the work of Alexander Maconochie, a captain in the Royal Army who was appointed as warden of Norfolk Island, a British penal colony located 900 miles off the northeast coast of Sidney, Australia. Maconochie implemented a new approach to punishment when he appointed, as warden in 1840, one that included a strong focus on reform. The penal colony had been characterized as one of the worst of England's, marked by brutality against the prisoners before Machonocie's arrival. Maconochie allowed for an indeterminate sentence, or an open sentence, in which prisoners had a chance of being released from prison. To further the open sentence structure, Maconochie developed a mark system whereby prisoners could earn marks for good behavior and later apply those good marks toward early release when they accumulated enough good marks. Does this sound familiar? We typically refer to it now as "good time" credits in our field, but the concept is the same, and so parole was born with Maconochie's vision of blending rehabilitation and humanity with punishment.

In 1854, Sir Walter Crofton developed a similar system in his capacity as administrator of the Irish prison system. Modeled after Maconochie's mark system, Crofton developed the Irish ticket-of-leave system whereby prisoners were gradually released back into society through a three-stage process beginning with solitary confinement, followed by group work, and then ending with a stay at a halfway house. Prisoners who successfully completed the process earned a ticket of leave, or conditional pardon, and were released back into the community. Ze-

---

18. Ibid.

bulon Brockway is usually credited with bringing this system to the U. S. prison system. More specifically, in 1876, as superintendent of Elmira Reformatory, Brockway instituted a system of early release at Elmira whereby prisoners could earn good time credits toward early release. By 1890, 20 states had adopted parole system, and by 1942, every state and the federal government had adopted parole.[19] The use of parole was very popular for almost 30 years, but the 1970s brought with it the beginning of massive changes to parole. The movement away from rehabilitation and toward more punitive sentencing resulted in the elimination of parole and where parole schemes survived, massive changes to the way parole is used.

Modern-Day Parole

There are approximately 853,000 Americans currently on parole.[20] A sentence of probation is determined by a judge, but the decision to parole an offender is typically decided in one of two ways: discretionary or mandatory release. Discretionary release means that a parole board makes the decision. This is what most people think of when they hear that someone has been paroled. Historically, this was the predominant method of release. In 1976, 65% of parolees were released by a parole board, which is a panel of anywhere from 3 to 12 members (traditionally 3 members) appointed by the state's governor.[21] The process of appointment has been highly criticized, as it results in a lack of uniformity in educational standards and other professional qualifications, but it remains the predominant method for choosing a state's parole board. Most parole hearings are private, but recently, the public was given access to the parole hearing of OJ Simpson, convicted of robbery in Nevada in October 2008 exactly 13 years after his acquittal for the murders of Nicole Simpson and Ronald Goldman. The four-person parole board asked Simpson questions about his conduct while in prison and feelings of remorse about his crimes. Parole boards typically assess factors including an inmate's conduct in prison, criminal history, and remorse, or lack thereof, about past crimes. Victims are allowed to speak at parole board hearings as well as those who wish to support a parole petition. In Simpson's hearing, one of his daughters spoke about how much she has missed her father and how much they would like to have him return home. Dexter Tyson's story will also give you an insight into the process of parole and what happens after release. If you recall, Dexter was convicted of felony murder, and several other felony charges, following a trial.

---

19. Travis, J. (2002). *But they all come back: Facing the challenges of prisoner reentry. Washington, DC: Urban Institute Press.*

20. Bureau of Justice Statistics. (2017). *Probation and Parole in the United States, 2013.* Retrieved from https://www.bjs.gov/content/pub/pdf/ppus13.pdf

21. Travis, J., & Lawrence, S. (2002). *Beyond the prison gates: The state of parole in America.* Washington, DC: Urban Institute.

Narrative: Dexter Tyson

The year 2016 marked my thirty-first year of imprisonment, but more importantly, my first eligibility for parole. I needed to convince 7 people out of a 12-man parole panel that I was not the same person who was responsible for taking someone's life. This panel looks for one to articulate the 4Rs: remorse, redemption, responsibility, and rehabilitation. Of course, the institutional record, plus one's criminal history, is crucially relevant. My juvenile record was not good and it had me very worried; however, I was hopeful March 3 as the shackles and handcuffs were fastened on me to be transported to New Jersey State Prison for my parole hearing. Everyone who has a life sentence has to be paroled by this panel.

After less than an hour of stern questioning, particularly about my juvenile history, all members voted for me to be paroled. Tears of joy dropped out of my eyes: I was given another chance at life. It is rare for the board to grant parole on their first eligibility, especially for the crime I committed. I can never forget how fortunate I am for getting this privilege.

April 19, 2016, was my release date to a halfway house, which is a setup to assist people with their transition back into society. I was given a 90-day stay there. However, after three weeks, I became eligible to leave the place, unescorted and without being stripped searched, which is common in prisons. This place allowed one to wear regular clothing and to have no more than $50 in one's possession. There were from two to eight-man rooms without any locks on the room doors.

As I stood on the corner to catch the bus to a job assistance center, I was in awe, feeling suspended in animation, and at the same time, overjoyed. Cars, buses, and people who passed by made me say "wow" as I took it all in. The bus ride to downtown Newark, NJ had the same effect despite it being overcrowded. As I looked out the bus window, everything seemed new. I felt as if I was lost in the same city that I grew up in. I constantly had to ask for directions as if I was a tourist.

To this day, I sometimes feel lost, especially now that I am driving. I am improving though. This is part of readjusting back into a world that has changed with its infrastructure. Something inside of me compelled me to hug a tree as I walked into the social security office to get a new social security card.

The job that I got from a temp agency allowed me to leave the halfway house at three in the morning and return at five in the evening. I was blown away with merely being outside at that time of day. I was accompanied by a few people who worked at the same warehouse located in Jersey City, Edison, and Carteret, New Jersey. Working inside the warehouses paid $9 per hour to load and unload 18-wheeler trucks. I did not mind because it was a way to be out in society. Temp agencies that helped get the jobs charged $10 per day to transport us back and forth to the location. After work, I was dropped off in Elizabeth, New Jersey, which is where I would walk the downtown area to sight see before I hopped on the bus. I window-shopped to look at fashions. I went into food places like McDonald's, Burger King, and the likes to eat foods that I had not eaten in decades. Despite the price change, I enjoyed my newfound freedom.

July 19, 2016, was the day for me to leave the halfway house. Two cars came to take me home: one with my second oldest sister and brother I had not seen for years and a second car with my childhood friend. There was a house full of family members and friends and a spread of food awaiting my arrival. After the mandates report to the parole office building, which lasted over an hour, I arrived at my new home. My sisters, nieces, family friends, and cousins embraced me. The food was professionally prepared by my nephew, who runs a catering business. There was lasagna, turkey meatballs and spaghetti, seafood salad, baked and fried chicken, yellow rice and beans, string beans, cabbage, and greens. For dessert was homemade chocolate and banana cakes and pies.

After a few hours in Orange, New Jersey, where I was paroled, and in a caravan of at least five cars, we headed to Plainfield, New Jersey, to visit my other sister's house. The grill in the backyard was grilling more chicken, burgers, and steaks, and there was more food being cooked in the kitchen. It was a hot day, so the in ground pool was open for our enjoyment. There was a question if I could swim by members of the family, so I just jumped in to answer the question. The deepest part of the pool was nine feet. The thunderstorm that came did not stop the celebration. Programmed music continued to blast out of the huge speakers.

My homecoming celebration lasted into the late hours. I am very fortunate to have the family support I continue to enjoy. I was treated to food buffets, shopping, and given money and gifts that include an iPhone without having to pay the bill to this day. To lay on a full size bed and watch a 50-inch television are a few amenities I enjoy. I was wise enough to save money while I was incarcerated along with the money I earned from working in the warehouses. Currently, I work for the City of Newark Sanitation Department, not permanently as of yet, but I get 80 hours.

Besides my family, there are other people who have been supportive of me and my transition back into society. I managed to get my driver's license within a year, went to see a professional football game, went to a Broadway show in New York City, and I have eaten at many restaurants. I like driving at night, going to the movies, and to the mall. I still have not mastered technology as far as using the computer. Without the help of my niece, I would be the worst. It is sister, my niece, and me who reside in this comfortable two-family home.

> It is great to enjoy the company of the opposite sex and eat what I want and when I want. If I want to stay overnight somewhere, I have to text the address to my parole officer. Besides New York, I have not traveled out of the State of New Jersey. My parole officer comes to my home once a month. I have to do a swab test to make sure that I am drug and alcohol free. The three decades of imprisonment sometime affects my thought process. I have had a few dreams of me being inside a prison, but I am fine. Being on parole for life, as it is right now, is so much better than being inside the confines of a prison.

Dexter faced a 12-person parole board who unanimously voted to parole him. Dexter had a long record of good behavior, including taking educational courses and serving as a member of the Lifers' Group in Rahway prison. Dexter was remorseful about his crime, but in his 31-year period of incarceration, Dexter did the work to rehabilitate himself, and that became evident to the parole board.

Dexter discusses the various conditions of his parole. If you recall, we also discussed the conditions of release under probation. These conditions are very similar to probationers, though they are usually more restrictive when it comes to parolees. As a reminder, standard conditions are those that apply to all parolees upon release. They include reporting to one's parole officer, requesting permission to travel, and finding gainful employment, as Dexter discussed in his story. Parolees cannot possess firearms and cannot associate with felons. They are banned from certain professions that require licenses, and in most states, they cannot vote. Special conditions also apply to parolees but are often applied as standard conditions. As Dexter mentioned, he is subject to monthly drug testing. He is also prohibited from consuming alcohol, and with many other parolees, curfews are standard. Parolees have less freedom because they are considered more dangerous. They have all served prison terms and some for serious violent felonies including robbery, assault, and murder. Parolees are subject to many restrictions, and they face a number of obstacles, which we will discuss soon. Before we get there, we want to return to our previous topic of the two ways in which inmates are paroled. The first method, as we discussed in some detail, is the parole board. The second method of release is known as mandatory release

Mandatory release is currently the more common form of parole. It means that a prisoner is released early by a mathematical calculation that subtracts good time credits from the prisoner's original sentence. The release date is mandatory because the prisoner has earned enough credits for automatic release from prison. The parole board is not involved, which is a vast departure from the 1970s. In 1976, about 65% of all prisoners were released by a parole board, but by 1999, that number dropped to just 24% of releases. In fact, by 2002, the movement away from indeterminate sentencing had grown so strong that 16 states abolished their parole boards.[22] The federal system abolished parole in favor of mandatory sentencing in 1984 when it passed the SRA of 1984. Many of the states followed in the footsteps of the federal system in abolishing or substantially limiting parole for several offenses and for various types of offenders.

Parole Revocation

Whether a prisoner is released via a parole board or via mandatory release, one thing remains the same: the release is conditional. The release is predicated on a person's abiding by the conditions set by a court. We just reviewed the many conditions of parole, both standard and special. If Dexter, for example, consumes alcohol which would violate his conditions of parole, his parole officer can choose to file a violation report with the court. Many of you might be wondering what happens to someone if they violate parole, so let us explain. This is not one of those clear-cut areas. Technically, a parole officer should file a violation report with the court if any parolee violates parole, but this is similar to the fact that a police officer should arrest any person who commits a crime, and we know that is not always the case. Similar to a police officer, a parole officer must use his or her discretion to decide which violations to bring to the court. The court's calendars are full and prisons are overcrowding, which makes judges less tolerant of hearings for minor violations. If however, a parolee commits a serious violation, such as a new offense, an officer will request a violation hearing with the court, and the court will place the case on its docket.

Similar to a probation violation hearing, a preliminary hearing to establish probable cause is the first step in the process, though as we discussed earlier, most cases will go to a full hearing. There are a few differences in the process between probation and parole violation hearings, though. First, where a judge presides over probation hearings, it is usually the parole board or a neutral parole hearing officer who decides parole revocation cases. Parolees are entitled to due process rights, many, but not all, of which are the same as those afforded to probationers. In *Morrissey v. Brewer*, the U.S. Supreme Court said that the amount of liberty a person stands to lose should be proportionate to their due process rights under the law. In this case, John Morrissey was paroled after a 7-month sentence of incarceration for writing fraudulent checks. He was arrested for a parole violation after his release, and his parole officer submitted a violation report to the Iowa Board of Parole, who revoked Morrissey's parole without a hearing. Morrissey's appeal went to the U.S. Supreme Court. In their final decision, they afforded parolees with the right to receive notice of violation charges, the right to be heard in a hearing, the right to present evidence and witnesses, and the right to be

22. Travis, J. (2005). *But they all come back: Facing the challenges of prisoner reentry.* Washington, DC: Urban Institute Press.

heard by a neutral party. These rights are afforded to all parolees facing possible revocation of parole.[23] The last questions we address in this chapter then is how many people complete parole successfully, and what do the numbers mean? Does parole work?

Does Parole Work?

Does parole reduce recidivism? Are parolees successful when they reenter society? The truth is that the numbers are not very encouraging. A national study of prisoners released from 30 states in 2005 found that 76% of all released inmates were rearrested for a new crime or parole violation within five years of release.[24] According to the American Probation and Parole Association, only 46% of parolees discharged completed the term of their parole supervision successfully.[25] The numbers alone though do not explain the reason why parolees are not more successful. Dexter's story illustrates a successful transition to society, but for many parolees, the transition is much more difficult. Dexter had a lot of family support, a home to live in, and he found steady employment quickly. However, many parolees are not so lucky. They face tremendous obstacles in reentering society. Felony convictions block many former inmates from employment, housing, and educational opportunities. Many parolees have medical problems, suffer from mental illness or substance abuse, and have little family support. While the odds do not favor success, the prisoner reentry movement has made progress.

Prisoner reentry is the successful transition of a person from prison back to society. The goal is to reintegrate former inmates into communities where they can secure housing and gainful employment and become productive members of society. There are now several prisoner reentry institutes devoted to identifying successful programs and policies to reduce recidivism among parolees. Researchers, policy analysts, and academics alike began to focus on this issue in the early 2000s. The Second Chance Act, signed into law in 2008, provides funding for state and federal programs that offer services to the men and women returning to society. Not every state offers these programs, and they vary from state to state, but certain programs and certain prisons show real promise. For example, San Quentin Prison in California has the largest in-prison college program. New Jersey's Education in Prison Consortium, which is housed at Rutgers University, has partnered with the New Jersey Department of Corrections (NJDOC) and New Jersey Parole Board to offer college courses in several New Jersey prisons. Education is one of the predictors of successful prisoner reentry, but other pro-

---

23. Morrissey v. Brewer, 408 U.S. 471 (1972)

24. Durose, M., Cooper, A., & Snyder, H. (2014). *Recidivism of Prisoners Released in 30 States in 2005.* Washington, DC: Bureau of Justice Statistics.

25. American Probation and Parole Association. *Probation and parole FAQs.* Retrieved on November 27, 2017 from https://www.appanet.org/eweb/DynamicPage.aspx?WebCode=VB_FAQ.]

grams focus on job placement, vocational training, and housing, which also predict successful reentry.

Many academics and other critics of mass incarceration argue that we should simply stop incarcerating our citizens by the masses, but until we see substantial decreases in the rate of incarceration in the United States, we hope that the prisoner reentry movement will grow in strength. Dexter Tyson is a strong example of someone who has successfully returned to society and who shares his experiences with students, academics, and policymakers. It is also one of the core tenets of prison reentry that we design programs with input from the prisoners, otherwise known as people, who are returning to society.

Chapter 6

Community Corrections

We hope that you are now familiar with the history of probation and parole and the purpose and the practical side of these forms of punishment. Probation, parole, and prisons (the three Ps) are the most common forms of punishment in the United States, with probation being the most widely used. However, there is another category of punishments that encompasses everything in between probation and prison. Referred to as intermediate punishment, this group includes a range of punishments that are more punitive than traditional probation but less restrictive than prison. These sanctions allow offenders to serve a sentence in the community while subjected to a greater level of control than probationers. There are several different sanctions in this category. In this chapter, we will our best to cover them. You will also read true accounts from those who have served this type of sentence. First, we will briefly discuss the history of the intermediate sanction.

The rehabilitative ideal that had prevailed in the United States beginning in the 1940s fell out of favor by the 1970s and 1980s. As we have discussed, the incarceration rate began to soar and prisons filled. Some notable scholars in this field called for a punishment rationale based on retribution, with a new focus as well on proportionality in punishments. Prisons and probation could not be the only forms of punishment in this new paradigm, particularly as many critics claimed that probation was not punitive enough. Rooted in the idea of rehabilitation but with a stronger focus on control and punishment, a system of scaled punishments emerged, including intensive supervision probation (ISP), boot camps, shock incarceration, house arrest, and more. These in-between punishments, once stemming from philosophies rooted in both rehabilitation and proportionality, became a practical method to deal with prison overcrowdings of the 1990s and cost savings.

Intensive Supervision Probation

ISP is a form of probation that is more restrictive than traditional probation but still allows an offender to remain free from incarceration. This intermediate punishment became popular in the 1980s when the incarceration rate began to soar and our focus on rehabilitation began to fade. Prior to the 1980s, some probation departments experimented with smaller caseloads to determine if closer supervision and contact between probationers and their officers would result in lower recidivism rates.[1] When the results did not show decreases in recidivism, the goal of ISP became more punitive in nature and focused on practical goals of reducing prison overcrowding and cost savings.

Modern ISP programs utilize increased contact in the form of home visits, office visits, and phone calls. Though there is considerable variation in the program design and specific requirements across jurisdictions, the focus on punishment and cost savings through increased surveillance and control is similar to most ISP programs.[2] Caseloads for ISP officers range from about 25 to 40 probationers[3] compared to the more typical caseload of around 100 probationers in traditional probation. Along with increased visits, offenders are subjected to more frequent drug and alcohol testing, stricter enforcement of financial penalties, and other conditions of probation. Does this increased supervision work? Does it reduce recidivism?

The evidence is not encouraging. Earlier studies of ISP programs show that offenders in these programs have high recidivism rates.[4] Increased recidivism rates lead critics to question if these programs can achieve cost savings. New arrests, technical violations, and revocation of supervision are costs not always accounted in evaluations. In truth, ISP programs are much more costly than originally thought and have been found to have a limited effect on prison overcrowding.[5] While most of the research is not favorable to these programs, some positive findings can help shape ISP program designs going forward. Studies have shown that programs that are not focused on surveillance have been more successful.

---

1. Tonry, M., & Lynch, M. (1996). Intermediate Sanctions. *Crime and Justice, 20,* 99–144.

2. Lowencamp, C. T., Flores, A. W., Holsinger, A. M., Makarios, M. D., & Latessa, E. J. (2010). Intensive supervision programs: Does program philosophy and the principles of effective intervention matter? *Journal of Criminal Justice, 38,* 368–375.

3. Tonry, (1996). Why are U.S. incarceration rates so high? *Crime and Delinquency, 45,* 419–437.

4. Lowencamp, C. T., Flores, A. W., Holsinger, A. M., Makarios, M. D., & Latessa, E. J. (2010). Intensive supervision programs: Does program philosophy and the principles of effective intervention matter? *Journal of Criminal Justice, 38,* 368–375.

5. Ibid.

ISP programs that focus on human service and appropriate risk and need are more successful those that focus solely on punish and control.[6] In essence, those programs that are treatment oriented have higher success rates, but reading this fact does not provide the real picture. That is why we include Amanda's story here.

Narrative: On Becoming Sober, by Amanda Finck

My name is Amanda. I am 28 years old. I grew up in the suburbs of northern New Jersey with both parents, an older brother, a younger sister, a little Chihuahua, and pretty much everything a little girl could ever have asked for in her childhood. I am a 3-time convicted felon and a recovering heroin addict with three years of sobriety. I was released from Edna Mahon Correctional Facility in July of 2012. I was sentenced to two 3-year prison terms. Where did I go wrong? Or optimistically, where did I go right?

When I was a kid, I remember from a very, very young age not feeling comfortable in my own skin. On the outside, I was loud, outgoing, funny, the "life of the party," opinionated, and a little rebellious. I mean, who actually enjoys being told what to do? On the inside, I was depressed, insecure, anxiety ridden, afraid, uncomfortable, and very, very self-conscious. I never showed those qualities. I always, always kept them stuffed down. It's exhausting putting on a show for everybody all the time, when inside you're screaming.

I began using drugs at the age of 14. I had followed the DARE program of what not to do to a "T." I started out with alcohol, then marijuana, then cocaine! See, I loved cocaine because I was ready for anything! I was happy and invincible. Most of all, I was getting skinny. That made my mother very happy. In turn, that made me feel happy. After bingeing on cocaine for far too long and feeling like I was going to die, someone offered me a bag of dope. Heroin. I had held off on heroin because I knew. . . I just knew. If I did heroin, I was going to be in huge trouble.

I did heroin that night. I was in big trouble. But I had absolutely no idea how much trouble this measly, stupid, powder was going to bring into my life. I stayed addicted to heroin for nine years, plunging deeper and deeper into hell. I had become a sack of bones, a shell of the person I used to be. But I was numb. I didn't feel anything. I wasn't hurting, I wasn't afraid, I wasn't depressed; I wasn't anything. Just a living dead girl.

My life had become living and breathing for heroin. I woke up immediately needing heroin. I had stolen, broken into homes for items to sell, sold all of my own items, just anything to get enough money to make sure I did not withdraw. I had figured out a way to keep myself high and make money doing so. I would go down below to Paterson, NJ and buy a massive amount

---

6. Ibid.

of heroin for cheap and come back up here to the suburbs and sell it for double the amount. I took the risk in driving into the hood and copping the drugs, so you pay the extra. I could do half the drugs and sell the other half to make back the same amount and pick up again.

Eventually, you run out of luck. But lucky for me, I didn't lose my life in this daily gamble of addiction. I was pulled over and arrested for possession of heroin, crack pipes, needles, a marijuana pipe (from high school stuffed under my seat), and rubber band paraphernalia. Thus began my career in the criminal justice system. I was placed on probation, which I ran from within the first week. Not necessarily because I did not want to comply, but because I couldn't stop using heroin. At this point, this lifestyle was taking a toll on me. I was at 98 pounds. I did not eat; I did not do anything at all except pick up, sell, and shoot heroin. Eventually I was arrested and spent some time in the jail where I was forced to withdraw for the first time. With officers that out right called me a dirty junkie. . . I thought I hit my "rock bottom."

I was placed on probation again with an extended period of time. I believe I lasted about two months before I relapsed and threw myself right back into the game. Now, I was on the run. And doing illegal activity on a daily basis. Luck runs out.

I was arrested again with heroin on me. I was sent to jail once again. Years of heroin abuse along with alcohol, Xanax, and whatever else I could get my hands on really does a number on the body and the nervous system. I developed a seizure disorder. The officers in the jail had decided that my seizures were "fake" so I could get myself some drugs while in jail. I remember waking up dazed and confused and immediately reaching for my breasts, which were killing me, to a group of officers giggling around me. Come to find out after seizing another inmate informed me that a female paramedic twisted my nipples to see if I was "faking my seizure." Normal people don't give a shit about addicts. I ended up spending almost four months in the hospital while they tried to figure out what was wrong with me physically. My internal organs were shutting down; my body literally could not function without opiates. I had to be shackled to the hospital bed with two officers bedside the entire time. I had the warden of the jail who got stuck spending an overnight at the hospital with me, ask me for my life story, and how I got mixed up in drugs. After I explained everything he turned to me, stared dead in my eyes, and said, "when you finally get out of here, if you don't die in this bed, you should get as much heroin as you can and shoot it, and shoot it, and shoot it until you turn green in the face and drop dead." Normal people just do not care for addicts. The stigma is crippling.

I took a plea deal at the end of this jail stay, which ended up being 270 days, and signed a deal for drug court in the amount to five years. I really gave it a shot. I thought I was done. I agreed to a long-term treatment program for adults with behavioral problems and addiction treatment. I truly excelled in that program. I met a lot of great women, I had a great counselor and for the first time... I felt like my life might be worth fighting for. I spent six months in that program and transferred to a halfway house in south Jersey near Atlantic city. I began working and truly thinking I could make this happen. I could live.

Until I met my officer. I knew from the very start this woman was in this field for all of the wrong reasons. She also referred to us as "junkies." There is nothing worse than truly feeling good about yourself and what you're doing and then have someone come and stomp all over you. No matter what I did, it wasn't good enough for her. I couldn't work at ANY of the jobs I had applied because they were 10 minutes past curfew. I couldn't go to meetings in my area because they were past curfew. She was pushing for me to remain in a program that I was near completing. I had just completed 12 months of programming. I was ready to come home and start over. Every step of the way I was being trashed, talked down to, shamed, and embarrassed, and most of all never given a damn chance. A probation officer can truly make or break an addict. This woman broke me over a course of four months. I gave up. I left the remainder of the program and jumped right back into my game. I started getting high again and was on the run from the law.

But this time it was different because I had had a taste of what sobriety was like. I was so paranoid and ashamed, and I felt guilty. My family was so damn proud, so damn happy, and here I am, missing. I just wanted to call that officer and tell her, "you win," and kill myself.

Spare everyone the pain of having to love me. What a dark time in my life. I was arrested a short time thereafter. I was afraid to be sick, so I hid my bundles of heroin and managed to sneak them into the jail. When I got into the jail, it turns out, it's extremely hard to hide drugs from a bunch of withdrawing women. I ended up giving a few bags to the women who were in the room with me, as they saw me doing it and I wanted them to shut up. Regardless of all my efforts, the word spread pretty quickly. I even had men from the upstairs yelling down in the vents to leave them bags in the library!!!!!! Oh boy! I knew it was coming! Within a few hours they ran down on the tier and found my drugs hidden on me. Everyone was given a urine screen so they could find out who was given the heroin. I received street charges of distribution of controlled dangerous substance within an institution, within a school zone, and within 25 feet of a state park. I knew I was getting my boots smoked off.

I was sentenced to two 3-year state prison terms in Edna Mahon Correctional Facility, the only female prison in the state of New Jersey. Prison was one of the most eye-opening experiences of my life. I met 200 different women with the same exact story. There were a handful of women that were NOT there for drugs. I stared into the eyes of a 56-year-old woman speaking of her next high when she was to be released, and I saw myself. I did not want to be in prison at 56 years old with nothing and no one but a career in prison terms and a busted up body from abusing myself. I didn't want to be her. I truly decided right there that when I finally got home. I was going to fight for my life.

I signed up for ISP and had a few interviews with people about why I wanted ISP, and Honestly, I almost didn't because of my last officer. I was terrified that was going to happen to me again. I convinced myself that it wasn't her, that it was me. I could do this if I really, truly wanted to despite who is in charge of me.

Months went by and I finally had my ISP hearing! I was accepted into the program and that was the day my life changed. I met my officer who was very tough on the outside. I was very nervous; she barely cracked a smile. She explained to me everything I had to do, and I did everything I had to do, plus some. She was an amazing woman who was there for me every single step of the way. She was moderating but nurturing and encouraging. She was everything I needed to get myself back together. She was adamant on the "no cell phone rule." The first 60 days (or more if need be) I couldn't have a cell phone. Now at first, I'm not gonna lie this rule kinda chapped my ass. Obviously I wanted a cell phone, I went into prison with a flip phone, texting on T9, and got out of prison, and people had damn laptops as phones!! Staring at the person on the other end!! It was pretty amazing! I remember giving her a bit of a hard time about that and instead of shutting me down with "you don't like it, you can go back." She drove ALL the way out to my house and sat outside with me and spoke to me. She spoke to me as if I was a normal human being. She explained to me why this rule is so important for an addict. She explained to me that she wasn't there to boss me around; she was there because she wanted me to succeed. She was there to help me in the ways I needed help, whether I could see them at that moment, or down the road. I stared in her face and I cried. I KNEW she meant every word.

The next 16 months spent with her guidance couldn't have been better if I scripted it myself. Obviously, there were tough times. There were moments I questioned all of my efforts. Even though I was a model participant, sometimes she said NO. She said no to gage my reaction. She made sure that in building a trusting, good working relationship with me I wasn't going to take advantage. Sad to say, addicts will do that, especially if we know we can get away with it. I couldn't take advantage. She remained impartial, although caring deeply for me, the rules had to be followed. When she said no, it was no. Was I going to stomp my feet, give up, and get high, run away? Yell that the world hates me? No. I wasn't. I was going to swallow that "no" and hope for a "yes" next time around. Try harder. Do better. She was teaching me how to survive in the real world. The real world tosses you lemons on a daily basis; she taught me how to make lemonade with those lemons. She taught me how to be a confident, respected, classy, and straightforward woman. A real woman. She would answer her phone every single time I called; I never felt like an annoyance to her. She listened. She heard me. Even though she never truly understood my struggle of wanting heroin so badly, she fought me WITH me. I would call my officer if I wanted to get high. I would tell my officer if I wanted to get high, and she would be ready. She slipped the gloves on and was in my corner every single time fighting my battle with me. She was integral to my success. If it wasn't for her, I don't know where I would be right now.

I just celebrated three years of sobriety in March. I am in college full time pursuing a REAL CAREER! I've got a side business of some of my talents that are beginning to show themselves, and I work part time at a toy store! I run events with children! I'm mending my relationship with my family, with my mother especially. And I still to this day speak regularly with my officer. And still to this day she'll slip on the gloves if need be. She's my wingman and I love her dearly.

I could say that I made the decision to stay clean and sober myself, but honestly, an officer can make or break an addict. Which one would you rather be? I know my life depended on an officer at one point, and I am so grateful she was a great person and truly cared about all of us. I'm forever grateful to her.

Amanda has a very common background to many of the people who fill our prisons and criminal justice system. Her criminal justice offenses were heavily entwined with her drug abuse, and this is a story we hear often in this field. Amanda was punished by the criminal justice system, but the punishments often did not deter her nor did they help rehabilitate her. Her experience with her first probation officer was a demoralizing and dehumanizing experience that left her feeling resentful and hopeless. It was not until she met her ISP officer that Amanda felt that the system was working to help her rather than hurt her. Amanda's ISP officer was firm with her rules but explained why those rules were important to Amanda's success. She was under a higher form of control, but Amanda's officer was also engaged with her as a person. She was encouraging and supportive. Amanda's officer demonstrated a real strength in human services and Amanda, sober, happy, and currently working in cosmetology, credits this human touch as the main reason for her success. Unfortunately, not all of the intermediate sanctions we will cover next have this component of human services.

Shock Programs

There are many programs that are meant to shock offenders into behaving. Boot camp programs are those that use military style training as a punishment in lieu of incarceration. Boot camps are generally offered to juveniles or nonviolent offenders with short jail or prison sentences. The original shock program is famously known as "Scared Straight," originated in New Jersey with the Lifers' Group in East Jersey State Prison in 1978 (you may have noticed that some of the narratives contained in this book were written by current and former members of the Lifers' Group at Rahway Prison, renamed later as East Jersey State Prison).

The Lifers' Group first gained notoriety in 1979 when the documentary *Scared Straight* aired on television. The documentary was a unique insight into prison life and a group of criminal offenders serving long sentences for violent crimes— mainly murder. The Lifer's Group met with at-risk youth in an attempt to scare them from committing crime. They yelled profanities at these teenagers and described the horrors of prison life, including the violence. The hope of the group was that by demonstrating the atrocities of prison life and having these potential delinquent teenagers see this up close and personal, they would be deterred from committing crime because they feared going to prison. The documentary received instant accolades, winning both an Emmy and Oscar, and catapulting the program to the forefront of criminal justice programs. The program claimed success in deterring juvenile offenders, but almost all subsequent research has conclusively shown that these programs actually increase delinquency for the teenagers involved and therefore do more harm than good.[7]

The shock program appeal extended from Scared Straight programs to boot camps in the 1980s. Though Scared Straight programs may not have been successful, they were popular and opened the door for boot camp programs, which are geared toward juvenile and low-level offenders. The first boot camp programs were developed in Oklahoma and Georgia in 1983, and by 1993, boot camps could be found in 30 states.[8] Boot camps offered the promise of punishment and deterrence. They were another intermediate sanction that could serve to reduce prison overcrowding and cut costs. Boot camps programs vary, but they typically have a paramilitary organization with a focus on discipline, routine, and hard work. They have extensive drills, physical training, and work, characteristics that are very appealing to both policymakers and the public, but do they work?

The answer is overwhelmingly no! The boot camp popularity hit its peak in the 1990s with promises of reduced recidivism and lower costs. Though boot camps received bipartisan support initially and enjoyed immediate popularity, critics ar-

---

7. Petrosino, A., Turpin-Petrosino, C., Hollis-Peel, M., & Lavenberg, J. G. (2013). 'Scared Straight' and other juvenile awareness programs for preventing delinquency. *Campbell Systematics Reviews*, DOI: 10.1002/14651858.CD002796.pub2.

8. Tonry, M., & Lynch, M. (1996). Intermediate Sanctions. *Crime and Justice, 20*, 99–143.

gued that this type of punishment would not work, as fear tactics and confrontation had not worked in correctional rehabilitation before. Opponents pointed out that boot camp programs did not employ prosocial modeling, individualization, or supportive treatment providers.[9] The studies were clear on this issue, though. While a few programs provided some positive benefits, most of the evaluations showed that boot camp programs do not reduce recidivism.[10] Even worse, though, were the lawsuits, which alleged physical brutality and abuse in many of the camps. In a few instances, these abuses resulted in the death of several participants.

It was the death of a 14-year-old boy in a Florida boot camp for juveniles, in fact, that prompted Governor Jeb Bush to sign a law closing down these programs in 2007. Martin Lee Andersen was sentenced to a term in a boot camp program after he stole his grandmother's car, a violation of his sentence of probation at the time. When Anderson stopped running during a drill at the boot camp, on his first day, several guards punched and kicked him until he lost consciousness. The guards then attempted to revive him by forcing him to inhale ammonia. The awful act was caught on videotape, which also revealed that a nurse at the program watched as the guards beat Andersen to death. The medical examiner first ruled that Andersen died of a complication related to an undiagnosed sickle cell trait but later concluded that Andersen had died of suffocation. When the guards held the boy's mouth closed and forced him to inhale ammonia, they caused his vocal cords to spasm and block his airway, which ultimately caused his death. Though a jury acquitted the seven guards and nurse responsible for Andersen's death, Governor Bush responded to outrage by the state's citizens and closed the juvenile boot camp programs remaining in the state.[11] To date, only a handful of boot camp programs remain.

House Arrest and Electronic Monitoring

House arrest, also known as home confinement, is another type of intermediate punishment that allows an offender to serve a sentence in his or her home residence. A court sets the length of the sentence, and an offender must abide by the conditions set by a court as well. This does not mean that a person on home confinement is on lockdown all of the time, though. In more serious cases, an offender might be restricted solely to their home, but even in those cases, there are exceptions, such as medical visits. In cases that are less serious, offenders can usually leave their home for work or school purposes so long as they have per-

---

9. Bottcher, J., & Ezell, M. E. (2005). Examining the effectiveness of boot camps: A randomized experiment with a long-term follow up. *Journal of Research in Crime and Delinquency, 42,* 309–332.

10. Ibid.

11. Goodnough, A. (2007, Oct. 13). 8 Acquitted in Death of Boy, 14, in Florida. *The New York Times.* Retrieved from http://www.nytimes.com/2007/10/13/us/13bootcamp.html

mission from a court. An officer from the pretrial division (if the release is prior to trial), probation, or parole supervises offenders on home confinement. In cases where offenders pose a higher risk, a court may order electronic monitoring as a condition of home confinement. There are a few types of electronic monitoring devices that are most commonly used. The offender is responsible for the costs of such devices.

Recent technology has allowed for advances in the types of devices uses for electronic monitoring (EM), but prior to some recent developments, a programmed contact system was commonly employed in which a computer would contact an offender to ensure that he or she was at home. The computer is programmed to ask an offender a few questions for a voice match verification. If the voice is not a match or an offender does not answer the phone, their supervising officer is alerted immediately. More popularly used, though, and well known to the public is the continuously signaling system. For this type of monitoring, an offender wears a transmitting device, usually in the form of an ankle bracelet, which transmits signals to a receiver. The receiver, placed in an offender's home, picks us signals from the transmitting device. A computer system monitored by a supervising officer records these transmissions, and in the event that a signal fails to transmit, that supervising officer is alerted that an offender is out of range. Some celebrities, such as Martha Stewart, have worn an ankle bracelet monitor as part of their home confinement sentence, and while the public may view this punishment as an easy one, there may be a counter argument. One anonymous author provided his account of what it was like to wear an ankle bracelet.

Narrative: What It's Like to Live with an Ankle Bracelet[12]

I cannot sleep. There is a device on my leg.

It requires that I wake up an hour early so I can plug it into a charger and stand next to the outlet, like a cell phone charging up for the day. Not the day, actually, but 12 hours. After that, the device runs out of juice. Wherever I am, I have to find an outlet to plug myself into. If I don't, I'm likely to be thrown back onto Rikers Island.

The device is my ankle bracelet, which I've now been wearing for 63 days. I wear it afraid that someone at work will notice the bulge. When I go to

---

12. So as not to violate the terms of his parole, the author asked that he be identified by his initials. M. M. is a full-time student and employee at a law firm in New York City. He has been on parole for more than three years on multiple charges stemming from an altercation when he was 22 and his subsequent re-arrest for driving while intoxicated. This story was originally published by the Marshall Project, a non-profit news organization that covers the U.S. criminal justice system and was retrieved from https://www.vice.com/en_ca/article/dp57kx/what-its-like -to-live-with-an-ankle-bracelet-717.

school, I worry my friends will spot it and leave me. I push it up into my jeans, hoping they won't see. But the higher up I push it, the more it starts to hurt; most days, my feet go numb. I try wearing bell-bottoms.

At the age of 22, I landed in prison. Though I had grown up around violence, it was my first time in trouble. I'd taken the law into my own hands during an altercation because where I come from, we don't dial 911 for help—we see how badly police officers treat people like us.

When I came home, I wasn't the same "I," and "home" wasn't home anymore. For the rest of my life, I would have to live with a mistake I made at 22. I would never belong to myself again; parole dictates everything that I do.

I'd been on parole for three years. I work full time at a law firm, attend college, and I am close to attaining my bachelor's degree. For three years, I never violated any rules, which included not leaving the five boroughs and returning home before 9:00 p.m. every night.

I don't have the luxury of the "college experience," of going to concerts, or hanging out with friends after class. And I learned from experience not to discuss my past with my classmates, at least not until they get to know me. People become fearful when they hear I was in jail.

Then I had a run-in with the police again and was charged with a DWI. I spent 30 days in Rikers and came frightfully close to losing everything I'd spent three years working for: my college semester and GPA, job, and post-prison healing. I woke up in cold sweats at night, traumatized by the experience of being caged again. And even though I am pleading not guilty and my case is still pending, my parole officer called me up after I left Rikers and asked me to come in to speak with his supervisor.

Details weren't discussed. They never are: a call is made and a probation officer (PO) appointment is scheduled.

The day of the meeting, I was in a panic. Entering that building—the office of parole—is guaranteed. Leaving it is not.

I was greeted by metal detectors and a throng of fellow parolees, mostly Black and Hispanic, many in work uniforms, all waiting up to six hours to be seen. When my PO finally saw me, he explained right off that an EM device would be placed on my leg for a year to enforce my curfew, though it would come off sooner if I was "compliant."

"But I have already been compliant, for years," I said. As I had many times, I explained to my PO that I was in school, have a full-time job, and maintain good behavior. "Am I a flight risk? Or a frequent violator?"

The more I spoke, the more hostile he became.

Later on the bus, looking down and seeing the bulge on my leg, I cried.

This is what summer under surveillance looks like: I can no longer wear shorts. I cannot visit a beach without enduring public humiliation. I asked my parole officer whether I could attend a Yankee game for my birthday, but he turned me down because it may have lasted past curfew. I usually spend Independence Day with my family in Long Island, but this year, I couldn't dare ask my PO for permission to leave the borough.

I have been alternating three pairs of pants for almost three months now—the only pants that can accommodate the device. When I'm with my coworkers, I stand out as the only person wearing jeans; dress slacks are too much of a risk, because when I sit down, pants like those hike up. At home, unexpected visitors have me scrambling to put on pants.

Throughout the day, the device becomes heavier and more painful, causing me to bleed. I push it down on my ankle to let my blood circulate— but then the pain becomes unbearable, and I can't plant my feet without crying out.

The device has me strapped, too, to a mistake I made at the age of 22. The device is, both literally and metaphorically, my greatest source of pain.

But every day I rise, stand by the socket, and charge my ankle to go to work.

The story you just read may have given you another perspective on EM. While it may not be a sentence of incarceration, there are certainly physical and stigmatic pains that accompany this type of sentence. The more recent technology we referenced in the beginning of this section, however; has resulted in the use of a satellite tracking system. More specifically, and as many of you have already guessed, the use of global positioning satellite (GPS) tracking has become more common. The GPS system uses satellite signals to track an offender's exact location, but this information is transmitted to a centralized computer system by way of a cellular phone system. But as such, the system also fails when large buildings, vehicles, local terrain, and other obstructions block cell phone signals. When the signal fails, the supervising officer is alerted, but it is difficult for officers to decipher which violations are a real danger and which are just failings of modern-day technology. For this reason, some agencies still rely on the original monitoring programs.

One area of EM that has utilized advances in technology pertains to alcohol-related offenses. The use of interlock ignition systems has become popular in recent years, at a cost to offenders of course. This system requires an individual to breathe into a breathalyzer before operating a motor vehicle. If the blood alcohol concentration (BAC) exceeds that allowed by law or by an offender's supervising agency, the vehicle will not start. The second device, made popular by celebrities, such as Lindsay Lohan, Tracy Morgan, and Jayson Williams, is a Secure Continuous Remote Alcohol Monitoring, otherwise known as a SCRAM ankle bracelet. This system monitors a person's BAC level, as well through skin perspiration, and reports this information to a monitoring agency. Offenders pay an initial installation fee of $50 to $100 and then pay approximately $10 to $12 daily for the device,[13] for an approximately total of $280 to $340 per month for this type of electronic supervision. We remind you that this is a cost that most poor offenders cannot afford.

Day Reporting Centers

Day Reporting Centers (DRCs) were first introduced in Great Britain in the late 1960s and first used in the United States in Connecticut and Massachusetts in the mid-1980s, when intermediate forms of punishment gained in popularity. Day Reporting Centers became popular rather quickly. By 1990, there were 13 DRCs operating around the United States, but within four years, that number jumped to 114 programs across 22 states.[14] The DRCs, or centers where offenders report during the daytime, are used for different types of offender populations: those released to pretrial diversion programs, those serving a term of probation with additional conditions, and parolees. There are also a variety of these types of programs offered, and they are referred to not only as DRCs but also as community resource centers and day treatment centers. Though not all programs are built the same, they typically share a number of characteristics.

DRCs usually serve as an alternative to incarceration, but they also seek to address the main problems facing those people who are coming out of prison or who have previous criminal convictions. What are some of these problems? Take a moment before you keep reading and try to imagine a few of these obstacles. You are all college students, but quite often offenders are uneducated, not just lacking in college education but also lacking in high school completion. With little formal education and a criminal record, many offenders have a difficult time finding gainful employment, which is often a condition of probation or parole. This means that even if they are trying and it is not their fault, these individuals may be penalized because they cannot find a job. Even when they can get job interviews, many offenders do not have a formal resume or possess formal interviewing skills. They face other obstacles, including lack of steady housing, drug abuse, and health problems. So how do DRCs help with these issues?

The DRC helps address prisoner reentry issues by providing a number of services to offenders who are court ordered to attend. Most DRCs will conduct an initial risk assessment analysis to determine which factors indicate that specific offenders are a low or high risk for reoffending. The risk assessment also helps

---

13. SCRAM Systems. (n.d.). SCRAM Systems Media Kit. Retrieved on January 15, 2018 from https://www.scramsystems.com/images/uploads/general/media-pdf/media-kits/scram-mediakit-camFAQ.pdf

14. Boyle, D. J., Ragusa-Salerno, L. M., Lanterman, J. L., & Marcus, A. F. (2013). An evaluation of Day Reporting Centers for Parolees. *Criminology & Public Policy, 12,* 119–143.

provide a plan for rehabilitation, which is one of the goals of day reporting centers. Treatment plans vary by offender, but the DRCs typically offer educational courses, vocational training, resume building workshops, job placement training, drug and alcohol treatment, and general life skills training. These programs also provide protection for the public through monitoring and surveillance mechanisms. Offenders must sign in, meet with counselors, submit to random drug testing, and comply with other court-ordered conditions. The DRCs therefore serve both the offenders and the greater community, but do they work?

On the surface, DRCs seem to positively serve all parties involved, but we need to measure its effectiveness as well. So, what does the research show? Unfortunately, most of the research is focused on probationers and those mandated to report during the pretrial phase, two groups who generally pose less of a threat than parolees. Nevertheless, several studies have demonstrated the obvious cost-savings benefits of these programs when compared with traditional incarceration, but the results are mixed when it comes to program effectiveness in terms of reducing recidivism.[15] While not all studies show success, some day reporting centers seem to be positively impacting their participants. Deputy Director Frank Scherer of the Alleghany County Adult Probation reports success in his Pittsburgh DRCs, stating, "What we were not good at is actually helping people and getting them out of the system."[16] He added though, they are starting to improve.

> Case in point: a longtime heroin user, Sandi A., 45, of Whitehall—who requested that her last name not be used—spent about a month in the Allegheny County Jail last year after she was arrested for drug possession, access device fraud, and theft by unlawful taking.
>
> Released from jail eight months ago, she was on probation for the fifth time in her life. She said the difference this time was that she went to a Day Reporting Center to get help in doing a job search.
>
> "There were real helpful in helping me get my resume together because I hadn't had one in 20 years," she said.
>
> Clean for eight months, she attended Narcotics Anonymous meetings at the center, and still visits the East Liberty site regularly for mandated drug testing. Earlier this month, she landed a job working for a market research firm.
>
> "Nobody's ever put in any time to try to help me succeed, except at this center," she said.[17]

---

15. Ibid.

16. Riely, K. (2014, Feb. 23). Study: New Day Reporting Centers are reducing relapses. *Pittsburgh Post-Gazette,* Retrieved from http://www.post-gazette.com/local/city/2014/02/24/Study-New-probation-Day-Reporting-Centers-reducing-relapses/stories/201402240108

17. Ibid.

Not all programs are built equally, and just as Amanda found her ISP officer to be helpful, the aforementioned former offender found her DRC to be instrumental to her success. The verdict is still out, however, when it comes to the effectiveness of DRCs for parolees. There are only two studies to date to report on this issue, one of which found that DRCs were effective at reducing recidivism for its participants, while the second concluded that DRCs do not produce better recidivism results than traditional parole supervision.[18] With just two studies, it is too soon to reach any conclusions. We would be remiss, though, not to remind you that parolees tend to have higher recidivism rates than probationers for many of the reasons previously discussed.

Community Service

The last form of intermediate sanction we will discuss in this chapter is community service. Many of you might already know about this sanction, and some may have already even performed it at some point! Community service is a punishment in which an offender is sentenced to provide some type of free labor to the community for a specified number of hours. This punishment emerged as a viable alternative to incarceration in the 1960s, before some of the other sanctions we just discussed. Community service can be used in lieu of a sentence to jail time but is rarely used solely as an alternative to prison time (stop here and think about why this is true). Prison time is used for felony offenders, while jail is more typically used for misdemeanor offenders, who commit lower level offenses.

Community service is usually reserved for lower level and nonviolent offenders. Often times, though, community service is also assigned in addition to a sentence of probation and/or fines. So what types of work constitute community service? Well, the most common type of community service involves cleaning up the community. Offenders will be assigned to trash pick-up, vandalism scrubbing, building repair, and other types of jobs that will benefit the surrounding community. There are other forms of service as well, though. Offenders can volunteer their time to several nonprofit agencies, including American Red Cross, Girls Scouts of America, Goodwill, homeless shelters, domestic violence shelters, and other organizations, which also include performing art theater groups, artisan festivals, and even farmer's markets.

Community service varies by jurisdiction, but its use is intended for many of the same purposes of other intermediate sanctions. First, it is a cost-savings measure that alleviates jail overcrowding. Second, it allows offenders to remain in the community while serving a sentence, indicating that it is a form of rehabilitation as well. We will discuss a court that offers rehabilitative services, such as

---

18. Boyle, D. J., Ragusa-Salerno, L. M., Lanterman, J. L., & Marcus, A. F. (2013). An evaluation of Day Reporting Centers for Parolees. *Criminology & Public Policy, 12,* 119–143.

counseling and access to social welfare programs, in a few paragraphs. Community service also provides an immediate punishment that also serves the goal of restorative justice. An offender is not simply punished, but rather they are held accountable and made to take part in making the wrong right. They are made to restore the community, in many instances where the offender's crime was against the community.

This approach was most notably employed first in 1993 in New York City with the development of the first community court. The Midtown Community Court (MCC) targets quality-of-life offenses committed around the Times Square Area in New York City, which was an epicenter for drugs, prostitution, and robbery-related offenses until the 1990s. More specifically, the offenses targeted by this court included prostitution, graffiti, shoplifting, and subway fare evasion.[19] When offenders are caught committing these crimes and processed in the MCC, they are sentenced to perform community restitution by cleaning up trash, graffiti, and debris in parks, in an effort to repay the community they have harmed. The premise is that the crime is not victimless when the community is victimized. Offenders are also connected with resources, such as drug treatment, health care, and other social services.[20]

Another such court that is reporting successful outcomes is the Orange County Community Court (OCC), located in Santa Ana, California. Founded in 2008, this court offers an array of services to offenders, but unlike the other 50 or so community courts in the United States, the OCC offers these services to anyone who lives in the jurisdiction in need of assistance. The services include mental health treatment, drug counseling and treatment, assistance to veterans, and other social services.[21] According to the presiding Judge Joe Perez, "The idea is for everyone to get together to try to figure out the best way to keep people from coming back. We try to provide them with the treatment that is needed, and the structure that is needed, because many of them have had no structure."[22] Community courts have many resources to make this type of sentence viable, but for the traditional community service sentence, it is often in the criminal courts for low-level offenders with no history of violence.

In sum, the dramatic rise in the American incarceration rate resulted in an increased use of probation, parole and other forms of community corrections. Intermediate sanctions became popular as a cost-savings alternative to incarceration. These sanctions vary, but most of them combine some type of punishment

---

19. Denckla, D. A. (1999). Forgiveness as a problem-solving tool in the courts: A brief response to the panel on forgiveness in criminal law. *Fordham Urban Law Journal, 27,* 1613–1619.

20. Ibid.

21. Latigua-Williams, J. (2016, June 19). When prison is not the answer. *The Atlantic.* Retrieved from https://www.theatlantic.com/politics/archive/2016/06/when-prison-is-not-the-answer/487703/

22. Ibid.

with the goal of rehabilitation. We introduced you to a number of these sanctions in this chapter, many of which the court relies heavily on. Most of the sanctions discussed in this chapter have shown mixed success, with boot camps as the exception. Though boot camps were very popular with politicians and the public, they were not an effective punishment, and in some cases, had devastating consequences. The remaining intermediate sanctions, while not always tremendously successful, have shown positive impacts. In fact, as you read, some participants of ISP and DRCs are grateful for the rehabilitative approach employed in community corrections. While others may find these punishments restricting, and in some cases physically painful (the ankle bracelet), community corrections provide a method for lowering exorbitant correctional costs, and that means we can expect them to remain popular for quite some time.

Chapter 7

Correctional Facility Life

As we documented in Chapter 4, prisons and jails come in a lot of different forms. These facilities not only vary in size, but perhaps most importantly, also by security level. Security level and whether men or women are kept in a correctional facility are the greatest predictors of not only levels of violence within these facilities but also how inmates interact with one another. Popular culture is full of depictions of life in correctional facilities. Among the most popular stories are full of drama, violence, sexual assault, and lawlessness. At the same time, many federal facilities or lower security facilities are deemed to be cushy places that are not much worse than a bad vacation. Within this chapter, we will discuss the various ways in which inmates in correctional facilities interact.

A Total Institution

For most people, their life is spent among many places. On a weekday, a typical day can consist of waking up at home and then later going to work. During a day, there may be various errands to run or children to take places. Weekends may be full of a variety of different activities. People also can take vacations or travel. Life can take them many places. Yet, for some people, life is not spent going from place to place. Instead, life is spent only at one place. Erving Goffman referred to these places as total institutions. He described these institutions as "places of residence and work where a large number of like-situated individuals, cut off from the wider society for an appreciable period of time, together lead an enclosed, formally administered round of life." Within prison, inmates have most of their life choices dictated to them. When inmates eat, where they must be at any given time, and a host of other things are dictated to them.[1] For anyone who has seen *The Shawshank Redemption*, Morgan Freeman's character Ellis Boyd "Red" Redding provides a prime example of the effects of a total institution. As he noted, he could not seem to go the bathroom unless someone told him he was allowed to go. Within the movie, Red referred to this process as being "institutionalized."

As we have discussed, many forms or systems of incarceration sought to re-train inmates. Whether inmates in the Pennsylvania system were supposed to stop sinning, or inmates in Auburn were supposed to learn a work ethic, correctional facility rules are designed to not only reform inmates but provide security to the institution as well. The process through which inmates are supposed to learn how to act in prison is referred to by many correctional scholars as the prisonization process. Such a process can be difficult to learn, including how to manage relationships with other inmates as well as interactions with correctional staff. Within correctional facilities, there are both formal and informal rules, and learning these rules and navigating them can be a difficult process.[2] One example of this comes from Dexter. He notes:

> Prison also strips one's identity, self-respect, and freedom of choices. Prisoners are told what to do, often in a vile tone by prison officials. A person's humanity is disregarded when he or she becomes an inmate. The use of the word "inmate" toward someone in incarceration carries a subhuman connotation. Not only is a person's freedom to exist lost when he or she is locked up, but they risk experiencing a psychological deterioration due to the stressful environment behind prison walls.

The Defects of Total Power

In his study of a maximum-security prison, Gresham Sykes noted something of a paradox. Correctional officers have been notorious for using brutality to manage inmates. However, as society became more aware of prison conditions and courts of law began to intervene, correctional officers and officials could no longer just rely on brute force to ensure inmate compliance.[3] By the end of the 1960s, all states had either abolished policies that officially allowed corporal punishment, or in states that did not make such prohibitions, these policies were deemed by the courts as cruel and unusual punishment. Certainly, there are still instances in which correctional officers initiate corporal punishment of inmates,

---

1. Goffman, E. (1961). *Asylums: Essays on the social situation of mental patients and other inmates.* New York, NY: Anchor Books. Quote on Page xiii.

2. Clear, T. R., Reisig, M. D., & Cole, G. F. (2015). *American Corrections* (11th ed.). Boston, MA: Cengage.

3. Sykes, G. M. (1958). *The society of captives: A study of a maximum security prison.* Princeton, NJ: Princeton University Press.

but these occurrences are no longer sanctioned by official state-sponsored pol-icies.[4] Additionally, while the legacy of the Pennsylvania system lives on today in supermax prisons and solitary confinement, only extreme disciplinary cases are supposed to be housed in this form of custody.[5] Furthermore, correctional officers live with a constant fear that the inmates can take over a facility or riot. For every correctional officer, there are many more inmates. Thus, correctional officers and inmates often have a give and take relationship. Correctional officers also know that they cannot write up every inmate for every infraction. Not only do correctional officials frown upon such actions, but they can only punish so many inmates at a time. This often presents correctional officers with a quandary. If they write disciplinary reports on inmates who will not be punished, this will diminish their power in the eyes of inmates. For these reasons, many inmates will test correctional officers, especially new employees, to see how far inmates can bend the rules without getting in trouble.[6] Political scientist John DiIulio has argued that the presence of violence in prisons, and in some instances inmates essentially running correctional facilities, represents defects in prison manage-ment.[7] Regardless, in most medium and maximum security prisons, there will be somewhat of a give and take between correctional officers and inmates. Given the large number of prisons, correctional staff, and inmates throughout the United States, the relationship can vary considerably.

The Pains of Imprisonment

Before Charles Manson would go on to found a cult and inspire his followers to commit a series of horrific murders, he had spent more than half his life in var-ious correctional institutions. Due to his chaotic life, he actually came to enjoy prison life and the structure it provided. When up for parole while serving time at minimum security Federal Correctional Institution, Terminal Island in Cali-fornia, Manson actually requested to stay rather than being paroled. If only cor-rectional authorities had granted his request is one of the big what-ifs of history.[8] In the movie *Goodfellas* and the book *Wiseguy*, which the movie was based upon,

---

4. Gideon, L., & Griffin, O. H. (2017). *Correctional management and the law: A penological approach*. Durham, NC: Carolina Academic Press.

5. Clear, T. R., Reisig, M. D., & Cole, G. F. (2015). *American Corrections* (11th ed.). Boston, MA: Cengage.

6. Sykes, G. M. (1958). *The society of captives: A study of a maximum security prison*. Princeton, NJ: Princeton University Press.

7. DiIulio, J. J. (1987). *Governing prisons: A comparative study of correctional management*. New York, NY: The Free Press.

8. Bugliosi, V., & Gentry, C. (2001). *Helter skelter: The true story of the Manson murders*. New York, NY: W.W. Norton & Company.

mobster Henry Hill noted that gangsters had a good life in prison.[9] Beyond these outlier examples, for most inmates, they would rather be just about any place else. To many people, locking them up in paradise might become a bad thing. After all, even if you really like a place, sometimes you just want to be somewhere else.

Gresham Sykes identified several pains that inmates suffer upon their incarceration. The first pain is that inmates lose their liberty. In addition to the negative effects of being in a correctional facility, inmates are mostly cut off from family and friends. They are only allowed to see them during limited visiting hours, collect phone calls, and mail.[10] Some prisons are experimenting with computer messaging services (such as Skype), but these services are still limited.[11] Isolation and various restrictions can lead to a deterioration of relationships that can further isolate inmates. The second pain is a loss of goods and services. In correctional facilities, inmates either have to eat in the cafeteria or purchase food items from the commissary. If they do not have money in their inmate account, inmates can only eat at the cafeteria, which is usually a lesser version of the food available in a school cafeteria. In most correctional facilities, inmates are forced to wear uniforms, which are usually unflattering and ill-fitting. There are restrictions on the type and number of items can keep in their cells. Correctional officials are always on the lookout for any item that could be used as a weapon. The third pain is the loss of heterosexual relationships. We will discuss this topic in more depth a little later in the chapter, but one frustration that inmates must deal with is not being able to engage in physical contact much less engage in day-to-day heterosexual relationships. Even when visitors are allowed into prison, there are usually restrictions on physical contact.[12] Furthermore, correctional facilities in the United States have never really embraced the idea of allowing inmates to have conjugal visits. Thus, for many inmates, this creates a big void in their life while they are incarcerated.[13] The fourth pain is the loss of autonomy. Somewhat building upon the loss of liberty and that inmates are not allowed to go where they please, inmates must abide by the commands, whims, and wishes of correctional officers and officials. As Sykes noted, some inmates may welcome a structured lifestyle to help them rehabilitate, but few inmates actually enjoy being treated like children and having to abide by many rules that, in least in inmates' minds, are unreasonable. The fifth pain is the deprivation of security. This may seem a little weird to you. After all, inmates are held in secure facilities—what do they have to fear? As it turns out, plenty. While it is true that most inmates have committed some

---

9. Pileggi, N. (1985). *Wiseguy*. New York, NY: Simon and Schuster.

10. Sykes, G. M. (1958). *The society of captives: A study of a maximum security prison*. Princeton, NJ: Princeton University Press.

11. Hanser, R. D. (2017). *Introduction to corrections* (2nd ed.). Thousand Oaks, CA: Sage.

12. Sykes, G. M. (1958). *The society of captives: A study of a maximum security prison*. Princeton, NJ: Princeton University Press.

13. D'Alessio, S. J., Flexon, J., & Stolzenberg, L. (2013). The effect of conjugal visitation on sexual violence in prison. *American Journal of Criminal Justice, 38*, 13–26.

crime, that does not mean they do not fear other inmates. Inmates must always be on their guard.[14] Just like the fish in the ocean where it seems there is always a bigger or badder fish, the same is often true of prison life. Even if another inmate is not looking to attack another inmate, they should often be weary. Having to always be on your guard is exhausting, and the fear of being attacked may cause an inmate to attack first, even if it was not necessary in the moment.

For some, or for many, the pains are much more psychological in nature. Take, for example, Victor Muglia's feelings about his incarceration. He explains the negative effects, which range from psychological to spiritual pains, as well as feelings of mistrust.

Narrative: Victor's Story

The negative effects of my incarceration are mostly psychological. I cry myself to sleep quite often thinking about how much I loved my mother and how much she loved me. I don't see how the greatest mother alive was senselessly beaten to death, but her killer is allowed to live. I wish I could die when I have nightmares of my mother on her knees crying, hugging my legs, asking me why I did this to her. I would have ended my life long ago, but I couldn't take a brother away from his sister, especially after I had already taken away her mother. It is frustrating to know that the cause of my crime is well-known information about drugs that has been documented in medical and psychology journals for years, but that none of my mother's family would ever understand how a son could kill his own mother. It is frustrating to know that my father, who was the cause of most of me and my mother's emotional troubles, feels like he could have done better but is too prideful to ever admit it.

My incarceration has also had an effect on me that could be both negative and positive depending on the perspective. I have little respect for authority figures and am completely rigid when it comes to my view of correctional officers. For a correctional officer to convince me that he/she is pro-prisoner, they would have to risk their life for a prisoner, risk their job for a prisoner, or quit the job because they don't agree with their fellow officer's views of prisoners. So far, I've met two officers who fall into this category throughout my nine years of incarceration.

I don't put my faith in anything said by correctional officers: I've been told to do one thing by one officer, then told by another not do it, and was given a charge by the first officer for refusing a direct order. I question every word that is said by an officer and always try to interact with them around other

---

14. Sykes, G. M. (1958). *The society of captives: A study of a maximum security prison.* Princeton, NJ: Princeton University Press.

officers and other prisoners, if possible, so that I can have witnesses. I question the intentions behind any seemingly benevolent act of an officer. I can't stand prisons that help officers do a job for which they are paid $50,000+ a year. I can't stand prisoners who participate in the oppression of fellow prisoners. These are not misguided judgments but are sound guidelines based on empirical observation and experience. I've seen female officers "lead on" a prisoner, and the prisoner ended up getting jumped by several officers because he made a sexual advance toward the female officer. I've seem inmates plant contraband in the cells of others and then tell a supervising officer. I've seen good people go to the intensive care unit because they said the wrong thing to the wrong officer and ended up with internal physical damage. My views of correctional officers do not contradict the positive character trait of humanity that I have gained from my incarceration. I try my best to be humble, and that's why I'm so frustrated, but humility always saves me in the end. Without humility, I would impulsively respond to every instance of abuse and would find myself in a permanent state of solitary confinement.

A lot of us say that their incarceration changed their lives. My incarceration didn't change my life—it completely obliterated any notion of who I thought I was.

Inmate Culture

One of the biggest debates within the correctional literature is the nature of inmate culture within men's prisons. As we discuss a little later, inmate culture in women's prisons is very different. Within popular culture, men's prisons are often depicted as some version of *Lord of the Flies* on steroids. It is essentially depicted as a dog-eat-dog world full of predators and victims. Furthermore, as the television show *Gangland* depicted, which aired on History from 2007–2010, there is no shortage of prison gangs fighting for control of various correctional facilities. Yet, as we have discussed, there are a variety of prisons in different states, and among these state facilities, there are facilities with different security levels. Furthermore, since federal prisons have much higher rates of nonviolent offenders and the Federal Bureau of Prisons and has more funding than the states, these facilities are not as violent as some state facilities. Thus, although we cannot describe what the typical prison culture is in every facility, there are certainly patterns that present themselves.

In describing prison culture, there are essentially two competing ideas, although in many ways, they can be overlapping. Gresham Sykes discussed prison culture as essentially a society within itself. It was a culture of various rules and hierarchies that more or less was created within the vacuum of correctional environments. He believed that inmates essentially developed, while in prison, a convict code of "argot rules" among which prisoners learned to live. Among the many rules that inmates were supposed to live by was to do your own prison time, and do not get involved in the affairs of others. Perhaps most important was to refrain from snitching on other prisoners.[15] In general, a convict code will be a series of informal rules that dictate how inmates behave. Within this code is some sense of what constitutes acceptable behavior and what is not. Furthermore, there will be some general sense of what the proper retribution is for an inmate who violates the code.[16] Obviously, inmate codes can vary widely, and how a particular prison is organized, administered, and maintained can have a dramatic effect on the behavior of inmates, including when and how often they engage in violence.[17] In general, there are essentially five general rules by which inmates should abide: do not interfere in the interests of other inmates, do not argue with fellow inmates, do not exploit other inmates, keep to yourself, and do not trust correctional staff or any of their values.[18]

John Irwin saw correctional environments a bit differently and with good reason. Irwin earned a PhD in sociology and was a professor at San Francisco State University. Like Sykes, Irwin performed hands-on research of correctional facilities. However, Irwin's experience with correctional environments began much earlier through his own personal experience. Looking back on his younger years, Irwin described himself as "a thug, a drug addict," and he served time in prison after being convicted of armed robbery.[19] Irwin argued that convict codes were not created in prison but was instead an extension of the thief's code that was developed by groups of thieves before they landed in prison. Thus, rather than prison rules being created in prisons, many of the social norms are created by inmates before they arrive in prison.[20] Irwin's version of prison culture is often referred to as importation theory.[21]

In jails, there is certainly a possibility of violence or victimization. This is one of the reasons so many defendants receive bail. Many people believe a person

15. Sykes, G. M. (1958). *The society of captives: A study of a maximum security prison*. Princeton, NJ: Princeton University Press.

16. Copes, H., Brookman, F., & Brown, A. (2013). Accounting for violations of the convict code. *Deviant Behavior*, *34*, 841–858.

17. Steiner, B., Butler, H. D., & Ellison, J. M. (2014). Causes and correlates of prison inmate misconduct: A systematic review of the evidence. *Journal of Criminal Justice*, *42*, 462–470.

18. Sykes, G. M., & Messinger, S. L. (1960). The inmate social system. In Cloward, R. A. (Ed.), *Theoretical Studies in Social Organization of the Prison*, (pp. 5–19). New York, NY: Social Science Research Council.

19. Irwin, J. (2002). My life in 'crim.' In Geis, G. & Dodge, M. (Eds.), *Lessons of criminology* (pp. 149–164). Cincinnati, OH: Anderson Publishing Co.

20. Irwin, J., & Cressey, D. R. (1962). Thieves, convicts and the inmate culture. *Social Problems*, *10*, 142–155.

21. Hanser, R. D. (2017). *Introduction to corrections* (2nd ed.). Thousand Oaks, CA: Sage.

should not be subjected to a correctional facility until they are actually adjudged to belong in one of these facilities. John Irwin stated that jailhouse culture is a bit different from prison culture. As we discussed in Chapter 4, Irwin stated that many jail inmates are members of the so-called rabble class. While many members of this class might not get along, many members of the rabble often jailed together, and there were some levels of solidarity in their continual trips through these facilities. Additionally, since the majority of inmates were awaiting trial, their primary focus was getting ready for trial. The hope of many was that they would be found not guilty or have their charges dropped. Thus, they did not anticipate staying in jail and would not treat it as their home.[22] One danger that jail inmates face is the possibility of jailhouse snitches. In an effort to curry favor with jail officials or try to negotiate a better plea deal, many jail inmates will try to find out information from other inmates. Some inmates will simply try to keep alert or question other inmates to get useful details. Additionally, in some instances, prosecutors or police might send specific jails informants to gather information.[23] Ronald describes one instance of how this can occur:

> In May 1985, it was revealed that the state had recruited one of (unnamed attorney's) other clients as the star witness against me. (Name redacted) was a jailhouse witness who would be called to testify that I confessed the crimes to him in the county jail. It was a sloppy setup. In March 1985, all the inmates had moved from the old Atlantic County Jail to the new jail. The witness was not even in the plan to be in the same unit with me. This was changed at the last minute. The witness's unit at the old jail was first to move and the units at the new jail were filled from left to right. My unit was last to move, and I was sent to the unit on the far right. The witness was already in there. As the new jail was being filled from left to right, all the units in between were empty. But the witness was all the way down the end of the hallway, right in the unit that I would be placed in. This was where he could say that I confessed to him.

With the correctional population explosion that began in the 1980s, jails have especially been affected. Prison inmate lawsuits have largely resulted in reductions in prison populations. Many prisons, if beyond 120% capacity, have been ordered by the courts to reduce population.[24] While this has helped many prisons, many jails have had to bear the heaviest burden in this change in policy, and convicted jail inmates must wait longer periods of time before they can be transferred to

---

22. Irwin, J. (1985). *The Jail: Managing the underclass in American society*. Berkeley, CA: University of California Press.
23. Call, J. (2001). Judicial control of jailhouse snitches. *The Justice System Journal, 22,* 73–83.
24. Gideon, L., & Griffin, O. H. (2017). *Correctional management and the law: A penological approach*. Durham, NC: Carolina Academic Press.

prison.[25] This is problematic since most inmates would rather spend time in prison, which is generally a more stable and less chaotic environment and has greater programming opportunities and more ways for inmates to spend their time. In jails, inmates who are awaiting transfer spend a lot more time being bored.[26] For instance, Victor describes his problems in a county jail:

> The county jail, although probably one of the most loathsome stages of the criminal justice procedure, gave me a well-needed reality check. I stopped using all drugs, cold turkey: the environment was too hectic to risk not being alert for even a second. I had been in several fights throughout my approximately 2-year stay. Some were the result of my own ignorance, while some were the result of me trying to protect myself from oppression. Overall, the county jail was the worst experience of my incarceration. After being sentenced, I soon began the prison journey that would make or break me.

Prison inmates who are serving short sentences may try to do their time as quickly as possible and stay out of as many people's way as they can. However, prisoners who are serving longer sentences will need to come to terms with the fact that prison will be their home for a considerable length of time, if not for the rest of their life. Many inmates respond poorly to their initial entry into prison, and it can take a considerable length of time, if they ever come to any sort of peace with their existence at all, before they can establish a routine.[27] As Gennifer recounted, some "lifers" can make a positive adjustment:

> I think one of the most surprising things I learned from visiting prisons came from interacting with men serving life sentences. Prior to sitting down with my first group of lifers, I was expecting to meet a group of angry men. Instead, the men I met were uplifting and full of hope. I sat among a group of men who appeared to be in better spirits than myself on a day-to-day basis. I was awestruck by their inner strength; they all had a sense of optimism about their futures. They believed they could have their sentences commuted or otherwise have their sentences reduced. I learned that to live in prison you must have hope; without hope there would be no reason to continue to live.

To some inmates, especially in maximum security prisons, the length of their prison sentence is their sole focus when entering a correctional facility. Many inmates will feel the need to prove their masculinity. Exaggerated displays of mas-

---

25. Tartaro, C. (2002). The impact of density on jail violence. *Journal of Criminal Justice, 30*, 499–510.

26. Clear, T. R., Reisig, M. D., & Cole, G. F. (2015). *American Corrections* (11th ed.). Boston, MA: Cengage.

27. Johnson, R., & Dobrzanska, A. (2005). Mature coping among life-sentenced inmates: An exploratory study of adjustment dynamics. *Corrections Compendium, 30*, 8–9.

culinity can lead to violence among inmates.[28] This is especially prevalent among younger inmates, who are responsible for a large percentage of the violence in prisons.[29] Research has demonstrated that inmates who identify with a code of the street or are involved with gangs present a higher likelihood of engaging in prison violence.[30] Yet, some researchers have argued that gang affiliation, in and of itself, is not the greatest predictor of engaging in violent behavior. Indeed, some researchers have argued that chronic offending and a history of violence are greater predictors of violence.[31] It is probably no coincidence that people who display these types of behavior will join and be useful to gangs.

Many prisons are organized along racial lines, and that is among the most common organizing factors of prison gangs. Some inmates will simply carry in gang affiliations that preceded their entry into prisons. Other inmates will select to join gangs when they enter prison, often for protection. Joining a prison gang is usually a lifetime commitment, and gang members in prison can only in the rarest circumstances peacefully resign from a gang. One of the reasons that descriptions of inmate life has changed over the years is that before the 1950s, prison gangs were nonexistent. By the late 1970s, prison gangs were a huge force in most prison systems. Many prison gangs are highly organized and tight-knit organizations whose reach extends beyond prison walls. Their proliferation within the American correctional system has upset and, in some instances, replaced various tenets of the convict code. While members of gangs will protect their own members, they will also punish their own members when they violate gang rules.[32] Thus, while gang members will punish their own members for violations within the gang, a nonaffiliated inmate, if victimized by a gang member, may be inhibited in enforcing the convict code out of fear that he might upset an entire gang.

As we have discussed, male prison society is highly organized by race, ethnicity, and age. One exception to this is the case of older inmates. Nearly one quarter of inmates serve a sentence of 25 years or longer. With the expansion of prison populations and harsher sentencing laws, many correctional facilities are

---

28. Lutze, F. E., & Murphy, D. W. (1999). Ultramasculine prison environments and inmates' adjustment: It's time to move beyond the "boys will be boys" paradigm. *Justice Quarterly, 16,* 709–733.

29. Lahm, K. F. (2008). Inmate-on-inmate assault: A multilevel examination of prison violence. *Criminal Justice and Behavior, 35,* 120–137.

30. Mears, D. P., Steward, E. A., Siennick, S. E., & Simons, R. L. (2013). The code of the street and inmate violence: Investigating the salience of imported belief systems. *Criminology, 51,* 695–728.

31. DeLisi, M., Berg, M. T., & Hochstetler, A. (2004). Gang members, career criminals, and prison violence: Further specification of the importation model of inmate behavior. *Criminal Justice Studies, 17,* 369–383.

32. Skarbek, D. (2014). *The social order of the underworld: How prison gangs govern the American penal system.* New York, NY: Oxford University Press.

experiencing greater numbers of aging inmates.[33] In many facilities, the elder inmates will hang out together, in many cases ignoring the racial barriers that often prevent many younger inmates from hanging out together. Elder inmates, often referred to as greyhounds, are usually afforded greater levels of respect among inmates. Attacking or taking advantage of these inmates is often viewed as taboo.[34] Beating up an older inmate will not provide a tough image for which many inmates, especially younger or new inmates, are hoping to acquire. Separate from these older inmates, most inmates, if not in a gang, will hang out among other inmates who share common characteristics.

For some inmates, prison life can be more difficult. Perhaps the most vilified groups of inmates are those labeled rats or squealers. As we mentioned, the inmate code dictates that you are not supposed to inform on other inmates. Informants may have different motivations, from simply seeking justice they cannot obtain on their own or informing on other inmates for personal gain. For instance, if an inmate has their own hustle and has competing inmates, some inmates will inform on those competitors, hoping to remove them from that hustle. In some instances, inmates will do this anonymously. In other instances, inmates will identify themselves to correctional authorities. This can pose a great danger. In just about any inmate or convict subculture, informants are vilified and are the source for inmate retribution.[35] Some inmates will become vilified by the crimes in which they engage. One of the most well-known groups of disrespected inmates are sex offenders and especially pedophiles. These inmates are often shunned and, in many instances, victimized by other inmates. Additionally, inmates who are either developmentally disabled or mentally ill may face rough treatment. Developmentally disabled inmates may suffer a tough time because they are perceived as gullible to predatory inmates, and those inmates may take some perverse pleasure into convincing these inmates to engage in a wide range of activities. Mentally ill inmates, which represents a wide spectrum, can have trouble getting along with other inmates and may be perceived as crazy or loose cannons. Some mentally ill inmates may find themselves in fights because of misunderstandings or because stressful correctional facilities may exacerbate diminished coping mechanisms.[36] Given their problems with both adjusting to prison life and interacting with other inmates, mentally ill inmates pose a quandary to correctional administers, and how to best manage this population is still a work in progress.[37]

---

33. Clear, T. R., Reisig, M. D., & Cole, G. F. (2015). *American Corrections* (11th ed.). Boston, MA: Cengage.

34. Hanser, R. D. (2017). *Introduction to corrections* (2nd ed.). Thousand Oaks, CA: Sage.

35. Sykes, G. M. (1958). *The society of captives: A study of a maximum security prison*. Princeton, NJ: Princeton University Press.

36. Hanser, R. D. (2017). *Introduction to corrections* (2nd ed.) Thousand Oaks, CA: Sage.

37. Adams, K., & Ferrandino, J. (2008). Managing mentally ill inmates in prison. *Criminal Justice and Behavior, 35*, 913–927.

Not only is fighting depicted as a common incurrence within correctional environments, but sexual assault is often depicted as prevalent as well. Certainly, sexual assault occurs and many cases go unreported, but some researchers have claimed that a seeming mythology has been created regarding sexuality in correctional facilities. Within correctional environments, three types of sexual interactions occur among inmates: bartered sex, coerced sex, and consensual sex. To some inmates, sexual identity can become fluid, and many inmates, who do not identify themselves as either homosexual or even bisexual, will engage in homosexual relationships while in correctional facilities.[38] According to Sykes, many inmates will distinguish between inmates with sexual perversions (a term he used in the 1950s) and inmates who were merely engaging in homosexual relationships because they were denied access to heterosexual relationships. Some inmates would play the role of either sexual predator or sexual aggressor. Within correctional environments, it can sometimes be difficult to define the difference. Some inmates would be submissive because they identified as homosexual, while others engaged in these types of relationships for protection or to obtain goods and services. Some inmates who did not identify as transsexual will even groom themselves in a feminine manner to exaggerate these relationships.[39] Inmates who are either transsexual or identify as homosexual report higher rates of sexual victimization while in correctional facilities than heterosexual inmates. Women are less likely to suffer sexual abuse from other inmates than men.[40] However, as we discussed in Chapter 4, women in prison are more likely to be sexually victimized by correctional staff than other inmates.

Until recently, sexual activity in women's correctional facilities, within popular culture, were predominantly depicted in various sexploitation films.[41] While these forms of entertainment have not ceased, more balanced accounts, such as *Orange is the New Black* and *Wentworth* have been produced. While violence does occur in women's facilities, it is not nearly as prevalent as within men's facilities. One of the reasons for this is because of the population of inmates themselves. Only one third of women are held in prison for violent crimes, and in many instances, their violent crime was targeted against an abusive partner or spouse.[42] Amanda,

---

38. Hensley, C., & Tewksbury, R. (2002). Inmate-to-inmate prison sexuality: A review of empirical studies. *Trauma, Violence, and Abuse, 3*, 226–243.

39. Sykes, G. M. (1958). *The society of captives: A study of a maximum security prison*. Princeton, NJ: Princeton University Press.

40. Tewksbury, R., & Navarro, J. C. (2018). Sexuality in correctional facilities. In Griffin, O. H. & Woodward, V. H. (Eds.), *Routledge Handbook of Corrections in the United States* (pp. 420–431). New York, NY: Routledge.

41. Cecil, D. K. (2007). Looking beyond caged heath: Media images of women in prison. *Feminist Criminology, 2*, 304–326.

42. Kajstura, A. (2017, October 19). *Women's mass incarceration: The whole pie 2017*. Prison Policy Initiative. Retrieved on July 27, 2018 from https://www.prisonpolicy.org/reports/pie2017women.html

who ended up in prison after years of drug abuse described the women she encountered in prison.

> I was sentenced to two, 3-year state prison terms in Edna Mahon Correctional Facility, the only female prison in the state of New Jersey. Prison was one of the most eye-opening experiences of my life. I met 200 different women with the same exact story. There were a handful of women that were NOT there for drugs. I stared into the eyes of a 56-year-old woman speaking of her next high when she was to be released, and I saw myself. I did not want to be in prison at 56 years old with nothing and no one but a career in prison terms and a busted up body from abusing myself. I didn't want to be her. I truly decided right there that when I finally got home. I was going to fight for my life.

Women do not tend to endorse the notions of a convict code.[43] Perhaps the most interesting aspect of women's correctional environments is that many women will gather into pseudo-families, complete with a mother, sometimes a father figure, and children.[44] One example of this comes from *Orange is the New Black*, with the characters of Galina "Red" Reznikov and Gloria Mendoza, both of whom at different times are entrusted with running the prison kitchen, seem to have a matriarchal sway over different groups of inmates. For these women, it seems like they are trying to create familial relationships that they were not able to create among general society.

One of the common problems regarding women inmates is that they are often known as forgotten offenders. Since they are less violent and provide far less security risks than male inmates, women inmates are often a neglected group, both by researchers and state officials. Furthermore, since there are fewer women offenders, there are fewer women's facilities. Thus, in many states, there may be only one facility for all women. This means that not only are women offenders not segregated by security levels, but if the facility in which they are housed is in a remote part of the state far away from family, they might not receive any visitors. Many male inmates, who may have less stable relationships, may be indifferent to any children they have. On the other hand, not only are many women offenders mothers, but being a mother is often a large part of their identity. In some instances, it might be the only positive thing in their life. Being so far from loved ones may further aggravate the pain of being incarcerated and exacerbate low feelings of self-worth. To counteract these effects, some states provide special visiting areas for children or allow overnight visits. Some facilities will even allow children born in correctional facilities to remain with their mothers for some

---

43. Ward, D. A., & Kassebaum, G. G. (2010). *Women's prison: Sex and social structure.* New Brunswick, NJ: Aldine Transaction.

44. Hensley, C., & Tewksbury, R. (2002). Inmate-to-inmate prison sexuality: A review of empirical studies. *Trauma, Violence & Abuse, 3*, 226–243.

period of time.[45] To some people this might seem crazy; yet, think back on your own life, and ponder how many memories you have before you were five years old or younger. Maintaining a relationship and the bonding experience with one's mother, especially if that inmate is not serving a long sentence, is usually more important than where that actual relationship occurred.

45. Clear, T. R., Reisig, M. D., & Cole, G. F. (2015). *American Corrections* (11th ed.). Boston, MA: Cengage.

Chapter 8

Juvenile Corrections

History of Juvenile Justice System

The tight-knit colonial landscape that marked America in the late 1700s was radically transformed in the early 1800s with the growth of American cities. Manufacturing jobs became abundant in the cities and drew a mass influx of immigration. The city became the hub for work but without regulations. Manufacturing jobs paid low wages, and many of them were located in factories that were filthy, diseased, and unsafe. While cities became the center of a booming and prosperous new economy, not all classes were part of the success. Immigrants who came to the city seeking work became part of a poor urban underclass, forced to work and live in squalor. The traditional agrarian family of the United States was transformed by rapid industrialization and city growth.

The old days where families lived and worked together all day on farms was now supplanted by competition of factory jobs. Remember, this was prior to the establishment of unions that regulate working conditions and protect workers, which meant that the people willing to work in the worst of conditions would often be the ones to work. The city solved the problem of overcrowding of poor urban workers by building "tenement" housing, which were large rundown apartment buildings that could accommodate the mass working class. The buildings were overcrowded, and waste and trash disposal was not yet systematized so that the cities, and in particular the tenements, were polluted and disease ridden. The dream of the big city lights and romanticism that was real for the middle and upper classes was all but a mirage for the lower class.

The lower-class workers who found jobs worked very long hours and for those children who did not also work in factories, they were often left unsupervised and even abandoned when families could not afford to take care of their own. The depression of the poverty among the poor urban class was often followed by alcoholism, drug use, gambling, and prostitution. For some, these were escapes from depressed conditions, while for others they were means of survival. These social ills became widespread in cities, where poverty was also becoming rampant. The fact that crime is correlated with poverty is not a new phenomenon. The crime rates were escalating, and the cities were wearing down the poor, especially the children.

The same conditions that led adults to crime led their children to it as well. They were children of awful circumstances, affected also by poverty, diseases, malnutrition, abuse, and abandonment. We will cover this later in this chapter, but many of the same factors that lead children to juvenile delinquency today are the same as those that led children to crime historically: abuse, neglect, and substance abuse. Many of the homeless children began to steal, beg, and prostitute for money. They were committing crimes of survival, and when they were arrested and convicted of crimes, they were imprisoned in the same squalid prisons as adults, with no protections from these adult offenders. There was no separate juvenile justice system at that time so these children, many of whom committed petty crimes, were sentenced to serve hard time with no opportunities for rehabilitation. Many of these children were not criminal at all, but since they had no parents and the state had nowhere else to place them, for the poor and abandoned children, prison it was. Ah, the promise of the city. . .

As conditions deteriorated in the cities and child abandonment, labor abuse and juvenile delinquency increased, a child savers movement took ahold. The child savers are well known as a progressive group, comprised primarily of women, who took steps to help these children. They were concerned with children living on the streets and those who were arrested and serving time with hardened adult offenders. They advocated for child labor laws, humane conditions for children in housing, and education for these children. They implored the government to protect these children and establish reforms so that these children would not become hardened criminals. By most accounts, the child savers were motivated by a genuine desire to help orphaned and abandoned children, but there was also a growing intolerance of these children, who seemingly threatened the existing social order. Charles Loring Brace, Founder of the New York Children's Aid Society in 1853, wrote the following:

> For the most part, the boys grow up utterly by themselves. No one cares for them, and they care for no one. Some live by begging, by petty pilfering, by bold robbery; some earn an honest support by peddling matches, or apples, or newspapers; others gather bones and rags in the street to sell. They sleep on steps, in cellars, in old barns, and in markets, or they hire a bed in filthy and low lodging-houses. They cannot read; they do not go to school

or attend a church. . . . The girls, too often, grow up even more pitiable and deserted. . . . They are the cross-walk sweepers, the little apple peddlers, and candy-sellers of our city; or, by more questionable means, they earn their scanty bread. They traverse the low, vile streets alone, and live without mother or friends, or any share in what we should call a *home*.[1]

In his book, Brace detailed conditions of the cities that lead to children becoming offenders. He discussed the disease and filth the lower classes lived in and the demoralizing conditions that lead to the breakdown of most families, particularly among the families doomed to the overcrowded tenement housing:

Few girls can grow up to maturity in such dens as exists in the First, Sixth, Eleventh and Seventeenth wards to be virtuous; few boys can have such places as homes and not be thieves and vagabonds. In such places typhus and cholera will always be rife, and the death rate will reach its most terrible maximum. While the poorest population dwell in these cellars and crowded attics, neither Sunday schools, nor churches, nor charities, can accomplish a thorough reform.[2]

Motivated by concern for these children but also their fear of social harm to society, and other possible dangers, child savers and other reformers were instrumental in lobbying for the first separate institution for children. As previously mentioned, the children described in these passages were often found guilty of petty crimes such as thievery and vagrancy. Often described as wayward children, they were sent to prisons along with adults. However, in the 1820s, reformers were successful in securing the first separate facility for children. More specifically, the first House of Refuge opened its doors in New York in 1825. The House of Refuge was a facility for deviant children and not adults, whereby children would be separated from their corrupting social conditions and taught the value of obedience and discipline through hard work. Philadelphia and Boston were quick to follow New York's example, and by the 1840s, there were at least 25 more facilities throughout the United States.[3]

The Houses of Refuge, in other states known as Houses of Reform, were rooted in the English philosophy of rehabilitation, or reformation. Children should not serve time in prisons, as those institutions did not meet the needs of a child. The first crimes for which children could be punished though varied greatly. The two broad categories for commitment to a reformatory were crime or incorrigibility. The first category is self-explanatory, but the second is where the gray area lies.

---

1. Brace, C. L. (1872). *The dangerous classes of New York and twenty years' work among them*. New York, NY: Wynkoop and Hallenback.

2. Ibid, at 57.

3. Center on Juvenile and Criminal Justice. Juvenile justice history. Retrieved on July 19, 2018 from http://www.cjcj.org/education1/juvenile-justice-history.html

Incorrigibility includes mostly status offenses (which we will cover again later in this chapter). Status offenses are those that are wrong because of the age of a child. Acts of incorrigibility were vast, including acts such as truancy, breaking curfew, and disobedience.[4] Many of these cases were initiated by parents, frustrated with their incorrigible children, but the question that followed, and one that remains still today, is should children with behavioral issues be punished with those who have committed real crimes?

The debate over the institutionalization of "wayward" children went on for several years, with not much slowdown in the practice. In fact, many states had adopted provisions to commit incorrigible children. Connecticut, for example, in 1879, adopted a provision to commit a boy under the age of 16 who was in "danger of being brought up, or is brought up, to lead an idle or vicious life . . . [or] who is incorrigible or habitually disregards the commands of his father or mother or guardian, who leads a vagrant life, or resorts to immoral places or practices, or neglects or refuses to perform labor suitable to his years and condition, or to attend school."[5] Certain institutions, such as the Pennsylvania Reform School, routinely admitted more children for incorrigibility and vagrancy than actual crimes into the late 19th century.[6]

Concern for the conditions in these institutions was growing as well. The mayor of St. Louis reported that their House of Refuge was no more than a prison for juveniles. "Windows and doors had iron bars to prevent escapes, children wore uniforms, rules prevented talking at mealtime, and the children's heads were shaved. The children had no directed play and few opportunities for indoor or outdoor recreation."[7] The superintendent of the institution echoed serious concern for the conditions to city councilman in 1893: "We have 100 boys sleeping in one room 40 by 80 feet, low ceiling and the beds are "two story"; there are no bathroom privileges of any kind in the building . . . Can we not prevail upon this assembly to give us relief? In the name of humanity!"[8]

Well, shortly after these pleas for humanity came a major change in the system! Illinois became the first state to create a separate juvenile court in Chicago in 1899 so that children would be tried separate from adults. The courts were designed to address the many distinct emotional and cognitive needs of children. The idea of the progressive court was well received and spread quickly. The courts utilized the philosophy of *parens patriae*, as parent of, or acting in the best

---

4. Nelson, P. (2012). Early Days of the State Reform School, Juvenile Distress and Community Response in Minnesota, 1868–1891. *Staff Publications,* Paper 4.

5. Act of Mar. 28, 1879, ch. 125, § 1, 1879 Conn. Pub. Acts 478.

6. Garlock, P. (1979). Wayward children and the law, 1820–1900: The Genesis of the status offense jurisdiction of the juvenile court. *Georgia Law Review, 13,* 341–447.

7. Abrams, D. E. (2004). Lessons from juvenile history in the United States. *Journal of the Institute of Justice and International Studies, 4,* 7–24.

8. Ibid.

interest of the child. The focus in the new juvenile courts was rehabilitation. The terminology used was softer than that of the criminal courts. We will not cover the terminology extensively here, but we can provide some examples. Instead of the term conviction, adjudication is used for a finding of juvenile guilt. A trial in front of a judge in a juvenile court is referred to as a hearing, rather than a trial, and a sentence of incarceration is called detention in the juvenile court. While the terms are meant to reduce the idea of an adversarial system, the processes are very similar to those in the adult courts. The major initial difference was that juveniles had no due process rights. The court's philosophy was that of a parent trying to rehabilitate a child, and therefore the child would not need protections. The obvious flaw in this philosophy is that if a juvenile can receive a sentence of detention similar to an adult who might be incarcerated, should not he or she receive the same protections as an adult? This question (and many other similar issue) were not addressed in the court until the 1960s and beyond.

Due Process Revolution and Juvenile Rights

By 1925, almost every state had its own juvenile courts, but juveniles still were not entitled to any due process rights. Stop and think about this. Imagine you were arrested with no reading of the charges against you, no right to a lawyer or a hearing, but instead you were brought straight to a judge who would decide your fate based on the accusations brought against you. In addition, you might have to spend several years in a prison (detention center sounds nicer, right) but you still would have no right to defend yourself because ultimately this decision is in your best interest. Does that sound like your best interest or justice? The U.S. Supreme Court saw the problem with this logic as well, and in a series of landmark decisions in the 1960s, also known as the time of the Due Process Revolution, the Court gave juveniles due process protections. So did they receive all of the same rights as adults? We will provide the answer to this question using the actual cases.

Let us begin with one of the most pivotal decisions regarding juvenile justice. In 1961, 16-year-old Morris Kent was arrested for robbing and raping a woman in her own home in Washington, DC. Kent was known in the juvenile system, having been convicted for a number of burglaries when he was 14 years old. Kent was serving a sentence of probation in the juvenile court already, and therefore law enforcement had his fingerprints already, which they matched to the crime. Kent was arrested and interrogated for two days without a lawyer, during which time he confessed to his crimes. His mother hired an attorney for Kent, who challenged the court's intention to transfer Morris Kent from a juvenile court to a criminal court, a process known as a judicial transfer or waiver. We are going to cover waivers in the next section in more detail. For now, we just want to familiarize you with the legal requirements for a waiver. The judge dismissed the request and transferred Kent to a criminal court without a hearing and despite a psychological evaluation that Kent was mentally ill and rehabilitation could work for him.[9]

In the criminal court, Morris Kent was convicted of several charges and sentenced to a prison term of 30 to 90 years for robbery but acquitted on the rape charges by reason of insanity. Kent appealed his initial waiver from juvenile court all the way to the U.S. Supreme Court. In *Kent v. United States*, the U.S. Supreme Court decided in favor of Morris Kent, declaring that any juvenile subject to a potential waiver into criminal court is entitled to a waiver hearing, an attorney for the hearing, and a statement of reasons for the potential waiver. In its decision, the Court gave due process protections to juvenile for the first time. The Court also provided factors juvenile courts should consider for a waiver, including, but not limited to, age, prior juvenile record, the seriousness of the crime, and the potential for rehabilitating the juvenile. You might ask still, what happened to Morris Kent? Kent was committed to St. Elizabeth's Mental Hospital, where he was treated for mental illness. He was eventually released and subsequently married, had children, maintained steady employment, and did not have any further contact with the criminal justice system.[10]

The *Kent* case was the first to give juveniles due process rights in the waiver process, but arguably the most significant case in this area is *In re Gault*. In this case, 15-year-old Gerald Gault was arrested one day in June 1964 for making lewd phone calls to his neighbor. Gault was not a repeat offender like Morris Kent. He was a kid making prank phone calls, which makes this case even more compelling. Granted, he was on probation for six months because he was with a friend who stole a wallet, but he was far from a seasoned criminal. After Gault was arrested by the police, who did not attempt to inform his parents of his arrest, Gault was brought before a judge for a hearing the next day after spending a night in the county jail with adults. He did not have counsel or any notice of the charges against him. After the hearing, Gault was brought to detention for a few days and then released to his parents. Later that week, Gault was brought back in front of the juvenile judge presiding over his case. Gault had no counsel nor was the complaining witness present. He was not able to call any witnesses. In short, Gault had no defense, and the juvenile judge found him guilty and sentenced him to a term of six years in juvenile detention. That is right, six years for making an obscene prank call! Does that sound proportionate to you?

What if an adult was found guilty of making prank calls to a neighbor? The sentence, at that time, would have been no more than 60 days in jail, but Gault received a sentence of juvenile detention until his 21st birthday. In a rare public

---

9. Kent v. United States, 383 U.S. 541 (1966)
10. Sansbury, L. (2016, March). The 50th Anniversary of Kent: The decision that sparked the transformation of juvenile justice. *National Association for Public Defense*. Retrieved on July 22, 2018 from http://www-old.publicdefenders.us/?q=node/1026

speaking event to help reform juvenile justice, Gault discussed some of his experiences and his feelings about what happened so many years ago:[11]

> *In response to being arrested at his home*: "It was devastating. I mean, 14 years
> old. I've never been away from my parents. You don't know why you're being
> taken away. You don't know where you're going. It's devastating."

> *In describing the juvenile detention center he was taken to*: "It was a building.
> I mean, bars on the windows. You had the cell that I was in, just, I call it a
> closet... two bunks. One of the jail type potty things and that was it."

In describing his parents' reaction to the judge's decision: "What really set my
father off was, my mother asked the judge if she could kiss me goodbye. He told
her, no you don't deserve that right. My father stood up and said this is bullshit."

Gerald Gault's father consulted 6 to 10 lawyers, but none of them could help, as
juveniles were not entitled to adult representation in Arizona. Finally, someone
recommended an ACLU lawyer, the decision that would change Gault's life. His
lawyer, Amelia Dietrich Lewis, appealed to the Arizona courts, but after these
appeals were dismissed, she appealed to the U.S. Supreme Court, who decided to
hear Gault's case. Gault had already spent three years in a reform school when the
Court issued its landmark decision. The U.S. Supreme Court decided that juveniles were entitled to due process rights similar to adults. Specifically, the Court
gave juveniles the right to remain silent, have counsel, receive notice of charges
against them, and confront their accuser. Justice Fortas delivered the opinion of
the Court, stating,

> We confront the reality of that portion of the juvenile court process with
> which we deal in this case. A boy is charged with misconduct. The boy is
> committed to an institution where he may be restrained of liberty for years.
> It is of no constitutional consequence—and of limited practical meaning—
> that the institution to which he is committed is called an Industrial School.
> The fact of the matter is that, however euphemistic the title, a "receiving
> home" or an "industrial school" for juveniles is an institution of confinement
> in which the child is incarcerated for a greater or lesser time. His world
> becomes "a building with whitewashed walls, regimented routine and insti-
> tutional hours . . . ." Instead of mother and father and sisters and brothers
> and friends and classmates, his world is peopled by guards, custodians, state
> employees, and "delinquents" confined with him for anything from way-
> wardness to rape and homicide. In view of this, it would be extraordinary if
> our Constitution did not require the procedural regularity and the exercise

11. Gault, G. (2008, April). *40 years after In Re Gault: The role of juvenile defense counsel and
obstacles to zealous advocacy in DC.* Talk presented at the Georgetown University Law Juvenile
Justice Clinic, Washington, DC.

of care implied in the phrase "due process." Under our Constitution, the condition of being a boy does not justify a kangaroo court."[12]

There are a few more cases that were instrumental in giving juveniles more rights, but we will only cover one more in this section, as it was one of the only cases that did not award juveniles a similar standard to adults.

In *McKeiver v. Pennsylvania*, a few cases were consolidated into one in front of the Supreme Court. In this case, 16-year-old Joseph McKeiver and several other boys were charged with robbery, larceny, and possession of stolen goods after they chased and stole 25 cents from a few other boys. McKeiver, and the other boys who were charged, requested a jury trial. This request was denied, as Pennsylvania law did not allow jury trials for juveniles. McKeiver was subsequently adjudicated a delinquent by the judge and placed on probation. He appealed his case, but the Pennsylvania Supreme Court sided with the juvenile courts. The U.S. Supreme Court heard the case and agreed with the lower courts, declaring that juveniles are not entitled to a jury trial, as a jury trial would make their process fully adversarial, and that is not the purpose of juvenile courts.[13] Though this decision did not favor due process rights, many of the decisions did, and there was a clear movement toward protecting and rehabilitating juveniles in the 1960s and 1970s.

The lack of protections in both the law and in reform schools came to light during this time. Lawsuits addressed cruel conditions in reform schools, also referred to as training schools. For example, take this description of the Boonville Reform School in Missouri:

> In 1950, social worker Albert Deutsch called Boonville a 'hellhole' with a 'long-standing tradition of sadistic maltreatment.' Boonville's boys were 'mixed indiscriminately—the younger with the older, dangerous mental cases with the normal, the first offender with the hardened repeater, the frightened child with the sadistic hoodlum.' Deutsch repeated frequent beatings by the underpaid poorly trained guards. '[T]error-stricken and desperate boys had been escaping from the institution in great numbers,' about four hundred escapes in 1948 alone. In the 1950s and the 1960s, some Missouri juvenile court judges refused to send children to Boonville or Chillicothe because of beatings by staff, youth-on-youth violence and other dangers lurking there. . . . Boonville was in an uproar by the late 1960s. A 1969 federal report roundly condemned its quasi-penal-military atmosphere, lack of adequate rehabilitation programs, substandard educational opportunities, understaffing, outdated physical plant and deteriorated buildings.[14]

---

12. In Re Gault, 387 U.S. 1, 27–28 (1967)
13. McKeiver v. Pennsylvania, 403 U.S. 528 (1971)
14. See Abrams, p. 14.

The reported conditions in these juvenile facilities prompted a 5-year investigation by the Senate Judiciary Subcommittee, which resulted in the authorization of the Juvenile Justice and Delinquency Prevention Act (JJDPA) of 1974. This major piece of legislation set out several provisions to reform the juvenile justice system. One of goals was reserving the use of juvenile reformatories for serious or chronic offenders. The JJDPA would provide financial incentives to those states who moved toward deinstitutionalization for status offenders or those youthful offenders who committed minor acts such as truancy, drinking underage, violating curfew, etc. The Act encouraged alternatives to incarceration in lower level cases, again stressing that reformatories were important in punishment of those serious and repeat offenders. It was clear by the 1970s that there was strong support for rehabilitation of offenders and community-based alternatives. It seemed that major reform was on the horizon, and that the 1980s would mark a major shift in the treatment of juveniles; it certainly did, but not in the way that reformers expected.

Back to Tough on Crime

The promise of rehabilitation and reform in both the adult and juvenile systems in the 1970s was crushed with the advent of the get "tough on crime" movement. What led to this change in the criminal justice approach? Crime rates increased substantially in the 1970s following the civil rights movement and the anti-war protests and the "crack" epidemic of the early 1980s spurred a great deal of violence in many major cities as well. As these crime rates were increasing, we also had the conservative Republican President Ronald Reagan take office. There was a growing intolerance of groups that challenged government authority, and Republicans ran on a platform of being tough on crime. Reagan declared a "War on Drugs," which became a war on all crime. Legislation mandating much harsher punishment was passed countrywide, and instead of viewing crime as a medical problem in need of treatment, the new approach was to incapacitate offenders. The new attitude toward criminal offenders that marked the 1980s and 1990s reverberated through the juvenile justice system as well.

One of the most significant indicators of this change was the passage of waiver law, also known as transfer laws. We discussed this in the previous section, but as a reminder, this is when a juvenile court transfers a juvenile offender under the age of 18 to a criminal court to be tried for a crime as an adult. Though the *Kent* decision allowed for waivers, most states changed their transfer laws to make transfer easier to criminal courts. In fact, 46 states and the District of Columbia have transfer laws that allow judges to use their discretion in making transfer decisions. This is one manner in which juveniles can be waived into adult courts. In 14 states, there is a mandatory waiver, in which a juvenile will automatically be transferred to a criminal court if he or she has committed a specific offense. Finally, approximately 15 states allow for prosecutorial discretion in making transfer decisions. This means that the decision rests solely with the prosecutor, who we know by now is not typically an impartial actor.[15] Does this seem appropriate to you?

Several states have more than one mechanism for transfer, but before 1970, transfer in most states was ordered on a case-by-case basis by judicial discretion, as described in the *Kent* Court. What do you think about waiver laws? Should juveniles be tried as adults in certain circumstances or by certain offenses? Does the potential harm to juveniles weigh in your decision? Juveniles who are convicted in criminal courts may be housed in adult prisons, where they are easy targets for physical and sexual assault, where they learn more criminal behavior from older offenders, and where rehabilitative and educational options are very limited. The consequences to juveniles who are mixed with adult offenders are substantial, but not every offender has suffered because of a waiver. Take Dexter, for example. He describes his experience below.

Narrative: Dexter Tyson

I became a product of my environment. The constant exposure to drugs, guns, and crime negatively countered the moral values my parents encouraged me to incorporate into my life. I am from Newark, New Jersey, which is still one of the least safe cities in the state. Although my childhood environment was plagued with many social ills, I had a choice in what kind of person I could become, since I had positive role models to emulate. My father was a hard worker who never went to jail, my mother was and continues to be a caring parent, and my oldest sister is a college graduate. However, the criminal lifestyle that was present in the City of Newark was easy to get involved in, and it appealed to me.

I started at a young age. I was 12 years old when I began indulging in criminal activities and exhibiting at-risk behavior such as getting high (smoking marijuana, drinking beer). I also lost interest in school. My physical being was present in class, but my mind was occupied with the activities that occurred in my neighborhood. It was common to see older people hustling drugs (dope, cocaine, marijuana, and pills), committing robberies, and inflicting violence on each other. I must admit that I was stupid to choose to live the lifestyle of a hoodlum. Anyhow, the people who had no regard for the law: the drug-dealers, "stick-up kids," and similar malicious people were rewarded with respect in the streets. The people who exhibited legal char-

---

15. Thomas, J. M. (2017). *Raising the bar: State trends in keeping youth out of adult courts (2015–2017)*. Washington, DC: Campaign for Youth Justice.

acteristics were treated as "ghetto celebrities," and they received lucrative material gains and enjoyed a seemingly luxurious life, a life that I continuously sought to live.

I started with robbery, indiscriminately committing strong armed robberies against people for their jewelry (watches and necklaces) since it was a quick way to get some money. Those acts along with other criminal acts I committed helped me to gain a favorable reputation among the older criminals. The admiration I received bought me favor to borrow their guns, and sometimes I would go along with them to do robberies since they had stolen cars to assist us to travel to different places where we committed crimes.

The adrenaline that I received from the car chases by the police, and the power I felt from holstering an illegal firearm, and the "fear of respect" that I gained were some of the elements of the criminal lifestyle that made me continue to indulge in that kind of behavior. The excitement that I felt made me disregard the danger that the life of crime presented. I was shot at on several occasions, bullets whistling past my head as I fled from crime scenes, and I escaped being fatally wounded with a knife as I tried to rob someone.

I was apprehended numerous times, and I spent weeks and months in the juvenile detention center. I was placed on probation and eventually sentenced to a 3-year term at a youth correctional facility in Jamesburg, New Jersey, at the age of 14. Those experiences were not enough to curtail my criminal inclinations, though. The seemingly fun and perceived glamour that I though criminal life provided ended when I was convicted for killing someone during a robbery attempt.

By the time I reached 17, crime was normal to me. Committing crimes was a sport. The crime (murder) that I am guilty of wasn't something that I planned to do the night of March 12, 1985, but it happened when my colleagues and I decided to rob a man as he waited at a bus stop.

I was the person who pulled the gun on the victim and demanded the money that we figured he had from the wad that bulged from his front pants pocket. One of the people who I was with attempted to go into the victim's pocket as I held him at gunpoint; however, the man stopped us from robbing him. A struggle ensued between us, and I shot the man once in the stomach and again in the chest. We fled from the area to a nearby housing project where I used to live. It happened on a Friday night at about 8:00.

I wasn't aware that he died after I shot him, neither did I give any thought to what I had just done: robbed and killed a person in front of people who must have been traumatized from what they witnessed. I asked the person who went into the victim's pocket if he got anything from him, and he said that he didn't. However, from the police reports, no money was recovered from the victim. Even so, I'm responsible for viciously killing someone for protecting his hard-earned values. He was someone I didn't know—an older Black man in his late 40s.

I was arrested that same night but on separate charges (possession of a gun) approximately four hours after the crime (12:00 a.m.). While I was standing outside of a music club with a group of people, we were approached by undercover police officers as we "loitered" in front of the club. I tried to run because I knew that I had an illegal weapon on me, but I was caught and arrested after they recovered the gun from my waist. I learned of the murder while I was detained in the Essex County Youth House for the gun charges and was later charged as a suspect for the murder after one of my colleagues confessed to the events that night.

I was eventually waived up to adult court after seven days of trial. My two codefendants and I were found guilty of felony murder, robbery, possession of an illegal weapon, and possession of an illegal weapon with intent to use it. We were all given the same sentence: life with a 30-year parole ineligibility. I was 18 years old.

I had been convicted twice as a juvenile. The incentives to commit crimes—street credentials, fast money—were overshadowed by the "reality check" that imprisonment presented. The street celebrity reputation, money, material gains, and the women attracted to those elements are worthless when sentenced to a monotonous life behind a prison wall. The bathroom-sized cells, which were rat and roach infested, were startling. The 100-plus temperatures in the summer and the freezing temperatures in the winter deglamorized the "coolness" of my perception of doing time. I have seen many people lose their lives from violence, suicides, and the poor health that goes hand-in-hand with long durations of imprisonment.

Prison also strips one's identity, self-respect, and freedom of choices. Prisoners are told what to do, often in a vile tone by prison officials. A person's humanity is disregarded when he or she becomes an inmate. The use of the word "inmate" toward someone in incarceration carries a subhuman connotation. Not only is a person's freedom to exist lost when he or she is locked up, but they risk experiencing a psychological deterioration due to the stressful environment behind prison walls.

I did not stop to think of the harm that my criminal acts caused to those whom I victimized; however, my imprisonment inside a supermax environment gradually caused me to become accountable and mature. I have remorse for what I did, and I now know that it was due to the choices that I made to salvage my character, while incarcerated, which caused me to be an accountable person. I can honestly say that I detest my past criminal behavior because I am responsible for destroying someone's life and shattering the lives of the people who were connected to the man I killed.

The numerous bouts with law enforcement (going in and out of jail), carrying illegal weapons, using drugs, quitting school, and other illegal acts were ridiculously attached to the rites of passage. I erroneously accepted those fallacies. However, my sober and well-informed mind rejects those false ideas of manhood.

I am associated with a group—Lifers Group in Rahway States Prison—which gives me a platform to help at-risk youth think about the harm that they are doing to themselves and society. I also encourage those who I talk with to with the advice to choose another path besides gang culture and criminality.

I consider myself fortunate to have met positive people inside the prison environments where I exist(ed) who encouraged me to change. As I write this, I have now been in prison for 29 years and 9 months; however, I am confident that my imprisonment was not in vain. I am a better person than who I was before I was imprisoned. I refused to continue to be a product of my environment. My experiences and the formal and informal education I gained empowered me to resist the entrapments and dictations that the prison environments suggests how I should act.

Dexter did not regret being waived to the criminal courts when he was 17, even though it meant he spent 31 years in prison. Dexter received parole after his 31st year in prison, having received a unanimous decision by a 12-person parole board for release (look back at Chapter 5 if you need a refresher on parole release). He was a model prisoner in almost every way. He had a strong record of good behavior in prison. He became a mentor to younger inmates and an instrumental figure in the Lifer's Group, which helps at-risk youth and those students interested in working with prisoners. Living in the real world now, Dexter has a full-time job, resides with family, has a significant other, and partakes in many speaking engagements to help further the work he began several years ago with the Lifer's Group. For Dexter, juvenile detention did not work. It did not deter him, and he wound up committing a much more serious crime after his sentence at a juvenile detention center. For Dexter, a sentence of incarceration in prison was the right solution, but keep in mind that Dexter was also 18 when he was sent to prison. Many juveniles are younger, and we caution you to consider that Dexter is an exception and not the rule. Most juveniles will suffer tremendous setbacks when tried in criminal courts, which is why early reformers lobbied so hard for a separate system for juveniles. So where are we now? We will discuss some of the changing attitudes toward juvenile punishment in the next section. Scientific developments have been key in prompting some of these modern decisions.

The Supreme Court and Modern-Day Juvenile Justice Issues

Three cases since 2005 have indicated that the landscape of juvenile justice is changing again. In these three decisions, the U.S. Supreme Court has made it clear that juveniles are different from adults developmentally, and these differences must be acknowledged in the way juveniles are processed and punished by the criminal justice system. We will begin with the case of *Roper v. Simmons,*[16] in which the Court announced that juveniles under the age of 18 could not be subjected to the death penalty. The Court relied on scientific evidence that juveniles are developmentally different than adults in coming to its decision. Justice Kennedy delivered the opinion of the Court, quoting evidence from a science brief submitted to aid the Court. He stated the following in his opinion:

> First, as any parent knows and as the scientific and sociological studies respondent and his amici cite tend to confirm, "[a] lack of maturity and an underdeveloped sense of responsibility are found in youth more often than in adults and are more understandable among the young. These qualities often result in impetuous and ill-considered actions and decisions."[17]

The Court relied further on scientific evidence to support its decision, though not all members of the Supreme Court agreed with the majority opinion. The facts of this case might shed some light as to why some members did not find such a strong fundamental difference between a 17-year-old and an 18-year-old. Christopher Simmons was 17 at the time of his crime, and his premeditation and his callous nature were significant in Justice O'Connor's dissenting opinion (meaning she disagreed with the majority opinion of the Court). In her dissent, Justice O'Connor stated the following:

> Surely there is an age below which no offender, no matter what his crime, can be deemed to have the cognitive or emotional maturity necessary to warrant the death penalty. But at least at the margins between adolescence and adulthood—and especially for 17-year-olds such as respondent—the relevant differences between "adults" and "juveniles" appear to be a matter of degree, rather than of kind. It follows that a legislature may reasonably conclude that at least some 17-year-olds can act with sufficient moral culpability, and can be sufficiently deterred by the threat of execution, that capital punishment may be warranted in an appropriate case.
>
> Indeed, this appears to be just such a case. Christopher Simmons' murder of Shirley Crook was premeditated, wanton, and cruel in the extreme. Well before he committed this crime, Simmons declared that he wanted to kill someone. On several occasions, he discussed with two friends (ages 15

---

16. Roper v. Simmons, 543 U.S. 551 (2005)

17. Roper v. Simmons, 543 U.S. at 569 (2005) (quoting Johnson v Texas, 509 U.S. 350, 367 (1993)

and 16) his plan to burglarize a house and to murder the victim by tying the victim up and pushing her from a bridge. Simmons said they could "'get away with it'" because they were minors . . . . In accord with this plan, Simmons and his 15-year-old accomplice broke into Mrs. Crook's home in the middle of the night, forced her from her bed, bound her, and drove her to a state park. There, they walked her to a railroad trestle spanning a river, "hog-tied" her with electrical cable, bound her face completely with duct tape, and pushed her, still alive, from the trestle. She drowned in the water below . . . . One can scarcely imagine the terror that this woman must have suffered throughout the ordeal leading to her death. Whatever can be said about the comparative moral culpability of 17-year-olds as a general matter, Simmons' actions unquestionably reflect "'a consciousness materially more "depraved" than that of' . . . the average murderer."[18]

What do you think after reading the facts of this case? Christopher Simmons, a 17-year-old, planned and carried out the kidnapping and murder of Shirley Crook in a particularly cruel fashion because he wanted to know what it was like to kill someone. Do you think the Court made the right decision in regarding him as a juvenile who lacked the maturity to understand the consequences of his decision, or do you agree with Justice O'Connor that this case was one which warranted the death penalty? Would Simmons have acted differently if he thought he could be executed? He told his friends that they were minors and would get away with if after all. Does that difference even matter to you? Perhaps take some time and decide what your feelings are about both the death penalty and its application to minors before we move on to our next case.

Five years after the *Roper* decision, the Court addressed another controversial case involving juveniles. The issue in front of the Court in *Graham v. Florida* was whether a juvenile could be sentenced to a term of life in prison without the chance of parole for a crime other than homicide. In this case, 17-year-old Terrance Graham was sentenced to life without the chance of parole for his role in an armed home invasion robbery, in which Graham held a gun to the chest of one of his victims. Graham and his two accomplices forcibly entered the home of their victim and held both him and his friend at gunpoint while they ransacked his house looking for money. Before leaving the home, Graham and his accomplice barricaded their victims in a closet.[19]

Later that evening, Graham and his friends attempted a second robbery, but one of Graham's accomplices was shot. Using the car he borrowed from his father that night, Graham drove both men to the hospital and left them there, but as he left the hospital, a police officer attempted to pull him over, and Graham fled, crashing into a telephone pole. The police found three handguns in Graham's

---

18. Ibid. at 600–601.
19. Graham v. Florida, 560 U.S. 48 (2010)

vehicle, and Graham had a previous record. In fact, he was on probation during the time of his offenses for a previous attempted robbery, in which he and two accomplices attempted to rob a barbecue restaurant. Graham was charged as an adult and therefore eligible for a life sentence, but he accepted a plea and wrote a heartfelt letter to the judge, saying that he would never get into trouble again, and that if he had a second chance he would do whatever it took to work his way to the NFL. The judge gave him two terms of probation, in essence, a second chance, but six months later, Graham was arrested for the home invasion robbery, and the judge in his second case was not as forgiving. The judge found that Graham had violated the terms of his probation by committing a home invasion robbery, possessing firearms, and associating with persons engaging in criminal offenses. At the sentencing hearing, the judge sentenced Graham to life in prison without the possibility of parole. The judge stated the following in his decision:

> I don't understand why you would be given such a great opportunity to do something with your life and why you would throw it away. The only thing that I can rationalize is that you decided that this is how you were going to lead your life and that there is nothing that we can do for you. And as the state pointed out, that this is an escalating pattern of criminal conduct on your part and that we can't help you any further. We can't do anything to deter you. This is the way you are going to lead your life, and I don't know why you are going to. You've made that decision. I have no idea. But evidently, that is what you decided to do.
>
> So then it becomes a focus, if I can't do anything to help you, if I can't do anything to get you back on the right path, then I have to start focusing on the community and trying to protect the community from your actions. And, unfortunately, that is where we are today is I don't see where I can do anything to help you any further. You've evidently decided this is the direction you're going to take in life, and it's unfortunate that you made that choice.
>
> I have reviewed the statute. I don't see where any further juvenile sanctions would be appropriate. I don't see where any youthful offender sanctions would be appropriate. Given your escalating pattern of criminal conduct, it is apparent to the Court that you have decided that this is the way you are going to live your life and that the only thing I can do now is to try and protect the community from your actions.[20]

Graham filed an appeal, challenging his sentence by the Florida court judge, but the appellate court affirmed the judge's sentence, and the Florida Supreme Court denied hearing the case. The next stop for Graham was the U.S. Supreme Court, and they agreed with Graham that a sentence of life for a juvenile for a

---

20. Ibid at 56–57.

nonhomicide offense was indeed cruel and unusual. In delivering the opinion of the Court, Justice Kennedy stated the following:

> Terrance Graham's sentence guarantees he will die in prison without any meaningful opportunity to obtain release, no matter what he might do to demonstrate that the bad acts he committed as a teenager are not representative of his true character, even if he spends the next half century attempting to atone for his crimes and learn from his mistakes. The state has denied him any chance to later demonstrate that he is fit to rejoin society based solely on a nonhomicide crime that he committed while he was a child in the eyes of the law. This the Eighth Amendment does not permit.[21]

In this decision, the Court again indicated its concern for the developmental differences between adults and juveniles and signaled a future direction of the Court in relying on scientific evidence to support their decision. The third decision in 2012 took the *Graham* one step further. In *Miller v. Alabama*, the Supreme Court ruled that states could no longer have automatic life without parole (LWOP) sentences for juveniles. Juveniles can receive a LWOP sentence, but there must be some form of sentencing hearing for a court to make this determination. Essentially, juvenile sentencing for LWOP works in a similar manner to adult capital cases with a penalty phase. As intended, before a juvenile can be sentenced to LWOP, a court must consider any aggravating and mitigating factors that would indicate whether such a sentence was appropriate.[22] Four years later, in *Montgomery v. Louisiana*, the Supreme Court made the decision in Miller retroactive and granted new sentencing hearings to thousands of inmates who had been given automatic LWOP sentences.[23] Granted, many of these inmates will remain in prison for the rest of their lives, but some of these inmates are getting a second chance. One of the authors of this book has worked on juvenile resentencing cases following the *Miller* decision. He places the decision in the proper context of juvenile justice and discusses what the practical implications are following this landmark case.

Narrative: Hayden's Story

In the United States, people are not allowed to purchase alcohol until they are 21. They cannot vote until they are 18. While teenagers may begin driving at 16, we often place restrictions on them doing so, such as what hour of the day they may drive and how many passengers they may have in the car

---

21. Ibid. at 77.
22. Miller v. Alabama, 567 U.S. 460 (2012)
23. Montgomery v. Louisiana, 577 U.S. ___ (2016)

with them. At the same time, while juveniles are denied so many freedoms in the United States or at least have them heavily restricted, since the 1990s, there has been the growing trend to treat juvenile offenders as if they were adults. This included, for a brief period of time, executing juvenile offenders and sentencing juveniles to automatic terms of life in prison without parole. This has always been a conundrum. We want justice for the victims of crimes, yet juveniles are not fully formed people. Even the smartest kids will lack self-control, long-term thinking, and the ability to fully appreciate the consequences of their actions. Furthermore, juveniles can be heavily susceptible to peer pressure. Juveniles often have a tendency to do dumb things. Sure, there are plenty of adults who have these same flaws, but you are more often going to find these traits among young people. As the saying goes, experience can be the greatest teacher.

Yet, much like any new legislation, there is often the possibility of net-widening. This has frequently happened to juvenile offenders. For every straight-up cold killer juvenile who is completely incapable of changing (which are rare), being warehoused in a prison for the rest of their life are many other juveniles who were hanging out with friends or in some cases, friends of friends when something went bad. Many of the juveniles who were sentenced to LWOP were parties to brutal crimes but played lesser roles or in some instances, were only hanging out with people who committed these crimes. Recently, many of these offenders are getting a second chance in life. In *Miller v. Alabama*, the Supreme Court ruled that offenders who committed crimes as juveniles could no longer receive automatic LWOP sentences. There is still the possibility that juvenile offenders who receive LWOP, but unlike sentencing hearings for adults, a court must consider many different factors before doing so. Among these factors are the actual age of the defendants, their maturity level at the time of offense, if they seem impetuous, and if they show signs that would indicate that they had an inability to appreciate the consequences of their actions. A short while later, in *Montgomery v. Louisiana*,[24] the Supreme Court made the decision in *Miller* retroactive, which means that any person serving LWOP for crimes committed as a juvenile is entitled to a new sentencing hearing. This does not mean that all of these people are going to be released from prison. Many will stay in prison for the rest of their lives, and even those who are resentenced may not be paroled for a long time.

Over the last two years, I have been involved with three different resentencing cases. In each case, I met adult men who were with people who later murdered someone. There was no direct evidence that they had

---

24. Montgomery v. Louisiana, 136 S. Ct. 718 (2016)

participated in the killings and at best could be considered as accessories. Furthermore, there was no evidence presented that any of the killings were premeditated. All three men had aged considerably—one of is closely approaching his third decade spent in prison. At this time, it is unclear if any of them will ever be released from prison, but at least there will be some possibility of a chance for them.

We have covered the history of the juvenile justice system, beginning from its inception in the 1800s, through the due process revolution, the tough on crime movement, and up to recent Court decisions that have utilized science as a marker for juvenile punishment. The juvenile justice system was conceived to separate juveniles from adults, but in recent times, it seems we have reverted to a system that once again treats many juveniles like adults. While many states and the federal system have suffered the consequences of mass incarceration, so have juveniles, and while it is true that we got very tough on juveniles in the 1990s, there are signs now of a changing direction in the system: one that favors a more rehabilitative approach to juvenile justice.

First, we have the recent Court decisions discussed in the previous sections. These decisions signal a concern for the possibility of rehabilitation in the juvenile system and certainly a recognition of the developmental differences between juveniles and adults. Next, since 2005, 17 states have reformed their legislation to remove most youth from adult prisons and jails and substantially limit the use of adult incarceration for future juveniles in the system.[25] Several pieces of legislation helped support this shift, including the Prison Rape Elimination Act of 2002 and the reauthorization of the JJDPA. Under both acts, separation of juveniles from adults is a priority for protection of juveniles.

Next, though every state has at least one or more mechanisms for transferring juveniles to adult courts, many states are currently challenging the automatic transfer mechanism. There is also a movement to raise the age at which a juvenile can be transferred from juvenile court, also known as "raising the floor." In addition, 25 states have reverse transfer laws,[26] which allow a juvenile to be transferred back into juvenile courts from the adult system. Suggestions for reform includ: limiting transfer laws to allow only those most serious cases to proceed to the criminal courts; raising the age involving juvenile transfer cases; using scientific research to support legislative decisions regarding juvenile punishment; and focusing on treatment and rehabilitation for juveniles. While we are far from reaching these goals, there is certainly evidence that we are headed, albeit slowly, in this direction.

---

25. See, Thomas (2017).
26. Ibid.

Chapter 9

Correctional Facility Workers

To supervise the millions of people under correctional control in the United States, thousands of men and women are employed by counties, cities, states, and the federal government. Along with the growing diversity of criminal sanctions, so has the needed skills of these employees. Originally, just employed to keep offenders from escaping from correctional facilities, today, correctional workers have a host of additional duties, including supervision, counseling, and education. Furthermore, just like in any other organization, there are multiple levels of supervision, including a host of administrators who must oversee correctional agencies and employees. This chapter will discuss the different men and women within the field of corrections and the duties for which they are responsible.

Introduction

According to the Bureau of Labor Statistics, in May 2017, 428,870 people were employed in the United States as correctional officers and jailers. The highest numbers of these employees were employed by state governments in prisons (227,860) and local governments in jails (161,910). The average annual wage for these employees was $47,600. Among states, the four states that employed the most officers were Texas (48,600), California (36,730), New York (34,820), and Florida (33,730). Pennsylvania is a distant fifth and employs 17,380 correctional officers and jailers.[1] Due to these figures, and their corresponding high inmate

---

1. Bureau of Labor Statistics. *Correctional officers and jailers.* Retrieved on August 23, 2018 from https://www.bls.gov/oes/current/oes333012.htm#nat

populations, Texas, California, New York, and Florida are commonly referred to as the "Big Four" in corrections.[2]

In addition to people who are employed to work within or in support of correctional facilities, thousands of Americans are employed as probation and parole officers as well as correctional treatment specialists. According to the Bureau of Labor Statistics, 87,700 people are employed in this industry, most of whom are either employed by state governments (46,020) and local governments (38,680). The average annual wage for these employees was $56,630. Once again surveying the Big Four of corrections, California employed 11,890 workers, Texas 8,600 workers, New York 4,530 workers and Florida 3,580. While Pennsylvania lagged far behind Florida in correctional officers and jailers, Pennsylvania actually had 4,240 probation/parole officers and correctional treatment specialists.[3]

As you can tell, there are numerous jobs in criminal justice. One of the seeming benefits of mass incarceration is that thousands of people are needed to supervise the millions of Americans under correctional control. Some people have argued that such a situation can be self-fulfilling and can impede reform. Once many people become embedded in these professions, they want to maintain the status quo, and this has led many labor unions and lobbying groups that represent correctional workers to fight legal reforms that could potentially reduce correctional populations. After all, more people under control leads to more jobs.[4] Furthermore, the expansion of community corrections and the growing privatization of many correctional programs has led to more opportunities for corruption.[5] One recent example of this occurred when Chris Epps, a former correctional officer who served as the Mississippi Corrections Commissioner for 12 years pleaded guilty, in 2015, to bribery and filing a false income tax return. During his 12 years in charge, he was accused of receiving at least $1.4 million in bribes and kickbacks that involved more than $800 million in state prison contracts. In 2017, although prosecutors only recommended Epps serve 13 years in federal prison, a federal judge sentenced Epps to almost 20 years in federal prison.[6] This is not to say that the whole system is corrupt, rather that it is a huge business. For instance, Nils Christie described crime control as "an industry."[7] Within the rest of this chapter,

---

2. Hanser, R. D. (2017). *Introduction to corrections* (2nd ed.). Thousand Oaks, CA: Sage.

3. Bureau of Labor Statistics. *Probation officers and correctional treatment specialists.* Retrieved on August 23, 2018 from https://www.bls.gov/oes/current/oes211092.htm#st

4. Page, J. (2011). Prison officer unions and the perpetuation of the penal status quo. *Criminology & Public Policy, 10*, 735–770.

5. Griffin, O. H., Woodward, V. H., & Sloan, J. J. (2016). *The money and politics of criminal justice policy.* Durham, NC: Carolina Academic Press.

6. Gates, J. E. (2017, May 24). Chris Epps sentenced to almost 20 years. *The Clarion-Ledger.* Retrieved on August 25, 2018 from https://www.clarionledger.com/story/news/2017/05/24/chris-epps-sentencing/341916001/

7. Christie, N. (1999). *Crime control as industry: Towards gulags, western style* (3rd ed.) New York, NY: Routledge.

we will discuss both the organization of this industry and the jobs of the men and women within it.

Correctional Organizational Structure

Correctional organizations are found at all levels of government: federal, state, and local. While we can describe the operations of the federal system, we cannot provide completely generalizable information on the states and localities (primarily counties) because many states have different operations. Two agencies are primarily responsible for federal corrections: the Federal Bureau of Prisons and Probation and Pretrial Services. To some people, beginning with a discussion of the federal correctional system is a natural starting point; it actually serves a functional teaching point as well. The Bureau of Prisons was created in 1930 and has ever since been an administrative unit within the Department of Justice, which is part of the executive branch of government. Thus, ultimate authority is overseen by the president of the United States.[8] In the federal system, for many years, a system akin to probation existed in federal courts in which judges would suspend part or all of an offender's sentence so that they would still be under the jurisdiction of the court but would not be placed in the custody of a correctional institution. In 1916, the Supreme Court ended this practice, noting if a system of probation was desired, it must come through legislation. Nine years later, with the passage of the Probation Act of 1925, federal courts were officially allowed to place offenders on probation. Originally, probation was administered by the Bureau of Prisons. However, 15 years later, the administration of probation was transferred from the Bureau to the federal courts. Therefore, probation was administered by the judicial branch of government.[9]

Within states, prisons are administered by state-run agencies that are housed within the executive branches of those states. Jails are most commonly operated by counties; however, as previously mentioned, a growing trend has been the creation of regional jails. This is most often done among counties with small populations or operating budgets. To offset these constraints and better plan so that these facilities are not overcrowded, small counties may band together and build one jail to serve them all.[10] Probation and parole services are a little harder to generalize. For one, 16 states (Arizona, California, Delaware, Florida, Illinois, Indiana, Kansas, Maine, Minnesota, Mississippi, North Carolina, Ohio, Oregon,

---

8. Federal Bureau of Prisons. *Historical information.* Retrieved on August 25, 2018 from https://www.bop.gov/about/history/

9. United States Courts. *Probation and pretrial services history.* Retrieved on August 25, 2018 from http://www.uscourts.gov/services-forms/probation-and-pretrial-services/probation-and-pretrial-services-history

10. Griffin, O. H., Woodward, V. H., & Sloan, J. J. (2016). *The money and politics of criminal justice policy.* Durham, NC: Carolina Academic Press.

Virginia, Washington, and Wisconsin) do not have discretionary parole, and four states (Alaska, Louisiana, New York, and Tennessee) will not parole certain violent offenders.[11] Frank Hellum identified four models of these agencies that administer probation and parole. The first are states that have a single state agency that administers probation and parole services. The second are states with a primary state agency that oversees probation or parole and local agencies that will deliver the services. The third are states that have local agencies with primary authority and a secondary state agency. The fourth are states in which only local agencies administer probation or parole.[12]

A reasonable person might wonder why there are some many different ways to administer what are essentially the same services. Indeed, that is a good question. The essence of why this occurs is how much state control over these services is desired. Many different localities will have circumstances or phenomenon that will affect the delivery of probation and parole services. For instance, some urban areas will have very different issues than other urban areas, and various rural areas will be different as well. Typically, state agencies will be better funded, but they will have more bureaucracy, which inevitably means more red tape. Local agencies will not be as well funded, but they will have less regulations and state oversight; thus, these agencies may be able to better tailor their services to the needs of their unique clients.[13] In 2011, the National Center for State Courts (NCSC) conducted a survey of the states to determine how they delivered their probation services (five states—Iowa, Kentucky, New Hampshire, New Mexico, and Oregon did not complete the survey). The NCSC found that for juvenile probation, services 35% of states used executive agencies, 48% used judicial agencies, and 17% used some mix of the two. For adult misdemeanor offenders, 43% of states used executive agencies, 39% used judicial agencies, and 17% used a mix of the two. For adult felony offenders, 63% of states used executive agencies, 33% used judicial agencies, and 4% used a mix of the two.[14]

Correctional Facility Personnel

In jails and prisons, there are many different types of employees. Prisons will have a greater diversity in staff because their operations are more diverse and include a greater variety of institutional programs. For the most parts, jails only have those

11. Bureau of Justice Statistics. *Reentry trends in the US*. Retrieved on August 25, 2018 from https://www.bjs.gov/content/reentry/releases.cfm

12. Hellum, F. (1983). *Adult probation systems in the United States*. Washington, DC: National Institute of Corrections.

13. Clear, T. R., Cole, G. F., & Reisig, M. D. (2013). *American Corrections* (10th ed.). Belmont, CA: Cengage.

14. National Center for State Courts. *CCJ and COSCA survey of evidence-based practices in sentencing and probation: Branch responsible for probation*. Retrieved on August 25, 2018 from https://www.ncsc.org/~/media/Microsites/Files/CSI/Branch-Responsible-for-Probation.ashx

programs to alleviate inmates' immediate problems, such as treatment of drug withdrawal or mental illness. The first type of correctional facility employees are line personnel. These employees have direct contact with inmates. Among the most common duties are those employees who are entrusted with maintaining security of the institution. This can include guards that police cellblocks, monitor security stations, and guard towers. Another type of line personnel are correctional counselors. These correctional workers have a variety of duties. As the name implies, some inmates will seek advice and counseling from correctional counselors. Counselors are also entrusted with ensuring that inmates are in the correct rehabilitation programs. Depending upon the correctional facility, there are other types of line personnel. Among prisons that still have farms on the facility, there will be specific officers who supervise inmates while they perform farm work. The same is true if a prison has a machine shop or any other type of industrial facility.[15] While figures differ for each correctional facility, roughly two thirds of a correctional facility is composed of correctional officers.[16]

The next type of correctional facility workers is staff personnel. This is a diverse group as well, and while they may have a few interactions with inmates, these contacts are typically minimal. Running a correctional facility is a complex task and just like any large organization requires a lot of different people to operate.[17] One of the most basic tasks that any correctional facility must do is much like any other organization—pay its bills. Thus, there must be support staff and maybe even an accountant to make sure this occurs in a timely manner. While many correctional facilities will rely on some inmates to perform some maintenance work, there will need to be some staff to either supervise these activities or perform these repairs in areas where inmates should be prohibited. Although some prisons will have farms that produces food for the facility, in rare instances are facilities self-sufficient. Thus, somebody needs to keep track and order food for the facility. Furthermore, someone needs to keep track of and order equipment for the facility. While figures differ for each correctional facility, roughly one third of correctional staff are employed as support staff.[18]

Every organization needs managers and administrators. The chief executive of a prison is usually referred to as a warden. For jails, in counties with small populations, a sheriff may directly administer the jails themselves, and that may be their greatest job concern. In counties with larger populations, it is more likely that a sheriff may appoint a member of his staff to perform this duty, such as a

---

15. Clear, T. R., Cole, G. F., & Reisig, M. D. (2013). *American Corrections* (10th ed.). Belmont, CA: Cengage.

16. Krisberg, B., Marchionna, S., & Hartney, C. (2015). *American Corrections: Concepts and controversies*. Thousand Oaks, CA: Sage.

17. Clear, T. R., Cole, G. F., & Reisig, M. D. (2013). *American Corrections* (10th ed.). Belmont, CA: Cengage.

18. Krisberg, B., Marchionna, S., & Hartney, C. (2015). *American Corrections: Concepts and controversies*. Thousand Oaks, CA: Sage.

captain or an associate sheriff, depending upon the terminology of that county.[19] In some large correctional facilities, a warden will need to employ deputy wardens for specific management areas of the facility or hire other employees, such as public relation officers. Obviously, with jails, maintaining a jail is inherently a political activity since sheriffs are elected by the public. Wardens, who are often overseen by state departments of corrections, may not be directly politically appointed but will certainly need to navigate politics to perform their jobs.[20] While figures differ for each correctional facility, about 2% of employees are considered administrators.[21]

Correctional Management

As we have discussed, for many years, prisons and jails were managed by a powerful warden or sheriff. In some instances, these powerful men may have had a powerful group of subordinates who shared the power. This is typical of what is referred to as an authoritarian model of correctional management. In this type of system, not only does an individual or small group of individuals run the show, they usually do so with little to no say from outsiders. Within these correctional facilities there is usually a correct way of doing things, and that will usually be the only way of doing things. Furthermore, as we have noted, correctional facilities of this type are often managed according to the common saying "with an iron fist." Although a correctional facility can be effective in this manner for maintaining institutional control and minimizing violence, it is often antithetical to the rehabilitative ideal, as inmates within these facilities tend to feel downtrodden and beaten down.[22] Additionally, having so few people in power and a lack of diversity in viewpoints can often lead to a situation called groupthink in which people seek consensus rather than looking for different types of solutions to problems.[23]

Within representative governments, most public services are provided by a government agency. The public administration of these agencies is usually performed with a bureaucracy.[24] Many correctional facilities are administered with a bureaucratic model. Bureaucracies are systems of structure that have institutional

19. Clear, T. R., Cole, G. F., & Reisig, M. D. (2013). *American Corrections* (10th ed.). Belmont, CA: Cengage.

20. Hanser, R. D. (2017). *Introduction to Corrections* (2nd ed.). Thousand Oaks, CA: Sage.

21. Krisberg, B., Marchionna, S., & Hartney, C. (2015). *American Corrections: Concepts and controversies*. Thousand Oaks, CA: Sage.

22. Hanser, R. D. (2017). *Introduction to Corrections* (2nd ed.). Thousand Oaks, CA: Sage.

23. Ahonen, L., & Degner, J. (2014). Working with complex problem behaviors in juvenile institutional care: Staff's competence, organizational conditions and public value. *International Journal of Prisoner Health, 10*, 239–251.

24. Niskanen, W. A. (1971). *Bureaucracy and Representative gGovernment*. New York, NY: Routledge.

rules, assigned rules, and hierarchies.[25] Ever heard the phrase "crap rolls down-hill" or some variation thereof? The person who said that was probably part of some organization that had some form of bureaucracy. Certainly, since correctional agencies in the United States are an outgrowth of representative government, it was somewhat natural that they would eventually become bureaucracies. However, perhaps the greatest reason these agencies have become ruled by bureaucracies is out of necessity. As we discussed in Chapter 3, prisoner lawsuits are a nonstop part of the correctional system, and while some inmates might file lawsuits because they are bored, others have alleged and/or demonstrated chronic abuse within the system. The best way to comply with abuses in the system is to create legal directives, from either the courts or state legislatures, to regulate the behavior of correctional agencies.[26] Granted, if you have ever been an employee within a bureaucracy, you will figure out that the system is often rigorous and unwieldly, but chances are, somewhere within the endless regulations, there is the answer for which you are looking.

The third type of correctional management is the participative model. As we have discussed, correctional facilities are typically top-down organizations. Yet, some people have argued that to be administered more effectively, input from the inmates is needed. Many correctional facilities already have this, whether it is inmates discussing problems with correctional staff or passing along anonymous tips to correctional facilities. It is difficult to imagine a facility ever being run without any inmate input.[27] In some instances, this may be little more than a system of inmates having a suggestion box or dropping the dime on other prisoners for their own protection and/or personal gain. However, one of the effects of prisoner litigation and the federal government and states' response is that to avoid or delay many formal lawsuits, inmates must go through a formalized correctional facility grievance process. Some people have argued that this will silence many inmates; yet, at the same time, it is giving inmates a formalized process in which they can be heard in a correctional facility.[28] Some people believe that this process should be taken further. One of those was John Irwin. He argued that inmates should be allowed a greater role in administering prisons. According to Irwin, not only was this a more just arrangement, but the sense of responsibility and accomplishment would aid in their rehabilitation.[29]

Correctional management can come in many different forms and is vital to the operation of correctional facilities. While officers may let minor infractions go

25. Hanser, R. D. (2017). *Introduction to Corrections* (2nd ed.). Thousand Oaks, CA: Sage.

26. Gideon, L., & Griffin, O. H. (2017). *Correctional management and the law: A penological approach*. Durham, NC: Carolina Academic Press.

27. Hanser, R. D. (2017). *Introduction to corrections* (2nd ed.). Thousand Oaks, CA: Sage.

28. Gideon, L., & Griffin, O. H. (2017). *Correctional management and the law: A penological approach*. Durham, NC: Carolina Academic Press.

29. Irwin, J. (1980). *Prisons in turmoil*. Boston, MA: Little Brown and Company.

unpunished, correctional staff cannot lose control of a facility. At the same time, brutal punishments can lead to feelings among inmates that their confinement is unjust—something many inmates feel regardless of the conditions in which they are incarcerated. Officers need to be motivated and work in a just manner. A seemingly universal finding in correctional research is that leadership is vital to a facility, and the quality of the leadership will often be reflective of the performance of correctional staff within—both for better or worse.[30]

Life as a Correctional Officer

Being a correctional officer can be a rewarding profession. Furthermore, working for a federal, state, or local government can provide access to desirable job benefits. Additionally, in many correctional agencies, the only educational requirement for entry level jobs is a high school diploma. To obtain employment with the Federal of Bureau of Prisons though, officers need to have at least a bachelor's degree or one-to-three years of full-time experience in a field that provides counseling, assistance, or supervision to individuals. Many jobs will require officers to attend a training academy, but the length and rigor of the academy varies, and in some agencies, training occurs while on the job.[31]

In his narrative, Terry discusses many of the different aspects of working in a jail.

Narrative: My Experience in a Metro Atlanta County Jail, by Terry

I'm a retired deputy. I spent 21 years with a metro Atlanta sheriff's office, retiring at the rank of sergeant. I began my career there as a jailer, just as 99% of the new hires do. Unlike many sheriff's offices, this agency hires "deputies" and sends you to the academy within your first year of employment; 99% of those newly certified deputies go back to the jail to work. They'll be there from two to four years, depending on the needs of the agency and their particular qualifications, aptitudes, and performance. I did some interesting things I never would have imagined myself doing, dealt with some interesting people I never would have imagined myself dealing with, and saw some wild things. I saw a LOT of bad stuff and some good stuff, all in a days—or nights—work.

My assignments there began at the jail, then to administration (now referred to as "public outreach"), then field operations, where I served civil

30. Clear, T. R., Cole, G. F., and Reisig, M. D. (2013). *American Corrections* (10th ed.). Belmont, CA: Cengage.

31. Bureau of Labor Statistics. *How to become a correctional officer or bailiff.* Retrieved on August 26, 2018 from https://www.bls.gov/ooh/protective-service/correctional-officers.htm#tab-4

process, criminal arrest warrants, conducted inmate transports, and was assigned to many special details (elections, VIP security, etc.). Ultimately, I was selected as a field training officer, helping get new assignees up to speed and teaching them how to "be an officer": minimizing the risks when serving warrants, driving a high speeds in a marked car, and often simply how to deal with the public, who are usually not having their best day. Once promoted to sergeant, I returned to the jail as a supervisor and immediately had a fresh, new perspective on things. I reveled in the responsibility! It did have its drawbacks on occasion; for example, if the sergeant is there, the inmate immediately tunes the deputy out. He will speak with the sergeant and no one else. If he/she doesn't get the answer they want, they often demand to see another supervisor. I spent a year in court security as a supervisor, and found that very interesting as well! I was at work in juvenile court the day Brian Nichols got loose in Fulton County (Atlanta, GA) and murdered four people—including a judge—before he was recaptured. Only one of my four judges seemed nervous, but they all know each other. My people and I could do little more than be out and visible to reassure the public; I spent the day at the main entrance, again being visible.

If I calculate correctly, I spent roughly two thirds of my career with the sheriff's office assigned to the Detention Division or the jail. In any metro area sheriff's office, the greatest bulk of the resources—budget dollars, equipment, personnel, etc.—are earmarked for jail operations. "Metro area" means "large population," and that translates to "large jail population," and that was true for us. When I retired, the inmate count was something short of 2,000 inmates. During my time there, I had a variety of assignments; I handled court paperwork, which included computing some release dates, dealing with the state Department of Corrections, arranging for inmate transport, etc. A shift supervisor might work a housing area, intake, bonding, or the occasional detail outside the facility. I have also been the supervisor over inmate discipline and segregation; if an inmate couldn't behave, they came to me. I did that job for four years or so. I made a few enemies along the way because some inmates didn't appreciate being locked away, or that I wouldn't allow myself to be conned into an early release from lockdown. Funny how that works...

A couple stories from my experience that might illustrate the 'diversity of activity' within the jail on any given day or night. The first one has a better outcome than it could have been. One particular inmate—who I will call "David"—had been in and out of our jail many times over his life and had a well-earned reputation as a troublemaker, a known gang member, and a dangerous man (his criminal history included starting riots in the jail and attacking a prison guard in an Alabama prison). Many supervisors would simply lock him down when he came back to jail, no questions asked. They acted simply on his reputation alone, though many had firsthand knowledge of how dangerous he was. While I acknowledged their experience and his reputation, I disagreed with that practice. David had done nothing to deserve being locked down, at least during that visit. Today, I would also argue that he was being denied due process, but that didn't occur to me at the time. Doing so, David would immediately become unmanageable. In the way of history, another officer and I had picked David up from Reidsville State Prison back in the 90s; his mother had passed away while David was doing time there. We picked him up on a compassionate visit; we allowed David to visit with his father at casket-side for far more than our policy allowed, and he never forgot that. David and I had a rapport building simply because I had treated him with a little dignity and respect. That was not really my intention at the time. It just seemed the right thing to do. Anyway, years later David was back in jail for some domestic-related violent crime and now in general population. I ran across him, and we spoke privately for a few minutes. David is almost my age, and he finally said "I'm getting tired of being locked up. I'm getting too old for this, but I don't know how to stop," and that was a true statement. He'd spent most of his life in jail or prison! We spoke a bit longer, and I offered to have someone come talk to him. I gave him the option of talking to a mental health counselor, or a chaplain, or anyone else I could arrange; he thought for a minute and said "I'll talk to a chaplain" Personally, I found that to be an excellent choice. I arranged it, one of the chaplains came to visit, and the visits became regular. David became a model inmate and was ultimately moved to the "honor dorm," even with his serious charges. The biggest problem we had with David after that was being up after lockdown, and that was because he was leading the late-night Bible study. I told my guys to give them a gentle warning, then lock the rest of the dorms down. David and his group could go last.

Another story involves another inmate with serious charges—a 17-year-old—I'll use the name "Ricky"—with an armed robbery charge. My deputies in his housing area did their usual random cell search on night and found some magazines (allowed) in Ricky's property, but they were addressed to another inmate (not allowed); the deputies knew the inmate the magazines were addressed to was no longer in our custody. He had recently been transferred into the state prison system but had left his magazines in that dorm, now in Ricky's possession. The magazines were confiscated, and Ricky went off! He was pounding on the door and screaming "GIVE ME MY F-ING MAGAZINES!!!" One of the deputies—a former Marine—went back to the door and politely but firmly asked Ricky to back away from the door. This request, obviously, was refused and resulted in more screaming and profanities. The deputy asked the tower to open the cell block door to let Ricky out;

Ricky immediately became aggressive with the former Marine deputy, who was prepared for an attack. Ricky got a full dose of pepper spray in the face, and his disposition changed suddenly. He retreated back into the cell block, and the deputy noticed the orange outline of a human figure on the wall behind where Ricky had received his response. I'm in my office just outside the pod, oblivious to what was going on. I get a call asking me to step in the pod, and I immediately notice—and react to—the smell of the pepper spray. The deputy briefs me on the incident and tells me that Ricky had run back in the cell block while the door was open. They went in, restrained him in a waist chain, and bring him to the rec yard to begin decontamination procedures. While they were shuttling water back and forth, Ricky had calmed down enough for me to have a conversation with him. Finally, it was just he and I, so I asked him if he realized that he could have handled that issue a different way. He said "yes," and I told him "Don't tell me 'yes' just because that's what I want to hear. How could you have done it differently?" and I guided the conversation like that. Finally, I asked him what was so important about a few magazines that would set him off like that. His answer caught me a bit off guard: "I can't read, Sarge. I like to look at the pictures" I immediately felt for the kid, but I sure couldn't tolerate that kind of behavior.

One final story has a more humorous ending, though the beginning isn't at all funny. One night an inmate was arrested by the county police, but the arresting officer had no idea that the guy had swallowed his stash of drugs. Therefore, no one in the jail knew it either. The book-in process had just begun, and the arrestee collapsed and died. There was an immediate response by the deputies and medical staff, CPR was conducted, but the man died. An unintentional suicide, it would seem. Less than a month later, this is still fresh on everyone's mind. I am the housing supervisor for several areas, including the female inmates. I get a call from my lead deputy there advising me that they had just received a new female from intake that was still under the influence ("high") from drug use, even after several hours in book-in. They weren't sure if she had swallowed any drugs or not, but were advising me as a precaution. I told them to pull her out and put her in a waist chain, and I'd take her to the infirmary, just to be safe. Under policy, male officers do not individually escort female inmates, but in this case I was going against policy. The girl wasn't going to die on my watch if I could help it.

By now it's 1:00 a.m., and the girl is coming down from her "high" and "just wants to go to bed." As we were leaving the pod, a female supervisor came along, and I asked her if she would walk with us to the infirmary. She agreed, and the policy issue was averted. (Now, it should be noted here that this female supervisor has a wonderful personality and sense of humor, which contributes to the end of this story.) The jail in those days had an access card system that allowed you to scan your card, enter a PIN, and operate the door or the elevator. It worked well through the fabric of the uniform shirt, so most of the staff carried their card in their shirt pocket to keep from losing it. Whoever gets to the keypad first scans their card first—common, everyday practice, and this night was no different. We get to the infirmary after an elevator ride and going through several doors; the inmate's vital signs are checked by the nurse and they're fine, all normal. We leave to return to the pod, and the female supervisor scans her card. The young female inmate, who has said very little up to now, finally speaks: "Why did you stick your tit on that thing?" Well, that female supervisor is NOT one to miss such an opportunity. She turned around, and with an absolute straight, professional face, said "It's a boob scan. Have you ever heard of a retinal scan?" The coming down from her high inmate said "Yes!" The female sergeant said "It's the same sort of technology" and proceeded out the door. I reminded the inmate that "It works for me, too," though I was having a LOT of trouble keeping a straight face. We never told the girl any different. . .

Terry's story highlights many different aspects of working in a jail. As we mentioned, jails are administered by sheriff's offices; thus, many deputies simply see working in the jail as the price to pay for working in a sheriff's office and preferred working in law enforcement—although Terry seemed to enjoy the experience. As Terry mentions, jails can be chaotic places with large turnover, and in many instances, jailers will see the same people being arrested repeatedly. Furthermore, within the chaos of the high turnover, there are many dangers jailers have to look for with new inmates. Many people arrive to the jail either under the influence of alcohol or drugs. This is something that needs to be constantly monitored as well as any medical problems among the inmates. Lastly, something that occurs in jails that Terry briefly touched on is the possibility of suicide by people who are arrested. While the rabble class that John Irwin spoke of pretty much see the experience of being arrested and jailed as normal life, to many people it is not. Being arrested and jailed can be a traumatic experience, and some people, rather than deal with the shame and humiliation they are feeling, will decide to try to end their lives. Thus, jailers always need to be on the lookout for any of these warning signs.

For many years, prison life was only studied from the point of view of prisoners. Beginning in the 1980s, correctional researchers began to realize that correctional officers were a group of people who should be studied. Within much of the literature, officers were frequently depicted as cruel characters who lived to abuse prisoners. Among the emerging themes within the literature were the effects of the correctional environment on officers and the constant on-the-job stresses that officers faced. Many of these studies found that correctional officers suffer from high rates of burnout, and job turnover is a frequent problem for correctional agencies. Positive leadership is often crucial to the correctional environment and can aid in job satisfaction. The better training officers receive and the better leadership is, the more likely correctional officers are to work in an ethical manner.[32] Working as a correctional officer is not for everyone. It can be a stressful job, but there are many different capacities in which correctional officer can work. In Dave's narrative, he discusses the many different tasks he performed while working in a prison.

Narrative: Dave's Story

I never aspired to become a correctional officer. However, my time working in the prison system taught me more about people, life, and myself than any other experience. In the early 2000s, the factory at which I worked hit an economic bump. The company's response was to layoff around 150 people. I was one of them. During my subsequent job search, a friend informed me that the prison was hiring. At first, the thought of working in a prison did not seem like a good prospect. However, after putting more thought into it I began to see it as a stable place to work and it could be a stepping-stone to something else in law enforcement. The next day, I submitted my application and was hired within a week.

The memories of my first day working in the prison system are vivid. One of the first things I noticed was the smell. One would think that the smell of a place filled with felons living in close proximity would be less than pleasant. The truth is that when I walked through the secure door and entered the holding area, I was hit with a strong smell of bleach, floor wax, and paint. Over the course of my career, I visited many prisons, and each one had a very similar smell. As I walked through the corridor toward the central control room, I could feel hundreds of eyes fixed on me. Many of the inmates were standing in the windows of their dorms looking me over. They knew I was a new officer, and the inmates were already trying to figure me out. The only inmate interaction I had on my first day was with an inmate that was in the isolation unit. The officer leading me on the "walk around" took me in to the ISO/SEG unit, commonly known as the hole. As I walked past one of the doors, I looked into the cell. Staring back at me were two wide eyes of an inmate with an expressionless face. During my brief glance at him, he uttered the words "we going to get you." In a split second, a thousand things ran through my mind about how I should react to the inmate's comment. Before I could really think of what to do, I just simply gave him a smirk and walked off in a dismissive manner.

---

32. Cullen, F. T., Link, B. G., Wolfe, N. T., & Frank, J. (1985). The social dimensions of correctional officer stress. *Justice Quarterly*, *2*, 505–533.

The first two weeks of working in the prison system were mundane. I shadowed one of the officers as they went about their daily routine. This time was meant to get new officers familiar with the prison layout and get them used to being in the prison environment. After these two weeks, I was sent to Basic Correctional Officer Training (BCOT). This was the equivalent to a 5-week boot camp for correctional officers. Over the next five weeks, I experienced a paramilitary training program that covered everything from firearms certification to CPR. Cadets would have to gather in formation in the morning for physical training (PT) then attend classes and practical exercise throughout the day. In the evening, more PT, then lights out. The little time I had between the end of evening formation and lights out was spent shining my boots and studying for the next day's test and practicum. The purpose of this training was to push cadets as to prepare them for the stress of working in the prison system and obtain the various certifications needed for working as a correctional officer (CO). Several of the cadets dropped out due to not being able to handle the stress of training. Others were kicked out due to rules violations or not being able to pass one of the exams or practicums. The thinking behind this was that it was better to have a cadet fail during training than to have said cadet fail on the job. Overall, my BCOT experience was intense but not overly difficult. The two main points of advice I gave to later cadets to simply, one, keep your mouth shut. Two, do what they tell you to do.

Once BCOT was completed, my first job as a CO was to supervise an outside work detail. My inmate crew was comprised of 12 inmates. No amount of training could have prepared me for the feeling of taking 12 inmates out into the community and have them complete tasks while keeping the inmates secure and the public safe. One 24-year-old officer supervising 12 men that had been convicted of various crimes. As overwhelming as this seemed, it turned out not to be as bad as I had worried about. Instead of constantly being concerned about an inmate's escape attempt, the reality was that most of the inmates assigned to outside detail enjoyed the opportunity to be out of the confines of the prison and enjoyed working. It was during my time as an outside detail officer that I developed my communication skills. Working directly with the inmates allowed me to learn inmate culture and the argotic language of the prison.

After working as a detail officer for two years, I was offered a promotion and position working inside the prison. This was the point in my career that I began to realize that working in the prison could be a long-term opportunity rather than a mere stopping off point. The potential of more promotions encouraged me to complete my bachelor's degree. After earning my degree, I was offered the position of counselor. Working as an inmate counselor allowed me the opportunity to make a difference on their time while incarcerated and prepare them for life after parole.

As counselor, my job was to manage a 120 inmate caseload. My duties included, but were not limited to, things like intake orientation, case file assessment, treatment recommendations, classification, parole summaries, disciplinary hearing advocate, and grievance investigator. These were just a few. While working as a CO, my responsibilities were limited to keeping inmates confined and safe. Being a counselor allowed me to have an impact on inmate's lives. Some of the most rewarding times of my prison career was seeing an actual change in an inmate's mindset and motivation. This was achieved by doing a "needs/goals" assessment, which placed inmates in classes that were focused on the inmate's limitations. An inmate that completed a course that gave him a new skills set, like a welding certificate, gave said inmate the potential to leave prison and obtain gainful employment. Many times inmates on my caseload would leave prison with a job waiting on them due to having a vocational certificate they earned while incarcerated. This would greatly decrease their chance of recidivism. There were many occasions in which parolees would call or return to the prison, as a visitor, to thank me for helping them during their incarceration. Several times these parolees would bring their families with them to visit. Each time, the inmate would introduce me to their family and then tell their family how I had changed their life or helped them get through their time in prison. It was during these situations I would think back to how when I first considered working in the prison system, I was not convinced it was a good decision. However, after having a four-year-old daughter of a parolee look up at me and say "thank you for taking care of my daddy," it was clear that it was one of the best decisions of my life.

Many officers worked with me during my decade of prison work. Their motivations for being a CO were similar to mine. Some were just looking for a job, while others saw it as a gateway to a greater career in law enforcement. However, working in the prison system can be a rewarding and exciting experience. There are many jobs in the prison system besides being a CO. Once a person has completed basic training, he or she has the opportunity to go in many directions while working in the prison system, too many to list. The key to working in the prison system is that the job becomes what a person makes it, meaning that one's motivation becomes the thing that is the difference in a CO advancing through the ranks or becoming stagnate. Working in the prison system is a high stress job that is held in low regard by many. However, a person who is motivated and has good communication skills can have a career with many opportunities for advancement and will last until retirement age.

There are many lessons from Dave's narrative. Among the first is that Dave was not initially looking for prison work, rather it was a good job that came along when he did not seem to have a lot of other opportunities. His narrative describes both the positive and negative interactions correctional staff can have with inmates. While Dave began his correctional career with a high school diploma, he soon learned the value of education in being promoted within the facility. There is a great diversity of tasks and roles and many different ways to interact and work with inmates. Dave found the experience rewarding and noted that not only were many inmates able to change, they were also grateful to Dave for helping them along the way.

Diversity in Correctional Staff

While corrections was, at one time, almost exclusively managed by White males, that has undergone some changes over the years. According to the Bureau of Labor Statistics, in 2017, women comprised 29.9% of correctional officers and 28.5% of bailiffs and jailers. In that same year, 13.1% of correctional officers and 29.1% of bailiffs and jailers were African Americans, 3.8% of correctional officers and 1.8% of bailiffs and jailers were Asian American, and 10.1% of correctional officers and 13.5% of bailiffs and jailers were Latino.[33] Today, women are still underrepresented, but the numbers for minority males are encouraging. According to U.S. Census population estimates for 2017, 76.5% of the population was White, 13.4% was African American, 5.8% was Asian American, and 18.1% were Latino.[34] While disparity certainly exists between the inmate population and the demographics of American society, at least the gap between the incarcerated and staff has shrunk. Diversity in correctional staff is not just important for lip service or public perception. Although prison riots occur for a variety of reasons, many of the riots from previous years could at least be partially blamed on the perception that racist captors were abusing inmates. It is difficult to imagine a correctional facility in which inmates will be happy or get along with their captors; evening out these ratios will seemingly help. Research has demonstrated that among African American correctional officers, they have tended to be less punitive and are more likely to embrace rehabilitation programs and the rehabilitative ideal.[35]

As we discussed in Chapter 4, for many years, the only way in which women could be employed in a correctional facility was if they were employed in a women's correctional facility. Even in those facilities, they were often criticized for

33. Bureau of Labor Statistics. *Labor force statistics from the current population survey.* Retrieved on August 26, 2018 from https://www.bls.gov/cps/cpsaat11.htm

34. United States Census Bureau. *Quick facts: United States.* Retrieved on August 26, 2018 from https://www.census.gov/quickfacts/fact/table/US/PST045217

35. Jackson, J. E., & Ammen, S. (1996). Race and correctional officers' punitive attitudes toward treatment programs for inmates. *Journal of Criminal Justice, 24,* 153–166.

being too soft on the inmates.[36] Today, there is still resistance to the role of women in the correctional field. If women are employed in the field, they are typically in low prestige jobs with less authority and opportunities for advancement.[37] Often, such a bias is focused upon outdated stereotypical views of women and especially that women tend to be less physically strong than men. While the latter point may have some credence, given the high disparities in officer to inmate ratios, even Chuck Norris might have difficulty if a large number of inmates decide to attack a correctional officer. Yet, research has demonstrated that in some instances, women officers may have skills that male officers lack. Among many traits, women were found to be better communicators and were more willing to display empathy to inmates. By trying to understand inmate complaints, rather than engaging in traditional male officer behavior, such as yelling at or threatening inmates, some women officers may be better able to manage inmates and potentially diffuse tough situations before they turn violent.[38] In Angela's narrative, she discusses the experiences of a woman working in corrections.

Narrative: Angela's Story

I have worked in prison, jails, reentry services and juvenile detention. I have worked as both a correctional officer and a therapist. I never meant to go into law enforcement, let alone corrections. I planned to work with children who have suffered abuse. While it seems as though my life went in a different direction, it really didn't. Working in corrections is in fact working with children, only those children who have experienced abuse are now grown up. My experience as a female working in corrections has been a unique and rewarding experience. I started as a correctional officer and later became a treatment specialist (therapist) in a high security penitentiary. While I have had other jobs in corrections, the time I spent as a therapist was the most interesting and rewarding. As a therapist, I got to know many inmates in a different and more personal way. I would do this job again in a heartbeat. Corrections is a male-dominated field, obviously. In male institutions, the inmates are men, the officers are mostly men, and the administration is made up nearly entirely of men. The institution is setup for men. My experiences as a female in this environment have been interesting, to say the least.

Most of my time has been spent in male institutions; in that respect, I generally consider being female an asset. The interactions between male

---

36. Freedman, E. B. (1981). *Their sisters' keepers: Women's prison reform in America, 1830–1930.* Ann Arbor, MI: University of Michigan Press.

37. Krisberg, B., Marchionna, S., & Hartney, C. (2015). *American corrections: Concepts and controversies.* Thousand Oaks, CA: Sage.

38. Cheeseman, K. A., Mullings, J. L., & Marquart, J. W. (2001). Inmate perceptions of security staff across various custody levels. *Corrections Management Quarterly, 5,* 41–48.

officers and inmates can and tend to have an adversarial and competitive nature to them. There is often a power struggle to see who can "out man" the other person. Yet, as a female, I have been able to avoid that whole mess. I am not the inmate's competition, I am not a threat, and they have nothing to prove to themselves or the other inmates when it comes to our interaction. No inmate ever gained status beating up a girl. Another observation that I have made is that fights occur less on units where female officers are working. Housing units tends to be calmer when the officer is a woman. I have responded to many fights but never had one on my unit. The one fight I nearly had on my unit was over the television, of course. However, by remaining calm and having a good preexisting relationship with the inmates, I was able to deescalate the situation by request rather than force. While there are always exceptions, I have found that I get more cooperation, as well as respectful behavior and attitudes, out of inmates because I am a woman.

I have been able to develop good working relationships with many inmates, both as a correctional officer and in the therapeutic program I ran. These working relationships have helped me avoid the more dangerous inmates. There have been many occasions when I have been warned about other "creeper" inmates, by the inmates who I worked with every day or those I did therapy with (my inmates). They also helped to keep "creepy inmates" away. A situation that would frequently occur would be a new or unfamiliar inmate monopolizing my time. If this were to happen, one of "my inmates" would come along and ask for my assistance elsewhere. After walking some distance away, my inmate would tell me he was just "helping me out with the creeper," referring to the unknown inmate having bad intentions. Working in a prison is a different experience for women and even more so for pregnant women. After a number of years working in this environment, I decided to grow my family and became pregnant. At this point, the relationships I had with "my inmates" changed. It was as if they became more, almost, protective of me. It was weird but not bad. The best example I can give is this. Numerous times a day, I was required to cross the yard to go to meetings. In the past, I may see "my inmates" on the 2000 yard walk, but it was rarely more than a "hello." Once I was pregnant and showing, I had what seemed like an escort when crossing the yard. There was always at least one of "my inmates" with me while walking across the yard, just making small talk. They never mentioned why, but it definitely kept the "creepers" away. After I returned from maternity leave, my escort was gone, and things returned to normal.

Despite the apparent consideration the inmates had for me when I was pregnant, not everything is good about being a woman in a male-dominated correctional environment. There are subtle forms of sexual harassment. While conducting pat-downs, inmates go out of their way so that they can be patted down by a woman. There are also those inmates who are "accidentally" changing their cloths every time you walk by their cell. Or inmates leaving pictures of naked women out in their cell when they know you are completing cell searches. Pornography is considered contraband, and officers are required to confiscate it. Yet, I have had male officers give me a hard time stating it is a "stupid rule" and inferring I only took issue because I am a woman.

There are also more clear forms of sexual harassment by inmates, such as "gunning." Gunning is essentially inmates exposing themselves while masturbating. While they do it to male staff as well, it is primarily a female staff issue. It is offending behavior that gets more prevalent in higher security institutions. It happens all over the institution regardless of department, and is especially bad in segregation. Inmates make up reasons to call you over to their cell, masturbate while speaking with you, and as soon as they think you are going to leave, they back up so that you can see what they have been up to. I had one particular incident where I was speaking with an inmate in my office. I had known him for months and thought we had a good working relationship. He seemed a bit jittery, when all of a sudden he stood up saying he had to leave, and it was clear what was going on. He was never allowed in my office again, which was unfortunate because otherwise he was a good guy. Dealing with "gunners" is most likely my least favorite part of being in corrections. The positive aspect of it is that my administration did take gunning seriously and the inmates normally go to segregation on the spot if caught.

I have worked in jails that house female inmates. This hosts a different set of pros and cons. While the staff is still mainly male, the needs of the institution and population are different. I personally find women more difficult for me to work with, possibly because I am a woman too. At any institution there is "visitation," which requires inmates to be strip searched. While working at an institution with females, I have had the unfortunate experience of having to strip search countless female inmates before and after visitation because I was the only female officer available during that shift.

The difficulties of being a woman in corrections do not end with the inmates. Women are looked at different by the inmates, by the staff, and the institutional setup itself. My first experience of sexism was the day I was interviewed. It was a panel interview including a psychologist, a captain and someone from HR. Nearing the end of the interview the captain looked at me and said "Why does a girl like you even want to work in this place?" I do not remember what my answer was, but I got the job. Another example of the sexism that exists is how assignments are handed out. I have witnessed male and female officers receiving generally different details or assignments. The "good ol' boys" receive more relaxed details, such as "monitoring the yard," while female staff get the more tedious tasks, such as completing pat-downs or searching property. Depending on the institution, it has appeared that male staff tend to get assigned tasks that enable them to promote more easily. This may not be everywhere but happens without a doubt. An issue I had with the architecture and planning of the institution happened after I returned from maternity leave. I was breast feeding and shockingly enough, the prison did not have anywhere for me to pump. I either had to walk 30 minutes to my car, or I could use the bathroom on our housing unit. As lovely as the cinderblock bathroom was, complete with sink, toilet, and urinal, it was also sandwiched between my coworkers office and an inmate cell. Neither of these worked particularly well, but at least my coworker was an awesome guy. Clearly, these institutions are not set up for women, let along those with babies.

Despite not intending to base my career in corrections, I would not change my experience for the world. I have found that while there are many unique challenges women face working in corrections, there are also many advantages. I have also found that it is more about who you are as an individual rather than whether you are a man or women. Everyone with a career in corrections will experience both negatives and positives; it is only the details and how you handle them that differ.

As Angela's narrative demonstrated, many of the inmates responded positively to her presence in the correctional facilities in which she worked. While she did receive some trouble from other staff, many of her experiences with inmates were positive. In many instances, inmates would tell her information that they most likely would not have shared with male staff. Unlike many male staff, who might respond to problems with inmates with threats or even violence, Angela would often calmly talk to inmates, and in many situations, it seemed she was better at deescalating bad situations than male officers. While it is difficult to see a future in which the number of women correctional officers roughly equals the general population, a greater inclusion of women and minorities among correctional staff highlights one of the growing shifts in the profession. Not only are new people getting in to the profession, but training and education levels have been improving as well. Some of the stereotypes of correctional officers remain the same, but the profession has evolved with the times and will continue to do so.

Chapter 10

Rehabilitation Programs

I n this chapter, we will discuss various rehabilitation programs that are used in the criminal justice system. Some programs will target a certain condition, such as substance abuse, mental illness, or a lack of education. Other programs strive to teach offenders new skills that will hopefully help their employment prospects. Additionally, programs can be administered in different forms, whether they are for incarcerated offenders or those serving their sentences in the community. Programs are usually designed to target one of two objectives. The first objective is to treat some immediate concern that will make an offender's life and/or incarceration problematic, such as mental illness or substance abuse. The second objective is to better prepare offenders for life outside of correctional facilities or if they are on some form of community corrections, give them life skills so that they no longer have to or are as likely to engage in criminal behavior.

Vocational Programs

As we have discussed throughout this textbook, historically, punishments have usually been retributive and/or deterrent. Corporal punishments and the death penalty were designed to bring pain to an offender and hopefully convey the message to everyone else that if you commit a crime(s), bad things will happen to you. Beyond putting an ugly image in a person's head and possibly creating a negative association with criminal behavior, punishment was not rehabilitative. While the results were not especially promising, many early supporters of incarceration sought to make prison punishment as well as rehabilitative. Whether it was the Pennsylvania system that encouraged offenders to reflect upon their misdeeds and sin no more or the Auburn system that sought to teach offenders a work ethic, prisoners were supposed to come out of prisons better than when they were admitted. Perhaps the ultimate example of a correctional facility seeking changes in inmates was the Elmira Reformatory.

The genesis of Elmira, and other reformatories with similar missions, was to make incarceration more humane and to include various rehabilitation programs. In addition to correctional officers and other traditional correctional staff, many of these institutions employed teachers and vocational instructors.[1] Yet, in many instances, calling prison labor rehabilitative, whether it was in factories, construction projects, or the prison farms of the south, was often a convenient excuse to legitimize the practice. Prison laborers were usually treated poorly and often worked in brutal conditions. With the prisoners in many instances out of sight and out of mind from general society, prison labor was able to pay for the correctional industry. Today, correctional budgets are huge, but in the time of big prison labor, the industry often paid for itself. As prison industries diminished due to it being considered exploitative and competing with organized labor in general society, a stigma has generally remained around vocational educational and any activities that involve inmate labor. Thus, prison administrators are often left with a quandary. How can they provide vocational programs or train inmates without it appearing exploitative or competition for labor industries outside of correctional facilities?[2]

There are four different types of systems in which correctional systems will utilize prison labor. The first is contract labor, piece price, and lease systems. In this type of system, private corporations will provide machinery and raw materials, and a correctional facility will use inmates to provide finished products to the corporation. The second system is the public account system in which a correctional system or facility will buy machinery or raw materials so that inmates can manufacture goods that can be sold. The third system, the state-use system is similar to the public account system, but goods produced by a correctional facility or system will only be purchased by state agencies or institutions. The fourth system, the public works and ways system, is a system in which the only projects inmates, or people in the correctional system, will only perform labor on public construction and maintenance projects.[3]

Perhaps the most well-known prison labor company in the United States is UNICOR. Originally called Federal Prison Industries, Inc., the organization was established by federal law in 1934. During World War II and the Korean War, UNICOR, using inmate labor, provided a variety of products that were useful to

---

1. Spillane, J. F. (2014). *Coxsackie: The life and death of prison reform*. Baltimore, MD: Johns Hopkins University Press.

2. Schlossman, S., & Spillane, J. (1992). *Bright hopes, dim realities: Vocational innovation in American correctional education*. Washington, DC: U.S. Department of Justice.

3. Clear, T. R., Cole, G. F., & Reisig, M. D. (2013). *American Corrections* (10th ed.). Belmont, CA: Cengage.

the war effort. While the company would provide materials at the beginning of the Vietnam War, by the end of the conflict, war production had largely ceased.[4] UNICOR acknowledges on its website "despite periods of criticism form detractors, increasingly constrictive procurement laws, misinformation and stigma associated with the value of inmate-made goods, prison industry work programs have endured."[5] UNICOR has many factories in the different correctional facilities in the federal system. Among the products inmates manufacture are clothing, electronic components, signs, and office furniture.[6]

One criticism of vocational training is that many prisoners are taught skills that do not make them readily employable upon their release. This is especially a concern for women inmates. As Merry Morash and colleagues noted, women's programming has often lagged behind that of men, and women are often taught skills that are stereotypically considered "women's works," such as cosmetology, sewing, and food preparation.[7] Among the biggest supporters of making prisons "factories with fences" was Warren Burger, who served as chief justice of the Supreme Court of the United States. Among the products he suggested inmates could make were ballpoint pens, hosiery, watch cases, automobile parts, lawnmowers, and computers.[8] Yet, the possibility that prisoners will find factory jobs upon their release from prison is increasing unlikely. In 1960, approximately 25% of Americans worked in manufacturing. In 2016, that number was less than 10%.[9] As if this was not bad enough, many jobs will have restrictions prohibiting convicted felons. Many of these restrictions, when challenged in courts of law, have been upheld.[10] Furthermore, many occupations that require special licensing (such as cosmetology) will have often have restrictions on obtaining these licenses that precludes people who have been convicted of a variety of crimes.[11]

As you can see, nothing in corrections is ever really simple. Many people want inmates to work so that the fruits of their labor can repay the state for incarcerating them. At the same time, many people argue that this is inherently exploitative

---

4. Hanser, R. D. (2017). *Introduction to corrections* (2nd ed.) Thousand Oaks, CA: Sage.

5. UNICOR. (n.d.). *Factories with fences: The history of UNICOR*. Retrieved on September 5, 2018 from https://www.unicor.gov/FPIHistory.aspx

6. UNICOR. (n.d.). *Products and services*. Retrieved on September 5, 2018 from https://www.unicor.gov/Category.aspx?iStore=UNI&idCategory=1

7. Morash, M., Haarr, R. N., & Rucker, L. (1994). A comparison of programming for women and men in U.S. prisons in the 1980s. *Crime and Delinquency*, *40*, 197–221.

8. Burger, W. E. (1985). Prison industries: Turning warehouses into factories with fences. *Public Administration Review*, *45*, 754–757.

9. Long, H. (2016, March 29). U.S. has lost 5 million manufacturing jobs since 2000. *CNN Money*. Retrieved on September 5, 2018 from https://money.cnn.com/2016/03/29/news/economy/us-manufacturing-jobs/index.html

10. Saxonhouse, E. (2004). Unequal protection: Comparing former felons' challenges to disenfranchisement and employment discrimination. *Stanford Law Review*, *56*, 1597–1639.

11. Wheelock, D. (2005). Collateral consequences and racial inequality: Felon status restrictions as a system of disadvantage. *Journal of Contemporary Criminal Justice*, *21*, 82–90.

of the inmates. Getting inmates to work can teach them valuable life skills and, in some instances, a trade. Yet, many of the jobs inmates do are either low paying or nonexistent in general society. Furthermore, inmates who return to the community will often have trouble getting jobs. Thus, putting inmates to work or training them is never a simple or unpolitic process.

Educational Programs

Researchers have generally found that people who are better educated are less likely to engage in crime. This principle generally works because better educated people are more likely to secure better employment.[12] In one survey of state and federal inmates, it was found that 41% of these men and women had not completed high school or obtained a GED prior to their admission to prison. By comparison, only 18% of the general population (over 18) had not completed high school of completed a GED.[13] Granted, Edwin Sutherland, when inventing the term "white collar crime," used the term to describe people in business and other professions who engaged in criminal behavior in their jobs, a group of people who were highly educated.[14] Furthermore, at one time, many scholars blamed rising levels of women committing crimes on their expanded employment opportunities and their broader opportunities in the American workforce. According to Meda Chesney-Lind, such a claim was relatively naive at the time and did not properly account for patriarchy and other forms of oppression.[15] Thus, there are some situations in which better educating people can lead to crime. However, among offenders, studies have found that when they are better educated, they are less likely to return to prison.[16] So, if this is true, why do we not simply provide educational opportunities to all prisoners? Well, just like vocational programs, it is not that simple.

One of the things that affects the implementation of education in prisons, and prison programming in general, is what many people have called the principle of least eligibility. While many people embrace the rehabilitative ideal, inmates are in prison to be punished as well. Many people argue that inmates should not receive special privileges and that inmates should receive no better treatment (or

12. Lochner, L., & Moretti, E. (2004). The effect of education on crime: Evidence from prison inmates, arrests, and self-reports. *American Economic Review, 94*, 155–189.

13. Harlow, C. W. (2003). *Educational and correctional populations.* Washington, DC: U.S. Department of Justice.

14. Sutherland, E. H. (1945). Is "white collar crime" crime? *American Sociological Review, 10*, 132–139.

15. Chesney-Lind, M. (1986). "Women and crime": The female offender. *Signs, 12*, 78–96.

16. Vacca, J. S. (2004). Educated prisoners are less likely to return to prison. *The Journal of Correctional Education, 55*, 297–305.

worse) than members of general society.[17] Prisoners are often viewed by general society as coddled, essentially layabouts who are being housed and fed at the state's expense. This combined with Robert Martinson led to less emphasis on correctional programming. While not an education program, the federal government and many states place restrictions on correctional facilities providing weights and other exercise equipment. This was done because many politicians did not want to provide the funds to inmates and the fear that jacked up inmates would later commit robberies and otherwise victimize people. Never mind that most of these types of crimes are committed with the use of a weapon.[18] One example of politics leading to less resources for inmates was in 1994 when Congress enacted legislation that prohibited inmates from accessing Pell Grants. This, for the most part, has ensured that inmates will not have access to college and university education.[19]

With limited resources and, in many instances, overcrowded correctional facilities, many prisons have limits on the services they can provide to inmates. Many correctional facilities require inmates without GEDs to enroll in basic literacy courses.[20] Yet, most prison resources are dedicated to reentry, essentially the last six months to a year of an inmate's sentence. In a recent survey of federal inmates, they seemed pleased by many of the programs available, but the inmates responded that there were long waiting lists for programs. Furthermore, not surprising in this digitized world, there are many available online and computer programs for inmates, but very few inmates have access to computers. Aggravating these problems is that there are few qualified teachers available. Many classes in prisons are taught by inmates, many of whom have little teaching experience.[21] One way to remedy this is through volunteer programs. One example of this is at the University of Alabama at Birmingham (UAB). Roughly 30 years ago, Ada Long, a professor and founder of UAB's honors program, began a lecture series at the nearby maximum-security prison Donaldson Correctional Facility. Throughout the years, many different professors at UAB have volunteered their time and taught single lectures and, in some cases, entire courses at the prison.[22]

---

17. Clear, T. R., Cole, G. F., & Reisig, M. D. (2013). *American Corrections* (10th ed.). Belmont, CA: Cengage.

18. Griffin, O. H., Woodward, V. H., & Sloan, J. J. (2016). *The Money and Politics of Criminal Justice Policy*. Durham, NC: Carolina Academic Press.

19. Ubah, C. B. (2004). Abolition of Pell Grants for higher education of prisoners: Examining antecedents and consequences. *Journal of Offender Rehabilitation, 39*, 73–85.

20. Hanser, R. D. (2017). *Introduction to Corrections* (2nd ed.). Thousand Oaks, CA: Sage.

21. George, J. (2017, May 31). *What are inmates learning in prison? Not much.* The Marshall Project. Retrieved on September 8, 2018 from https://www.themarshallproject.org/2017/05/31/what-are-inmates-learning-in-prison-not-much

22. Gunter, L. (2016, September 6). *Chapman is a national voice for reforming 'wasteland of the mind.'* UAB Reporter. Retrieved on September 8, 2018 from https://www.uab.edu/reporter/peo-

Drug Treatment

Studies have consistently found that a majority of jail and prison inmates committed their crimes while under the influence of alcohol and drugs. Additionally, many inmates will commit crimes to obtain money to purchase drugs.[23] Movie star Robert Downey Jr.[24] and musician David Crosby[25] often credit stints in prison as helpful to their recovery because it gave them a sense of hitting rock bottom and how their life should not turn out. For most people who do not have the ability to make millions of dollars acting or playing guitar, prison and a subsequent label as a convicted felon can actually make many people's lives significantly worse. Furthermore, despite being secured environments, drugs and alcohol can be obtained in many correctional facilities. Thus, many people have argued that people with drug problems need to either be diverted from correctional facilities or at least receive drug treatment while they are incarcerated.

Without going into a complete rabbit hole or tangent that is American drug policy, for our purposes here, the federal and state governments did not begin to punish drug users with incarceration until the early 1900s. Before then, drug use was generally legal, and since drugs were relatively cheap, there were not large numbers of people stealing to obtain money or goods for drugs. Prior to the 1900s, drug use was largely confined to middle-age, middle-class White women and veterans of the Civil War. In many instances, their drug use began through a physician proscribing or giving them drugs. As the 1900s began, a pharmaceutical revolution was occurring, and from then to the present day, more and more drugs have become available. While some drugs, such as aspirin or penicillin, are used to treat specific conditions and have no psychoactive properties, an increasing number of drugs have become available that people have used for recreational purposes. As America's drug problems began to spread, many physicians responded to their patient's drug misuse by proscribing small amounts of drugs to them to either maintain their habit or in attempt to wean them off drugs. This strategy is often referred to as addiction maintenance. In 1914, Congress passed the Harrison Narcotic Act, which essentially led to the first war on drugs. In its wake, physicians who prescribed drugs to patients in bad faith (not for a strict

ple/awards-honors/item/7226-chapman-has-been-a-national-voice-for-reform-of-wasteland-of-the-mind

23. Goode, E. (2015). *Drugs in American Society*. New York, NY: McGraw Hill.

24. Scott, P. (2013, May 23). From washed-up drug addict to the $100m man: How iron man star Robert Downey Jr. turned his life around from prison and cocaine. *Daily Mail*. Retrieved on September 9, 2018 from http://www.dailymail.co.uk/tvshowbiz/article-2330012/How-Iron-Man-star-Robert-Downey-Jr-turned-life-prison-cocaine.html

25. Greene, A. (2016, September 27). The last word: David Crosby talks Trump, Kanye, what prison taught him. *Rolling Stone*. Retrieved on September 9, 2018 from https://www.rolling-stone.com/music/music-features/the-last-word-david-crosby-talks-trump-kanye-what-prison-taught-him-125887/

medical condition) or users who did not obtain their drugs through a physician's prescription started to be arrested and incarcerated. At this point in time, the criminal justice system gave little concern to drug users.[26]

Incarceration as the primary punishment for drug users largely continued until the 1960s. During that decade, two innovations happened. The first, in 1964, was the opening of the first outpatient methadone clinic. Beginning in 1949, physicians at the U.S. Public Health Hospital in Lexington, Kentucky experimented by providing prisoners with histories of opiate misuse methadone. The physicians found that so long as the prisoners received regular controlled doses, it seemed an effective treatment. In 2000, Congress passed a law allowing physicians to prescribe the drug buprenorphine to substance misusers. While methadone is more stringently regulated than buprenorphine, people with substance abuse problems can receive methadone or buprenorphine both inside and outside of prison, although various states, counties, and municipalities have placed various restrictions on these drugs.[27] The second innovation was the use of civil commitment programs, originally developed for people with mental illness, for drug users. These programs were extended to drug users who were constantly in trouble with the criminal justice system. Essentially, drug users were held in secure facilities so they could receive treatment. By the mid-to-late 1970s, these programs were mostly replaced with drug treatment programs run by communities.[28] If you have ever watched *Intervention* or *Celebrity Rehab with Dr. Drew* you have probably seen these types of programs, often referred to as therapeutic communities. Although these types of group programs, or similarly Narcotics Anonymous, are often available in correctional facilities, the goal of therapeutic communities are usually to be a residential facility in which people can receive treatment in group settings.[29] While some people may be referred to a residential community as part of probation or specifically in lieu of being incarcerated, most people who seek treatment in these facilities are not under court order to do so.[30]

Another large part of drug treatment in the United States is the use of specialized courts for drug treatment. Beginning in the 1950s, Chicago and New York, facing large numbers of defendants with drug charges, established special court dockets for these defendants. In 1989, Dade County, Florida established the first

---

26. Griffin, O. H. (2014). The role of the United States Supreme Court in shaping federal drug policy. *American Journal of Criminal Justice, 39*, 660–679.

27. Miller, J. M., Griffin, O. H., & Gardner, C. M. (2016). Opiate treatment in the criminal justice system: A review of crimesolutions.gov evidence rated programs. *American Journal of Criminal Justice, 41*, 70–82.

28. Leukefeld, C. G., & Tims, F. W. (1988). *Compulsory treatment of drug abuse: Research and clinical practice.* Rockville, MD: National Institutes of Health.

29. Goode, E. (2015). *Drugs in American society.* New York, NY: McGraw Hill.

30. De Leon., G. (1988). Legal pressure in therapeutic communities. In Leukefeld, C. G. & Tims, F. W. (Eds.), *Compulsory treatment of drug abuse: Research and clinical practice (NIDA Research Monography, 86)*, pp. 160–177. Rockville, MD: National Institutes of Health.

modern version of a drug court.[31] The first court, and thousands of other courts in the country that have been established, are guided by the principles of therapeutic jurisprudence. Rather than being an adversarial proceeding, drug courts are meant to have a defense attorney, prosecutor, and judge work together for the betterment and treatment of defendants. Indeed, to avoid labeling defendants, they are instead referred to as "participants," "clients," or other variations thereof.[32] In most of these courts, defendants must plead guilty to the charges against them and will then undergo community-supervised treatment. If they complete treatment successfully, they will have their charges dropped.[33]

Mental Health Treatment

Perhaps no group is stigmatized more than people who suffer from mental illness. One of the traditional responses to dealing with people who suffered from mental illness was to lock these people up in asylums.[34] Within contemporary times, the peak period of admissions of mentally ill people to asylums or mental hospitals was the late-1950s. While some people may have benefited from this arrangement, the state-run hospitals of the early 1900s often became overcrowded and rundown. Furthermore, many patients were left isolated, and abuse of these patients occurred regularly. With the invention of several promising drugs that many people thought would be useful in the treatment of mental illness, the deinstitutionalization movement began. Rather than housing patients in these large broken-down hospitals, many politicians envisioned a future in which patients could be medicated and either returned to their communities or receive treatment in local facilities. Unfortunately, most of these new local facilities were not built.[35]

With no places to send mentally ill offenders, many of these people ended up incarcerated in local jails and prison. Avoiding such circumstances was behind the creation of state-run mental hospitals in the first place. Risdon Slate and colleagues have referred to this vast increase in mentally ill offenders into correctional facilities as the "criminalization of mental illness." This is unfortunate be-

31. Belenko, S. (1998). Research on drug courts: A critical review. *National Drug Court Institute Review, 1,* 1–42.

32. Hora, P. F., Schma, W. G., & Rosenthal, J. T. A. (1999). Therapeutic jurisprudence and the drug treatment court movement: Revolutionizing the criminal justice system's response to drug abuse and crime in America. *Notre Dame Law Review, 74,* 439–538.

33. Belenko, S. (1998). Research on drug courts: A critical review. *National Drug Court Institute Review, 1,* 1–42.

34. Link, B. G., Phelan, J. C., Bresnahan, M., Stueve, A., & Pescosolido, B. A. (1999). Public conceptions of mental illness: Labels, causes, dangerousness, and social distance. *American Journal of Public Health, 89,* 1328–1333.

35. Bassuk, E. L., & Gerson, G. (1978). Deinstitutionalization and mental health services. *Scientific American, 238,* 46–53.

cause not only are correctional facilities not the place where many of these people belong, but jails and prisons are usually ill-equipped to deal with many different types of mentally ill offenders. These facilities do not have the resources, and very few of the personnel have the proper training to work with these offenders.[36] While some mentally ill offenders can still secure places in mental hospitals, the majority of these people are often placed among violent offenders. In many instances, this can lead to them being abused, or in some instances, some mentally ill offenders may have diminished coping mechanisms and find themselves getting into violent confrontations with other inmates.[37] Some correctional facilities will place mentally ill offenders into protective or supermax custody, which can worsen existing mental illness. Some correctional facilities will dispense various drugs to mentally ill offenders and will provide psychological services, but in few cases do these offenders get the treatment they need.[38]

Faith-Based Programming

As we have discussed, many of the first prisons in America were founded by people who thought offenders needed more spirituality in their life. In most correctional facilities, inmates will have access to religious services, and most institutions will either employ a prison chaplain or allow volunteer religious leaders to enter correctional facilities and minister to inmates. Furthermore, correctional facilities need to provide reasonable accommodations so that inmates can practice their faith and religious diets are usually accommodated as well.[39] To some degree, correctional facilities will either make these accommodations so that they will not get sued or to give inmates a constructive activity in which to engage. However, a growing literature within corrections has demonstrated that inmates who practice religion and/or spirituality are often better behaved and less likely to engage in violence.[40] Both presidents Bill Clinton and George W. Bush were big proponents of getting charitable organizations and religious groups to help serve underserved populations, such as providing services to groups such as the homeless or prisoners. In particular, the Bush administration established the White House Faith-Based and Community Initiative that sought to greatly expand the availability of federal grant money to religious organizations that provided assistance to underserved people. Within corrections, these programs can take many forms, from treating prisoners with substance abuse problems to juvenile crime

---

36. Slate, R. N., Buffington-Vollum, J. K., & Johnson, W.W. (2013). *The criminalization of mental illness: Crisis and opportunity for the justice system.* Durham, NC: Carolina Academic Press.

37. Hanser, R. D. (2017). *Introduction to corrections* (2nd ed.). Thousand Oaks, CA: Sage.

38. Clear, T. R., Cole, G. F., and Reisig, M. D. (2013). *American Corrections* (10th ed.). Belmont, CA: Cengage.

39. Hanser, R. D. (2017). *Introduction to corrections* (2nd ed.). Thousand Oaks, CA: Sage.

40. Kerley, K. R., Matthews, T. L., & Blanchard, T. C. (2005). Religiosity, religious participation, and negative prison behaviors. *Journal for the Scientific Study of Religion, 44,* 443–457.

prevention programs to reentry services for offenders to many different types of community corrections programs.[41] In the following narrative, Dr. Angelita Clifton, an associate minister, discusses why she engages in prison ministry.

Narrative: Dr. Angelita Clifton

The prison system is the only "business" that succeeds because of its failure. As prison populations grow larger, prisons grow larger. Unfortunately, the cycle of recidivism is key to the repetitive cycle of incarceration. Reentry, reoffending and reincarceration challenges the current policy and requires a major shift in praxis. The answer is not more prisons. It is not locking people up and "throwing away the key." I am convinced the answer is in the Gospel of Jesus the Christ. Prisoners need more than rehabilitation; they need regeneration. Jesus has commissioned his followers to reach beyond the barbed wire fences touching lives with His transforming love. Answering my call to ministry providing Trauma Informed Correctional Care at several facilities in New Jersey is one of my greatest blessings. I am grateful to shed light in dark spaces.

Traumatic events, coupled with the intergenerational transmission of historical traumas experienced by the incarcerated, is quite obvious to some yet remains hidden in plain sight for most. In 2006, while working on a dual degree in seminary, a master of social work and master of divinity, I often questioned my direction. But in 2018, I understand my decision. While facilitating a group session at Northern State Prison, I heard a young man tell a familiar story. When he was still in high school, he lost four family members in a house fire. Unable to process the overwhelming grief and deeply traumatized, he began acting out. With each episode, his behavior was a cry for help with no response. Subsequently, he became more and more violent due to issues related to his grief. With no outlet and no counseling from the school system or the courts, he found himself standing in front of a judge and facing a long prison sentence. The judge sentenced him to the maximum time allowed for the crime, his justification being this young man was "incorrigible." Sadly, this deeply traumatized child of color, just barely 18 and struggling to navigate the various stages of grief on his own, was described as a depraved delinquent who was unredeemable.

Regrettably, this young man's story is not unique. There are many traumatized men and women trapped in the criminal justice system. The tragedy of his long prison sentence with little rehabilitation is the result of a society that is uninformed about trauma. I believe professional intervention, access

---

41. Dodson, K. D., Cabage, L. N., & Klenowski, P. M. (2011). An evidence-based assessment of faith-based programs: Do faith-based programs "work" to reduce recidivism? *Journal of Offender Rehabilitation, 50,* 367–383.

to trauma-informed therapists, would have changed the trajectory of his life. Society cannot afford these kinds of failures in the schools, social service agencies, churches, or the criminal justice system. Intervention at one or on all of these levels would have inevitably transformed his life.

I am often dismayed to discover many churches do not have a prison ministry. Transformation is the primary focus of the church. So the obvious question I pose to the church universal is if not now, then when? The church cannot fall into the trap set by society, labeling human beings as unredeemable. When will the followers of Christ recognize we are falling short? When will we begin meeting God's sons and daughters where they are? Prison ministry is not for the faint of heart; it requires a faith-filled heart. God is calling the body of Christ to minister to the needs of His people, and I hear Him asking if not now, then when?

Restorative Justice

In Chapter 2, we briefly discussed restorative justice. Victims are often a forgotten part of the corrections process. They may testify at trial or in a sentencing hearing, but that is generally it. Restorative justice seeks to accomplish two goals. The first goal is that a victim can approach their aggressor and tell them of the harm that he or she caused. This will essentially provide a victim some measure of taking their power back. This only works when an aggressor is willing to admit the harm that he or she caused. The second goal is that if restorative justice works properly, the aggressor will accept responsibility for the harm that he or she caused. The end result will hopefully be that the victim will ultimately provide some level of forgiveness to the aggressor, and that will hopefully help their rehabilitation process.[42] In her narrative, Alissa explains in more detail how this process can work.

Narrative: Alissa's Story

On a Saturday night in April of 1999, when I was just 16 years old, I was raped on a beach by a man I had just met at a party. Suffice to say, rape affected me in many ways. I was angry and reckless. I engaged in self-harming behavior. I drank heavily. I attempted suicide more than once. I stayed in unhealthy and abusive relationships. Experiencing rape led me down a path of self-destruction, brought about by a total loss of self-worth.

---

42. Zehr, H. (2014). *The little book of restorative justice: Revised and update*. New York, NY: Good Books.

Perhaps paradoxically, I became a sex crimes researcher and scholar. I wanted to learn everything I could about why sexual violence happens and how to prevent it. Yet, throughout my career I remained silent about the fact that I am a rape survivor. Fifteen years after my rape, I started disclosing and speaking publicly about my experience. I waited so long to speak out because I was afraid that people would not take my professional work seriously. I was worried that people would think that I could not be objective. That couldn't be farther from the truth.

Amazing things can happen when you stand in your truth. Two years after I began disclosing, a close friend and colleague, Dr. Jill Levenson, asked me if I would be willing to come speak with the men in her treatment program. The program is designed for people who have been convicted of a sexual offense. These offenses range from child pornography and exhibitionism (flashing) to child sexual abuse and rape and of course, everything in between. She requested that I come as Alissa, rape survivor, and not as Dr. Ackerman, sex crimes expert. I wasn't exactly sure what I was getting myself into, but I said yes.

The hot and humid south Florida air consumed me as I stepped out of the car and walked toward the building. Several men stood outside making small talk, smoking cigarettes, and biding their time before group started. I wondered what they were thinking as I reached for the door with my trembling hands. They had to know that I was the survivor coming to speak with them.

I've spent countless hours in rooms with people who have committed sexual offenses, but I have always done so with the Dr. Ackerman mask on. Walking into a space where I would knowingly take off that mask was terrifying. I agreed to do this as a favor to a friend to help her clients gain some empathy and insight. I had no idea how healing and life changing the experience would be for me.

The chairs were arranged around the perimeter of room. I sat toward the front of the room with the door directly to my right. It was a quick exit if I needed it. My friend and colleague, Jill, sat to my left. The men, who had now all taken their seats in the remaining chairs, trusted Jill. They knew she would not put them in a situation that was dangerous for them. I, too, trusted that I was safe in this space. Yet, we all had our defenses up as we began the session.

I had the opportunity to share about the impacts that rape had on my life, and they had the opportunity to ask questions of me. In turn, I asked questions of them. By the end of the session, we all learned the importance of sharing authentically and vulnerably. One man, who had served 20 years in prison for a rape that he committed when he was 19––and that was strikingly similar to the rape I experienced––approached me at the end of the evening.

"I'd really like to give you a hug if that's okay," he said cautiously. Before the words were fully out of his mouth, I threw my arms around him. I recognized in this moment that we were so much more similar than different. This hug was one of the most powerful moments of my life.

The following night, Jill drove me to the beach where I was raped. The temperature was cooler than I remembered, and the moon was brighter. I found the rocks where it had happened and inhaled the salty sea air. I felt no fear. It had been nearly 17 years since I was last there in the darkness. But now I was no longer wrestling a monster in my head. I had made peace with this place. With what happened to me. And with the man who raped me. I turned back toward my friend. "It's just a beach," I said with a smile.

I would never have been able to go back to this place at night without the connection I made with the men in Jill's treatment group.

As I thought about my time with these men and then values inherent in sharing space with them, I realized that what we were doing was a form of restorative justice.

Restorative justice is a framework that seeks to address the harms caused by wrongdoings rather than the statute violation that it broken. Restorative justice and restorative practices values the interconnectedness of all human beings. Doing so promotes healing and repair for all people involved in the harm. It is multifaceted in that it seeks to make reparations even when the needs of the various parties are different or even diametrically opposed. There is no one way to engage in restorative justice. In fact, because it is a framework built on specific values, there are multiple options for harm reduction, acknowledgment, accountability, and connection.

How could I create experiences like this for others who have experienced sexual abuse or who have perpetrated it?

I began volunteering my time participating in and facilitating what Jill and I have termed vicarious restorative justice. It is named as such, because I do not know any of the people—none of them perpetrated harm against me or any other survivors who come into these spaces.

I've now met with almost 400 men and women who have been convicted of a sexual offense. I've engaged other survivors with this process as well, and the results have been incredibly positive.

Restorative justice takes on many forms and can be used in all types of harm. Our criminal justice process makes it difficult for survivors of crime to get the healing and closure they deserve. Restorative justice, in conjunction with correctional policies, may be an answer to the injustices of the formal system.

Finally, we note that one of the key ways in which rehabilitative efforts have received significant attention is in the area of prisoner reentry. We discussed the prisoner reentry movement that has taken ahold in Chapter 7 when we covered parole. One of the distinguishing features of prisoner reentry is to focus on preparing prisoners for outside society before they are released from prison to improve their chances of success when they return home. A second feature of prisoner reentry is to include the population affected (prisoners and parolees) in the process of designing successful reentry programs. Their input is essential. In keeping with these core tenets, we offer John Dreher's narrative to conclude this book. John has been incarcerated at East Jersey State Prison for over 30 years. He was a highly successful businessman who has suggested that our current system of incarceration is not producing meaningful reform in prisoners. John proposes the following changes, which he suggests will have a positive impact on prisoner rehabilitation.

Narrative: John Dreher

I've always been inquisitive both about how the thinking behind physical processes and systemic procedures develop.

After leaving college in 1964, I first worked for Ocean Leather in Newark, NJ, a small leather tannery at the time. The name derived from there on a small secondary unique product line: leather made from shark hides. It was secondary due to the limited supply of hides. I was tasked with expanding existing resources and finding new ones. It turned out rather well, even getting co-featured in the December 9, 1968, *Sports Illustrated* article on shark fishing. (Years later, the tannery ceased basically because of new EPA regulations that impacted materials used in shark tanning.)

My reputation grew and in 1974, I was selected to be the keynote speaker at the first international leather symposium and trade show held in Moscow.

My continued success and growth was based on the usual traits necessary to run a successful business: attention to customer satisfaction and diligent attention to efficiency, innovation, quality control, and costs. Along the way, I was granted a patent in leather making technology.

The habits necessary for good management were carried over in to my imprisonment but only for use as a spectator. They showed me that a major opportunity is being wasted: no overall structure exists to encourage reform, turning the term Department of Corrections into an oxymoron.

Then in 1995, a chance conversation shocked me even further: a returning inmate said that he voluntarily committed a new crime in order to return to prison. For him, life behind the walls was more advantageous than in normal society. This was the straw that caused my anger. My family might be at risk because someone wants to go back to prison?!

Not resuming looking for a remedy for high recidivism rates makes as much sense as would abandoning cancer and malaria research only because a cure has not yet been found. Continuing the status quo actually encourages crime by omission.

The following provides a means to improve public safety by attacking the seeds of recidivism in prison throughout a convict's incarceration. No one changes without a reason. Here is a simple one.

PRISON INMATES NEED A POSITIVE MOTIVATION TO CHANGE: Previous efforts to produce fewer recidivists and more successful reentries did not succeed because of how data was gleaned and analyzed (inmates simply filled out forms with presumed proper responses, or data was used for gross populations that hid human variables) for the former and because of the latter following the principle of "locking the barn door after the horse had been stolen." Ignored or not recognized was that the ex-cons had become addicted to the prison lifestyle.

In 1995, a returning inmate mentioned that he "had to return to prison to get healthy." When I asked, "parole violation?," he replied, "no, I had to catch a new charge." This stunner led me to asking returnees, "what's it like out there?" Their replies centered around the normal costs and complexities of regular living. It soon became apparent they were comparing the real world to the predictable ease of the cost-free, fully catered prison lifestyle. When released and confronted with normality, they couldn't cope and had to commit fresh crimes in order to return to their prison homes. They had fallen prey to an induced addiction.

From the start of incarceration, inmates are steered toward focusing only on the day-to-day prison life and its unending Groundhog Day sameness. We are constantly pressured to obey and conform, just as in the military's basic training. The difference is that the military quickly starts a rebuilding process that imbues skill sets and positive attitudes so that after obligations are over they are better equipped to smoothly reenter society. The opposite is true for ex-cons. The majority who became addicted (institutionalized) exhibit the same tendencies that the PTSDs do when faced with the stresses of the real world. Other inmates refer to them as "doing life on the installment plan," while officers label them "frequent flyers."

Work and behavior credits designed to promote reform only enable those the parole boards reject as unfit for return to society to have their sentences shortened. For example, someone serving a 10 to 20 year sentence will max out around the 15th year, thanks to the credits that accrued, but not activated until the parole board's initial rejection.

Those who max out normally quickly commit fresh crimes, (thus validating parole board evaluations,) die, or are deported. Convincing them to focus on long-term goals is the key to reduced recidivism rates. This can be accomplished by offering a visible carrot and hard stick approach. Give those who self-improve an opportunity for earlier parole review (with NO guarantee of parole being granted, nor will the overall sentence be reduced; supervised parole periods would be commensurately extended). Give the unimproved a longer incarceration by eliminating the current work and behavior credits, which only truncate sentences. This change would not affect high parole board standards, nor lessen stringent psychological review.

The new structure still emphasizes behavior improvement but with a new formula. The work credits will be replaced by having achievements met as a criteria for evaluation. Augmenting these will be a requirement to take a variety of introspective programs. No such structured pressure currently exists. Those who fail to demonstrate improvement will be kept incarcerated longer by requiring their full sentence be served in prison, with no reduction possible (20 years in the above example) and no released earlier by the application of the current credit formula.

THE CARROT: For each educational degree obtained, vocation learned, and addiction shedding (minimum of five years drug free) the inmate will be reviewed 10% earlier than originally sentenced. Behavioral improvement will result in a 1-year earlier review based on a sliding scale of time values changing with age. For the 18–37 age group, require five years of proper behavior to earn each earlier year; for the 38–45 age group, require four years; for the 46–54 group, require three years; for the 55–60 group, require two years; and for the over 60s group, require one year.

THE HARD STICK: Those who fail to try to improve will be kept incarcerated longer (the full term the judge ordered). This will force inmates to evaluate their futures and make choices and long-term commitments. For the majority, it will probably be the first time they do so. Once the commitment is made, pressures will come to bear. Family and friends will constantly question what progress is being made, as they want to see them come home earlier with an improved outlook. Their fellow inmates who strive will supply competitive pressure, which will prevent lagging.

FOR THOSE WHOSE WHO BECAME INSTITUTIONALIZED: Understanding that they fear normal society without prison's largess, and continual guidance is the reason why they should be given the option to remain in prison longer than their court-imposed sentences. Many will take the option if an economic incentive is attached so that they can rationalize to themselves and others why they should stay. The amount would not have to be great, probably less than 1% of their annual cost to the taxpayer. This would be cheaper than the cost of the damage (crimes) they inflict on society in order to return to their prison homes.

Trying it has no downside!

In order to provide the right atmosphere for a cultural shift, the staff must be brought on board for the successful implementation of the program. A motivation for them to change their current approaches to work must be introduced. Set aside a portion of the monies saved by the state by each inmate who for five years does not reoffend or violate parole. The savings should be put in a newly created "earned income trust" that will not be comingled with the current troubled pension system.

Fixed and 85% sentences should be eliminated, as they disincentive reform. When convicts hear the judge say exactly which day they will be released, they tend to think they might as well relax and enjoy the ease of the prison lifestyle instead of changing for the better.

BENEFITS FOR THE PUBLIC: The unimproved will be fully exposed and kept in prison longer, resulting in short-term recidivism rates declining. Later, the long-term rates will be more drastically reduced because the incorrigibles will be released fewer times over their life spans.

Employers will now have a means for better evaluating which ex-cons have self-improved and worthy of hire, instead of the automatic rejection that is normal now. Gainful employment is necessary for the improved to be able to stay on the right side of the law.

Other less visible benefits will develop: fewer young people will be led astray by negative role models leaving prison too soon, social and economic activity will improve with less crime occurring, property insurance rates will decline, etc.

John Dreher, 402287B / 272498, New Jersey Prison System

As we have discussed throughout this textbook, the presence of rehabilitation has waxed and waned throughout American corrections. In some instances, although some naive, an entire correctional system was based upon principles of rehabilitation, usually with a one-size-fits-all approach. In other times, correctional programming has been targeted to specific inmate needs. Regardless, rehabilitation has been controversial. Some people believes it works, some people believe it does not, and others are somewhere in the middle. One of the biggest factors that affects rehabilitation, though, is the support levels of the federal and state government. Correctional agencies will usually prioritize security of rehabilitation, and if resources are not available, programs will not be implemented. One of the problems, both within politics and corrections, is that we often take a short-term view. People today seldom want to pay for a problem in the future.

Index